The Governance Report 2013
Hertie School of Governance

The Governance Report 2013

Hertie School of Governance

OXFORD
UNIVERSITY PRESS

OXFORD
UNIVERSITY PRESS

Great Clarendon Street, Oxford, OX2 6DP,
United Kingdom

Oxford University Press is a department of the University of Oxford.
It furthers the University's objective of excellence in research, scholarship,
and education by publishing worldwide. Oxford is a registered trade mark of
Oxford University Press in the UK and in certain other countries

© Hertie School of Governance 2013

The moral rights of the authors have been asserted

First Edition published in 2013

All rights reserved. No part of this publication may be reproduced, stored in
a retrieval system, or transmitted, in any form or by any means, without the
prior permission in writing of Oxford University Press, or as expressly permitted
by law, by licence or under terms agreed with the appropriate reprographics
rights organization. Enquiries concerning reproduction outside the scope of the
above should be sent to the Rights Department, Oxford University Press, at the
address above

You must not circulate this work in any other form
and you must impose this same condition on any acquirer

Published in the United States of America by Oxford University Press
198 Madison Avenue, New York, NY 10016, United States of America

British Library Cataloguing in Publication Data
Data available

Library of Congress Cataloging in Publication Data
Data available

ISBN 978-0-19-967442-8

Managing Editor: Regina List
Book design: Plural | Severin Wucher
Cover illustration: Emilia Birlo
Information graphics: Kilian Krug
Typeset in Publico and TheSans

Links to third party websites are provided by Oxford in good faith and
for information only. Oxford disclaims any responsibility for the materials
contained in any third party website referenced in this work.

Table of Contents

Foreword — 7
Acknowledgements — 9

1. Governance: What Are the Issues? — 11
HELMUT K ANHEIER

**2. Meeting Global Challenges:
Assessing Governance Readiness** — 33
INGE KAUL

**3. Governance Challenge in Focus:
Financial and Fiscal Governance** — 59
WILLIAM ROBERTS CLARK, MARK COPELOVITCH,
MARK HALLERBERG, LUCIA QUAGLIA, *and* STEFANIE WALTER

4. Governance Innovations — 83
HELMUT K ANHEIER *and* SABRINA KORRECK

5. Introducing a New Generation of Governance Indicators — 117
HELMUT K ANHEIER, PIERO STANIG, *and* MARK KAYSER

6. Recommendations and Conclusion — 149
HELMUT K ANHEIER

References — 163
About the Contributors — 173

Foreword

Governance is a relatively new word for a relatively new experience. The experience: There are more and more issues of national, international and even global concern that seem difficult to address and resolve with the institutions, rules and players we know–or used to know. For even these familiar institutions, rules and players seem to change rapidly, and new ones multiply so fast it is hard to keep track of all the changes. As the complexity of problems mounts, so does the intricacy of the search for adequate responses and for their implementation. Modern politics with its many fields and forces of interaction seems like a magic Rubik's Cube– almost intimidating to the beginner, but open to clever procedures, and yielding results that range from poor to optimal. To study governance is to look for preferably clever procedures and optimal results. And good governance is of key importance for shaping politics and policies so as to be legitimate and efficient and so as to achieve just and sustainable outcomes.

This Governance Report provides facts and analyses, cases and principles about how–and how well–governance works on different levels of problem solving: locally and statewide, globally and in transnational and international relations and organisations. The Report furnishes indicators for gauging the quality of governance and offers recommendations for improvement. It was written by the Hertie School of Governance, a renowned public policy school in Berlin, which stands for an international and interdisciplinary approach to current governance challenges. The Governance Report aims to bridge the gap between academia, policymakers and the many stakeholders involved in the thrill and tribulation of governance at all levels.

This Report is a premiere. It pays special attention to questions of economic and fiscal governance that are so pressing currently, and it highlights many choices and trade-offs decisionmakers face in that crucial area. But the Report casts its net much wider. It asks for the most promising roads to better governance in general, it shows why so often these roads are not being taken yet, and it argues convincingly that many obstacles on the way to better governance can be overcome, particularly by recognising that in the world of today, national sovereignty is best used and preserved multilaterally, by combining it with the sovereign rights of others.

There are many encouraging aspects in this Report. A new governance indicator system can help us to better understand the dynamics and relationships between the multiple levels and actors involved in governance processes. The Report discusses governance innovations which provide examples of how in difficult times, we can achieve more if we learn from each other. I am particularly impressed at how creative people have coped with problems not so distant from ours as we might think. They inspire us to think beyond a logic of necessity and think creatively about how to govern better. And the Report highlights 'the pronounced presence (...) of civil society in the innovations reviewed', not alone but in 'cooperation with governmental agencies and even business that brings about change' and better governance for all. Governance, then, is something we all can help to improve.

This Governance Report deserves many readers and a lively debate, and since it is a premiere, there is more to come. I am glad we have this new and clear view on issues of governance now, and I look forward to reading the next editions of the Governance Report.

PROF. DR. HORST KÖHLER
Former Federal President of Germany

Acknowledgements

Many people have been involved in developing this premiere edition of The Governance Report, in addition to the authors of the various chapters.

First, we would like to thank the members of our International Advisory Committee who offered input at various stages of the project:

CRAIG CALHOUN	London School of Economics
WILLIAM ROBERTS CLARK	University of Michigan
JOHN COATSWORTH	Columbia University
HERVÉ CRES	Sciences Po Paris
LINDA C CROMPTON	BoardSource
NABIL FAHMY	The American University in Cairo
ANN FLORINI	Singapore Management University & Brookings Institution
GEOFFREY GARRETT	University of Sydney
MARY KALDOR	London School of Economics
EDMUND J MALESKY	Duke University
HENRIETTA MOORE	Cambridge University
WOODY POWELL	Stanford University
BO ROTHSTEIN	Quality of Government Institute, University of Gothenburg
SHANKER SATYANATH	New York University
JAMES VREELAND	Georgetown University
KENT WEAVER	Georgetown University
ARNE WESTAD	IDEAS, London School of Economics
MICHAEL ZÜRN	Wissenschaftszentrum Berlin

In the process of developing the Report, we convened two thematic expert workshops and one general review meeting. We are grateful for the inputs received from participants in the June 2011 workshop on indicators, including Daniel Kaufmann (Brookings Institution), Alina Pippidi-Mungiu (Hertie School of Governance), Eddy Malesky (Duke University), Klaus Brocsamle (Hertie School of Governance), and Lorenzo Fioramonti (University of Pretoria), and from those participating in the September 2011 workshop on financial and fiscal governance, including the authors of the Report chapter and Henrik Enderlein, Jobst Fiedler, and Christoph Gandrud from the Hertie School community. The general review meeting in January 2012 brought together many members of the International Advisory Committee, including Michael Hoelscher, Shanker Satyanath, Kent Weaver and Michael Zürn, and members of the Hertie School faculty.

In our work on innovations, we benefitted from the input of a six-member International Steering Group consisting of Adriana Alberti (UN Public Services Award and InnovMediterranean), Jed Emerson (Blended Value), Laura Massoli (Department of Public Administration, Italian government), Caroline Oliver (Policy Governance), Thuli Radebe (Centre for Public Sector

Innovation), and Simon Zadek (Center for International Governance Innovation).

We thank the Hertie School community, especially the many faculty members who have contributed their ideas and constructive criticism. Working with the authors at various stages have been senior fellow Lorenzo Fioramonti and an active team of research assistants including Oriana Angelucci, Donald Blondin, Fang Duan, Mark Fliegauf, Luca Giacopelli, Ariane Goetz, Olga Konoykhina, Linnea Kreibohm, Christian Ruiz, Julia Schubert, Ramsey Wise, and Christopher Yetman. Thanks are also due to David Budde, Zora Chan, Regine Kreitz, and Dayna Sadow.

We also wish to thank the Board of the Hertie School of Governance for encouraging this Report, and for providing critical feedback and direction.

At OUP we thank Dominic Byatt for seeing the promise in this enterprise and to Lizzy Suffling for guiding us through.

For the Report's look we are grateful to the team of Severin Wucher and Kilian Krug at Plural in Berlin.

Finally, we are especially grateful to the Hertie Foundation for its support, and to Evonik and Stiftelsen Riksbankens Jubileumsfond for providing the additional financial resources that made the Report's development and production possible.

Whilst every effort has been made to contact the copyright holders of material in this book, in some cases we were unable to do so. If the copyright holders contact the authors or publisher, we shall be pleased to rectify any omission at the earliest opportunity.

I. Governance
What Are the Issues?

by HELMUT K ANHEIER

This Report is about the changing conditions of governance, the challenges and opportunities involved, and the implications and recommendations that present themselves to analysts and policymakers. Indeed, few would doubt that the demands put on existing governance systems have changed–and continue to change–as the early twenty-first century seems to enter a period of profound uncertainty. The aftermath of the 2008 financial crisis is a case in point, as is the inability of the international community to reach agreement on major issues such as the environment, freedom of information, or arms trade.

With established systems under pressure, and no realistic, visionary grand solutions to guide, the world is nonetheless alive with a seeming cacophony of approaches–old and new–on how to improve governance and, ultimately, policy outcomes. Not all are well grounded, let alone well guided. Some innovations would likely do more harm than good; others appear unfeasible, too self-serving, or fraught with unknown consequences. Some, however, do harbour potential for seeking better ways and means of governing the world's affairs, be they in terms of economic well-being, justice, financial stability, environmental protection, health or social welfare. They differ in how much actual good they would do; the extent to which they are sustainable and replicable; and, of course, how much legitimacy they do and could enjoy among stakeholders.

> *The world is alive with a seeming cacophony of approaches on how to improve governance and, ultimately, policy outcomes.*

These innovations take place in a complex world with a seemingly contradictory 'push and pull': cautious pooling of national sovereignty is met by attempts to repatriate monetary or environmental policy, with the euro and Rio+20 as cases in point; a greater openness of national borders confronts renewed emphases on safeguarding and policing frontiers, as exemplified by challenges to the Schengen Agreement; the growing volume of cross-border economic activity is threatened by protectionism, especially by emerging market economies; the free flow of information, so much facilitated by the rise of the Internet, faces the controlling hand of governments and private corporations alike; the ACTA Agreement and small arms treaty of 2012 join a growing list of treaty failures that includes the Mutual Agreement on Investments in the 1990s, and the Kyoto Protocol in the 2000s; social and political movements organise more easily across borders as part of a growing global civil society yet face many restrictions at national levels and find limited access in international organisations. Finally, although more examples could easily point to the 'back and forth' of today's world in other policy fields as well, international people movements, while growing in numbers, show increasing travel restrictions and more selective migration patterns.

Governance and Interdependence

These developments occur in the wake of deepening interdependencies among countries. Financial markets, global supply chains, and the Internet are as much indications of this deepening as are environmental issues, migration, health and social policies. Such interdependencies have opened up many opportunities but they also involve risk; they invite competition as well as cooperation–and not only among states but also among business corporations, public agencies, and civil society institutions.

As recent crises have amply demonstrated, risks and opportunities on the one hand and competition and cooperation on the other are more easily realised and established for private goods and services than for public goods generally, and for global public goods in particular. And it is in context of the latter–bringing about policy outcomes that involve cooperation and competition in public goods provision–that governance systems have shown the greatest strains and weaknesses.

Developments towards greater interdependence unfold in the context of major shifts in global power relations since 1989 and a politically weakened and cash-starved UN system. They gather force as many states find their capacity to respond to the developmental challenges of our times reduced, with limited state capacity in all but a very few countries and the persistence of failed states, in contrast to the continued rise of the transnational corporation as the likely dominant organisational form of the twenty-first century and a strengthened role of civil society actors at national and international levels.

We live in a complex, interdependent world, to be sure, so perfectly illustrated by the financial crisis of 2008, especially the tensions between risk and opportunity, and cooperation and conflict: weaknesses in national and international financial regulation created short-term opportunities and long-term risks, brought to extremes in the US housing market. At the height of the tumult, the solution to swap private for public debt pushed sovereign debt to crisis levels for countries such as Greece, putting pressure on interest rates for government bonds and the euro; others, like the US or the UK, through a policy of quantitative easing opted for higher inflation and loss of purchasing power. Austerity measures enacted by national governments to reduce public debt and ensure liquidity led to economic contraction, increased unemployment, and political instability. Ultimately, political and financial risks increased, as did opportunities and opportunism; and institutions meant to cooperate found themselves in conflict, e.g. the European Central Bank and national central banks, and countries until recently on the best of terms traded public insults, at times falling back onto old stereotypes.

It seems that the geopolitical dynamics unleashed by the end of the Cold War, the economic globalisation spurt that has gathered new momentum with the rise of emerging market economies, and the advances in information and communication technologies–all appear to threaten the very foundations of many of the successes they themselves helped bring about over recent decades. In an almost dialectic process that would require the pen of a Joseph Schumpeter or Max Weber to describe adequately, the affairs of the world–at the global and even local level–seem to be going backward and forward at the same time, leaving the observer at awe as to the speed and depth of the changes taking place.

> *By good governance we mean an effective, efficient, and reliable set of legitimate institutions and actors engaged in a process of dealing with a matter of public concern.*

These changes have not gone unnoticed, to be sure, as the uncertainties they generate lead to searches for new approaches to governance and policymaking. This pursuit involves new ways of thinking (e.g., the initiative to redesign economics by the Institute of New Economic Thinking; to rethink the very notion of sovereignty as a foundation of a future EU that is at the core of the various political design efforts proposed by think tanks around Europe), innovations of many kinds (e.g. constitutional reform to break political gridlock in California; social impact bonds in Britain; or Liquid Democracy in cyberspace), and also investigations of how weakened institutions and fragile organisations could be changed to perform better in the longer run (e.g. UN reform efforts, relationship between the European Central Bank, national banks and regulatory agencies, or the African Union).

New approaches are being explored and tested, not only by national governments and international agencies but also by local governments, corporations, think tanks and universities as well as civil society organisations. They reflect specific interests, to be sure, and serve different stakeholders, entangled in strategic games of power relations and positioning–be it in dealing with transnational issues such as the euro crisis, climate change, or intellectual property rights or with seemingly more local issues such as local government budget woes, water and air pollution, or crime.

This Report is not to lament the changes and uncertainties of today's world; nor is it to bemoan the complexity of the often contradictory movements and counter-movements that are taking place; rather the Report seeks to address the implications of the current state of the world in terms of governance–or 'good governance' to be precise. By good governance we mean an effective, efficient, and reliable set of legitimate institutions and actors engaged in a process of dealing with a matter of public concern, be it in the field of financial markets, health care, or migration, and across local, national and international levels.

While achieving good governance may be difficult during the best of times, it is certainly more difficult today–not only because there are more 'actors' involved, be they governments, regulatory agencies, corporations, political parties, or social movements. Furthermore, it is not more difficult only because there are more high risk issues at stake: be they climate change, demographic changes, financial markets, or health care costs. What ultimately lies behind the complex challenge of governance today is the increased interdependence among actors across policy fields and geopolitical borders.

Interdependence implies constraints as well as opportunities. What corporations have practiced for long is being taken up as explicit policy and a seemingly rational choice by nation states: cooperation when necessary to address matters of common concern; and competition whenever possible in order to secure access to human and natural resources. This implies, as Chapter 2 argues, free-riding, stalling and a zero-sum orientation when approaching international treaties and cooperation generally. One expression of this emerging trend towards intensifying competitiveness and rivalry among states, often together with corporations, is the growing interest in immigration policies aimed at attracting the world's best brains. Another is the use and abuse of copyright regimes by some countries and firms alike; a third, the purchase of vast tracts of African land by Arab and Asian countries to secure food supply; and a fourth, the routing of oil and gas pipelines.

> *The interdependencies of today's world go beyond governments and corporations but involve civil society and communities–and with these, religions and values.*

The interdependencies of today's world go beyond governments and corporations but involve civil society and communities–and with these, religions and values. The Danish cartoon crisis of the mid 2000s is a case in point: the public spheres of two regions, i.e. Denmark and then the 'West' on the one hand, and Iran and Afghanistan, later the Islamic world on the other hand, were brought into contact through migrant communities and cyberspace in a conflict over press freedom and religion, causing riots and leaving many dead (Albrow and Anheier 2006). So is the release of a video on the Prophet Mohammed and the fierce and often violent reactions it provoked in many Islamic countries in 2012. What is more, the Arab Spring of 2011 revealed how youth activism in several countries in the region, diaspora communities dispersed across Europe, the Internet and the international media succeeded in creating a public sphere on Tahrir Square and enacted deliberative politics that proved capable of regime change.

Interdependencies also involve goods and bads. That air or water pollution does not stop at political or geographical borders is as much a commonplace as it remains a largely unsolved problem in much of the world. That serious environmental pollution impacts other policy fields like food security, health and migration over time, too, seems a rather obvious statement; but such interdependencies or spillovers from one policy field to another remain easier stated than addressed, and remain frequently unsolved.

How, then, can we make sense of governance in a world that seems to be changing fast, not necessarily always for the better, and that seems to gain in complexity, even a certain 'messiness' und unpredictability as it moves seemingly forward and backward at the same time? What are the main issues and components of, and for, good governance? What governance innovations are taking place, what options emerge, and what policy recommendations come to mind? This is where the Governance Report comes in.

The Report focuses attention on institutional changes and innovations that state and non-state actors have adopted, or could adopt, in response to the structural shifts that have been occurring and are likely to become even more pronounced and entrenched in the future. Put differently, the Report does not deal with the purely technical and procedural aspects of today's policy challenges, e.g. the best technology to reduce greenhouse gases; how to introduce voucher systems in social welfare provision; or how to improve treaty compliance of UN conventions. Rather, it uses such policy challenges as a lens to see how different actor groups have adjusted and could adjust to the new types of challenges brought about by changed and changing governance conditions.

Take one example to illustrate the kind of interdependencies we have in mind: by mid-twentieth century, the extreme pollution of Europe's Rhine River System and damages caused by severe and frequent flooding finally pushed the countries, ministries, regional authorities, municipalities, manufacturers, mining companies, shipping agencies, and nongovernmental organisations into collective action. Any actor on its own would have been incapable of improving water quality and preventing floods; moral hazard, free-riding, fragmented constituencies and patchy regulation required a series of international conventions, especially the 1963 Berne Convention, to reduce water pollution by binding parties together. Today, the International Commission for the Protection of the Rhine, created on the basis of that Convention, is to develop its ecosystem in a sustainable manner; to ensure that river water is apt for drinking water production; to improve the quality of Rhine sediments such that dredged material may be deposited without causing environmental harm; to put in place a holistic flood prevention and protection system taking into account ecological requirements like flood plains rather than dams; and to provide ecological relief for the North Sea.

Turning the Rhine from an ecologically dead shipping canal back to a river with a water quality not seen in perhaps a century and to which many species of fish have returned and now flourish represents a successful example of governance, as would the Great Lakes Commission in North America. Other salient examples of such approaches to governance for achieving policy outcomes are innovations such as: the UNICEF-led project 'A Promise Renewed' to lower child mortality (UNICEF 2012)[1]; public budgeting to create transparency and thereby reduce corruption[2]; the acquis communautaire in the 1990s to regulate accession to EU by central and eastern European countries[3]; new ways of allocating risks and rewards in social markets (see social impact bonds in Chapter 4); approaches to public-private partnerships in addressing public healthcare problems[4]; forms of e-governance to improve citizen access to services and to offer greater voice (see, e.g. mySociety also reviewed in Chapter 4); ways and means of handling internal and external conflicts, including their legacy, as exemplified by the South African Truth Commission or the International Criminal Court in dealing with war crimes[5].

Why Governance?

Governance is a fairly new concept that has gained much currency in recent years.[6] Governance is a broader notion than government and its principal elements of legislature, executive and judiciary. The World Bank (1991) defines governance as the manner in which power is exercised in the management of a country's economic and social resources for development. Note the emphasis on power and management and the nation-state frame. The corporate governance perspective, in a similar way, views governance as a way of distributing rights and obligations among boards, managers, shareholders, unions and other stakeholders. We suggest that neither the power-based nor the rights and obligations approaches, and clearly no longer the nation-state framework alone, are sufficient to capture the complexity of modern governance.

By contrast, Enderlein et al. (2010: 2) suggest a generic definition of governance that denotes 'the sum of rules and regulations ..., processes as well as structures... justified with reference to a public problem' brought about by actors. In other words, governance is about how we approach and solve a recognised collective issue or problem such as public security, poverty or pollution; how we monitor the performance of corporations; and the role of civil society.

Kooiman and Jentoft (2009) distinguish between first and second order governance. The first is about deciding who can legitimately address what public problem for whom and how; and the second about the kinds of institutions, organisations and regulations needed for achieving desired policy outcomes. First order governance is more about politics; second order governance more about policies. However, first order governance is not necessarily a top-down approach, nor does it always come first. Frequently, the identification and framing of public problems are brought forward from below, from social movements and civil society institutions. The interaction of from-below activity with top-down legislation through parliaments or legitimated agencies brings about first order governance proposals.

But what do these rather abstract terms actually mean? Let's consider a hypothetical case first, and then look at a series of 'real' governance arrangements to begin to appreciate today's governance challenges and potentials.

Imagine a group of some 200 cruise ship passengers stranded on an isolated island. They vary by age, gender, education, occupation, and wealth. While most are able-bodied adults, there are a few children and frail-elderly among them. They managed to rescue food and medical supplies estimated to last three months and succeeded in obtaining basic tools for constructing shelter from the sinking ship. A source of fresh water supply was located, though its reliability is unknown. For some reason, and in the fog of frantic rescue efforts, some 100 cases of champagne and 10,000 packs of cigarettes were also uploaded and made it to the island's shore.

The stranded passenger case, familiar to generations of governance students, leads directly to the heart of what governance is about: how to govern what, for what, by or through whom, and according to what rules? This is the first order governance problem. How is the power to make decisions to be distributed in terms of rights and obligations? Should elections be held? Should all adults have equal vote, or should those most knowledgeable and

Table 1.1 **Governance orders and dimensions**

Governance Order	Dimension	Basic Questions	Main Tasks
First Order 'Politics'	Legitimacy	Who?	Power basis, allocation of rights and responsibilities
	Public Problem	What?	Definition, framing formulation
Second Order 'Policies'	Institutions and organisations	How?	Setting rules, designing, implementing
	Regulation and control	What if?	Monitoring, sanctioning, incentivising
Policy Outcome	Performance	So what?	Goal attainment, distributional effects

able to function have more influence? Then follow second order issues: should all receive equal portions of food? Who is to oversee the process of dividing and disbursing rations? How should we distribute medicines, and on what basis? Should trade be allowed so the ample but capped supply of cigarettes could serve as currency? Should those building shelter for others or those helping the injured be rewarded and enjoy privileges such as the conspicuous consumption of champagne?

In raising these questions, we implicitly address five distinct but related dimensions of governance (Table 1.1). First order governance is essentially about power and politics in the large sense as the interplay between the exercise of legitimate power and its support endowed by stakeholders, i.e. the extent to which a distribution of power and its rights and obligations obligations entailed are seen as legitimate. Who among the passengers has the right to assume power, how and why? Is power limited and checked? Is it established and maintained by threat of violence or given freely? First order governance is also about the issues at hand and the public problem that needs defining and framing–the other dimension. Is the use of cigarettes a public problem, one with the same priority as looking into water supply or medical care? Defining and framing are closely related to solving or at least suggest approaches on how to address the public problem.

Second order governance, too, includes two dimensions: first, what rules and regulations are needed, and, second, how are we to enact them? For example, should there be markets, hierarchies, or networks based on communal or family bonds when distributing food? Then there are issues about the regulations themselves, ways of monitoring them, the checks and balances needed to make sure that rules are observed, and, if violations occur, that sanctions can be applied, and redress and remedial action sought.

The final dimension is the outcome achieved by first and second order governance arrangements. It is about performance and achievement, and the extent to which the governance system in place has brought a solution, obtained a desired level of goal attainment and brought about intended redistribution outcomes, and, especially, the extent to which it enjoys the legitimacy among key stakeholders.[7]

Let's now look at some real-life governance cases, and begin with a rather mundane, seemingly trivial example: the hamburger, a near universal fast food item consumed by millions of people across the world each day. While a private good, it is also public in a profound sense from a governance perspective. Yet what precisely is the governance problem when it comes to hamburgers, and how is it governed?

Box 1.1 Governing the Burger

Behind every hamburger ordered as a meal for lunch is a process surrounding a complex set of rules and regulations that involves various agencies and organisations. Normally we do not think about this process at all, taking for granted that somehow consuming a hamburger in a fast food restaurant is as predictable as it is mundane and, presumably, safe. Yet how exactly is the burger governed as it is transformed from cattle on a ranch to patty on a plate?

Working backward through the production cycle, store policies would be the first aspect of regulation from storing, thawing and preparing the meat patty to how it is to be assembled into a hamburger, dressed and presented. Some of these policies are the rules of the fast food franchise while others are a matter of public governance, highlighting the public problem: hygiene and food safety.

Hamburger franchises cannot treat food in any way they like. They must adhere to certain standards of public hygiene. Accordingly, the store policies fall under the jurisdiction of food hygiene regulation—usually a municipal or state-level agency, which in turn is overseen by a national ministry or agency of agriculture. In Los Angeles, California, for example, food safety is monitored by an inspection agency run by Los Angeles County, which maintains several bureaus dealing in environmental matters that oversee regulations and maintain a restaurant rating list based on hygiene. In Germany, regulation is lodged with the Business Control Service (itself part of the state police). It randomly checks food stores and reports to the Federal Ministry of Food, Agriculture, and Consumer Protection.

However, if we assume that the franchise happens to be located in the European Union, there are also EU norms, which in turn provide a common framework for national food hygiene regulation and are administered by the EU's Directorate General for Health and Consumers. In addition, there is the global 'Codex Alimentarius' jointly overseen by the UN's Food and Agriculture Organisation and the World Health Organisation and to which EU, national and local regulations are to conform. Some of these regulations address meat marketing, transportation and, indeed, meat processing, and others the slaughtering of animals, the raising and breeding of cattle, and the food they consume. Ultimately, we will reach the germ cell that grew into the cow that provided the meat that eventually became the burger patty served on your plate.

The many rules and regulations around meat production are the result of long and bitter struggles not only between and within agencies, ministries, European institutions or even UN organisations, but also between producers, consumer protection organisations, and animal rights activists who clashed in the context of routine politics as well as in response to large-scale crises and scandals. So when looking at it from this angle, a simple burger patty thus aptly illustrates the enormous complexity of governance—regarding the multitude of institutions involved on various political levels as well as the numerous actors engaged in pressing for, passing, implementing, and enforcing the respective rules. The simple patty on your plate thus actually is the highly multi-level, multi-actor outcome of a complex process of governance.   *by* GREGOR WALTER-DROP

The core public problem in hamburger governance (see Box 1.1) is food safety along the production process of the main ingredients: meat, wheat, vegetables, and condiments. It involves local (e.g., food inspection agency), national (e.g., health authorities) and international agencies (e.g., EU and UN conventions), as well as corporate (e.g., restaurant) and civil society (e.g., consumer advocate organisation) actors. So when sitting down to appreciate a hamburger, we have, in fact, a multitude of institutions and organisations looking over our shoulder, and whose combined regulations and pressures made sure that the product–while not among the healthiest–is at least safe to consume.

The hamburger governance system evolved over time and is the result of failures (e.g., lack of hygiene and food poisoning) and ways to avoid them (e.g., food safety inspections); it involved many conflicts (e.g., meat producers vs. animal rights groups) that would have impacted franchises and their profits; and it meant calibrating corporate strategies with consumer preferences and public health demands for better nutrition. It continues to evolve as new issues such as obesity or genetically modified food come up and push against established interests.

That governance is the result of ongoing contests of political as well as economic power and interests becomes even clearer when taking a brief look at how the financial system is governed. Indeed, fiscal and financial governance is the thematic focus of this year's Report, as is, in the context of the 2008 financial crisis, the politics of global finance. That rules and institutions governing international markets have not kept pace with these rapid and substantial changes is clear even to the most ardent proponents of nation-state centred financial policy that seek to keep as much financial regulation as possible at the domestic level. The world is entering the fifth decade of the post-Bretton Woods era, which began in 1973, without a formal and functioning international monetary system in place.

As Chapter 3 makes clear, the current system of international financial regulation has not been lacking in complexity given the multitude of international organisations, statutes, committees, and agreements (Davies 2010). Besides the IMF and World Bank, roughly 20 organisations such as the Financial Stability Board, FATF, IAASB, Bank of International Settlements, Basel I to III, and IOSCO make for an interconnected web of regulatory responsibilities that is, even for the expert, hard to disentangle (highlighted through the purposeful use of acronyms).

Moreover, representation in these institutions has been heavily skewed toward Western countries in general and the United States in particular, which, in turn, has continued to pursue a primarily national economic policy through them. In addition, Europe may have arrived at a common currency but still lacks a common voice in the form of political-fiscal governance. The absence of an effective, international and comprehensive governance structure can be mainly attributed to the lacking willingness of national governments to transfer competencies from the national to the supranational level.

After the 2008 crisis, the reaction was to increase regulation, which in most instances meant greater reporting requirements imposed by national bodies. So far, proposals to reform the global financial architecture have

---

Box 1.2 Governing the Budget in California

As the California Department of Finance states: 'The budget process for California defies a simple concise definition. It is a process rather than a product' (http://www.dof.ca.gov/fisa/bag/process.htm). In terms of governance, it exemplifies how two of the most essential functions of government, taxing and spending, can be effectively halted by institutional constraints and spill-ins through voter interventions or global trends such as financial and economic crises. It also illustrates how established governance structures and processes can be trapped in a vicious circle of ineffectiveness, which undermines the efficacy and, ultimately, the legitimacy of governance.

At first glance, the process to pass the state budget in California is straightforward and follows a model embraced at all levels of the US government. The state's governor, as the elected chief executive officer, proposes a budget, which is introduced at a press conference with the governor highlighting special policy initiatives and the budget's overall principles. It is then promoted in the State of the State Address before being introduced in each chamber of the legislature. The governor's budget must be accompanied by a budget bill, itemising recommended expenditures. The Assembly and the Senate take up the budget bill and divide the sections among subcommittees, which report back to the Assembly Budget Committee and the Senate Budget and Fiscal Review Committee, which submit a recommendation to the respective chambers.

However, the final threshold for passing a budget is high. Since Proposition 58 was approved by California voters in 2004, the state has to pass a balanced budget each year and cannot finance its expenditures by taking on additional debt. Six years later, voters supported Proposition 25, allowing the legislature to pass the budget with a simple majority in both chambers—instead of the previous two-thirds majority. However, a two-thirds majority is still required to raise new revenues. Given that neither party is usually in control of such a majority in both chambers at any time, political majorities are almost impossible to organise for any increase in revenue.

California allows its citizens via direct initiative to propose and vote on constitutional amendments and laws, which is why California voters are frequently asked to vote on new taxes or tax increases at the ballot box whenever revenue increases are blocked or rejected in the legislature. Given the balanced budget requirement and California's burden of public debt, voters decide whether to increase taxes or face drastic spending cuts.

Unlike any legislature, the decision-makers in this case—the voters—are not required to engage in deliberation or compromise; they can only approve or reject propositions. With little technical knowledge of the complex budget measures before them and a barrage of special interest advertisement on the advent of the vote, citizens have to decide with little or distorted information. Their decisions impact directly the fate of teachers, firemen and street cleaners, as well as state programmes, such as for culture and the arts.

Each drastic spending cut that follows a failed proposal for a revenue increase to balance the budget further withdraws the means from local government to achieve good performance. Hence, while the California budget is governed on the local level, it is subject to external effects such as economic trends (e.g. the financial crisis and recession of 2008 and 2009) or the influx of special interest money to be spent on political advertisement. The governance structure in place lacks the appropriate mechanisms to achieve effective, efficient and legitimate decision making because it rewards political stalemate instead of providing incentives for deliberation and compromise.

aimed at establishing new agreements, statutes and committees but without either putting in place some new institutional framework or rationalising the existing ones to accommodate altered macroeconomic conditions. Indeed, there is confusion between first and second order governance decisions, and a consequent emphasis on technical fixes, as Chapter 3 argues.

Do financial matters look simpler at local or regional levels? Let's take fiscal governance in the US state of California as an example, and look at how the state's budget comes about (Box 1.2). Here, clearly delineated first order governance decisions are caught in spill-ins through the electoral process, namely the frequent use of referenda and propositions. The California budget is less about the budget and what the state requires in terms of public spending given its growing population; at its core, it is about taxes, and especially the politically willed enshrinement to limit and reduce direct taxation on income and wealth. It is an example of a governance system caught in a suboptimal political stalemate created by past policies and electoral outcomes, which leaves little room for manoeuvre for actual fiscal governance. As a result, second order governance is blocked.

Yet the California budget is not a California problem. First, as the world's seventh largest economy and centre of high technology innovation, it is connected to all corners of the globe, and a systemic failure of its public sector will have repercussions well beyond its borders and the US. Second, California debt is financed by the international bond market, and closely watched by rating agencies. In other words, California matters to the world just as the eurozone does; they are interdependent yet appear to be seemingly disconnected policy actors.

Could it be that we do better at governing newer domains like the Internet (Box 1.3) than entrenched budgetary problems? Here, too, we see

---

Box 1.3 **Governing the Internet**

'Internet governance is the development and application by governments, the private sector and civil society, in their respective roles, of shared principles, norms, rules, decision-making procedures, and programmes that shape the evolution and use of the Internet'.
Tunis Agenda for the Information Society, 2005

The Internet is a globally distributed network where information is decentrally stored on and communicated between interconnected computers. Its operation requires the smooth functioning and interaction of many layers, including physical infrastructure, codes, and content, and involves, among others, service providers, engineers, developers, and ultimately users.

A look at just one layer illustrates the complexity of Internet governance. When you enter 'www.hertie-school.org' as a URL (Unified Resource Locator) in your web browser, it is translated into an IP (Internet Protocol) address, or '212.77.229.145' in this case. The IP address is what your browser and your computer need to connect to another computer on the Internet and retrieve the requested information. Since such numerical IP addresses are not easy to remember, URLs like 'www.hertie-school.org' are used to make Internet navigation easier.

Valid URLs must comply with the Domain Naming System (DNS), which is at the heart of how the Internet appears to the everyday user. Allowing or not allowing Top Level Domains (TLDs) such as '.org' (for organisations, originally intended for non-profit ones), '.com' (commercial), or '.xxx' (adult entertainment) can make a big economic, political and moral difference.

The DNS and other essential technological and policy aspects of the Internet infrastructure are coordinated by the Internet Corporation for Assigned Names and Numbers (ICANN), a nonprofit, private organisation based in the United States. Essentially, ICANN allocates and maintains the unique identifiers that allow computers on the Internet to find one another. While, generally speaking, the Internet operates without a central governing body, the power over the DNS makes ICANN in fact one of very few authorities with global, centralised influence over the Internet (Mueller 2010).

ICANN is itself a complex entity with three supporting organisations, four advisory committees, a technical liaison group, and its international governing board contributing to decision-making. Among the advisory groups are the Governmental Advisory Committee, on which national governments and international treaty organisations are represented, and the 'At-Large' Advisory Committee representing normal everyday users. While final decisions on any changes are made by ICANN's Board of Directors, they come after a consensus-building process involving, in particular, the supporting organisations and advisory committees, as well as the general public.

ICANN's position in Internet governance is not uncontested. ICANN's operations were governed in large part by Memorandums of Understanding with the US Department of Commerce until 2009, when an 'affirmation of commitment' replaced the expired project agreement (MacKinnon 2012). Despite this change in overt control and efforts on ICANN's part to enhance transparency and participation, many voices—especially IBSA (India, Brazil, South Africa)—have called on the UN to create a new body to oversee the technical and operational functioning of the Internet and to arbitrate disputes. The governance questions at the moment for this layer of the Internet are whether it should continue to be the remit of a transnational, private sector led entity or of nation states and intergovernmental organisations and whether the US should maintain its privileged position through control of the DNS and IP addresses.

by BJÖRN NIEHAVES

a complexity developing that suggests unclear boundaries between first and second order responsibilities. How about the governance of fields like maritime and oceans policy? While ages-old, this field requires urgent attention due to pollution, rising sea levels, depleting fish stocks, and the prom-

Box 1.4 Governing Oceans

While oceans are areas devoid of statehood, they are by no means 'un-governed.' States may only claim authority over the ocean and the seabed within the twelve nautical miles (22 kilometres) of territorial waters. Beyond these territorial waters, states' powers become more limited: a coastal nation's sole exploitation rights over natural resources (e.g., minerals, oil and fish) extend 200 nautical miles (370 kilometres) from the baseline to form exclusive economic zones. Beyond these boundaries, multiple stakeholders assert claims over the ocean: Multinational corporations seek free and safe passage to transport goods and raw materials, as do the economies and consumers who demand them; local fishers and industrial fishing vessels struggle over fishing grounds; and global environmental activists seek to protect endangered ecosystems.

First order governance principles defining the rights and responsibilities of states are laid down in the United Nations Convention on the Law of the Sea (UNCLOS), which was signed in 1982 and entered into force in 1994. Among the Convention's main achievements are agreements on the areas of state authority, rights to resource exploitation, free passage, and obligations for safeguarding the marine environment. However, as continuing disputes over the reach of territorial waters and the continental shelf show, second order governance is crucial to enforcing the Law of the Sea. While the UN has no direct implementation role, the Convention establishes three UN bodies: the International Tribunal for the Law of the Sea to adjudicate disputes; the International Seabed Authority to control resource exploitation of the seabed; and the Commission on the Limits of the Continental Shelf to advise states in establishing limits. Other UN specialised agencies such as the UN Development Programme, UN Environment Programme and UNESCO are involved in addressing, but not regulating, specific governance challenges such as sustainable fishery, pollution and maritime livelihoods. In the European Union, the Commission's Directorate-General for Maritime Affairs and Fisheries oversees development and implementation of the common fisheries policy and the integrated maritime policy.

Other stakeholders engage in a variety of ways to influence and promote better governance of the ocean 'commons'. Nongovernmental organisations such as Conservation International and the World Wildlife Fund (WWF) are forming broad partnerships with governments and businesses to conduct research, educate the public, and develop new ways to manage marine ecosystems. On the side of business, many members of ocean industries are engaged in the World Ocean Council (WOC), an association aiming to stimulate 'corporate ocean responsibility' through research, education, and innovation. For its part, the Marine Stewardship Council, an independent NGO originally founded by WWF and Unilever, seeks to set and implement standards for sustainable fishery through product certification and education.

While the oceans have been governed by customary law for centuries and are nowadays subject to the Convention on the Law of the Sea, multiple actors must be involved to ensure the implementation of its principles. While the UN bodies established by the Convention have the power to advise and adjudicate the disputes of member states, it takes initiatives and actions of other governmental, civil society and business actors as well to hold stakeholders accountable for their actions and foster ideas for promoting ocean health as a global public good.

ise of raw materials (Box 1.4). Both ocean and Internet governance have the added challenge of managing both the protection of global commons and private commercial use, bringing into focus issues such as property rights and global public goods.

Chapter 2 of this Report revisits the management of interdependencies from a global public goods perspective, and clarifies how those involved in public policymaking nationally and internationally within the realm of the state, the market and civil society could resolve and properly balance risks and opportunities as well as cooperation and competition. Doubtlessly each of these strategies has its place. But it could be destabilising if competition–going it alone, if necessary, by using one's economic or military might–were chosen where international cooperation would be the preferable option for all. In fact, national and private interests can often be best achieved through cooperation–management of spillover effects; seeking policy buy-in of others; and, importantly, more participatory governance. Likewise, deterrence, coercion and exercise of power may have their place in addressing interdependencies, but the shadow of authority, strategic coalition building and trust building measures towards workable solutions may be more optimal in the end.

The Report does not start from a normative perspective. It recognises that we live in a world of diverse and differing policy priorities based on different normative foundations and deep-seated value dispositions that lend themselves to different interpretations of concepts such as democracy, human rights, justice and equity. Recognising such differences, the Report explores which policy thinking and rationales and organisational arrangements have emerged in response to today's changing realities; which seem to hold promise in different contexts; and what lessons can be drawn from these experiences that could help particular actor groups realise their policy goals while fostering global stability, growth and sustainability.

Governance Performance

The examples in the text boxes–and with greater analytic depth in Chapter 2 as a whole–show that governance is rarely some simple command-type structure where the exercise of power leads to predictable actions to achieve some desired outcome. It is not about some direct input-output relationship addressing well-defined and contained public problems. This may work in limited circumstances, but is in no way characteristic of contemporary governance challenges. Even the hamburger example revealed the interplay between different actors and the connections between policy fields.

Rather, governance includes multiple actors or stakeholders, multiple levels and policy fields, frequently contested problem frames and definitions. There are spill-ins and spill-outs across levels, actors and fields–the result of the interdependencies characteristic of a globalising world which is also evident at more local levels. In sum, governance is a system of related, nested parts whose interdependence in political, legal and economic terms implies shared scope of autonomy and responsibility. For some actors like governments, this addresses notions of sovereignty, as Chapter 2 discusses, and for others, degrees of independence and hierarchy. It is these kinds of systems that are of central interest to this Report.

How then are we to understand the performance of such systems in terms of good governance? What first and second order arrangements and ways of managing interdependencies bring about the effective, efficient, and reliable set of legitimate institutions and organisations dedicated to dealing with a matter of public concern? For this purpose, the Report adopts a conceptual model first introduced by Linz and Stepan (1978) to study the performance and stability of political regimes. While they looked at regime performance over time, the model proposed here (Figure 1.1), would look at governance systems and distinguish between:

- ***Legitimacy*** involves two mutually reinforcing components: it requires adherence to the institutional rules and regulations by both the majority of actors and those in position of authority based on first order allocations of responsibilities, rights and obligations; and it requires trust on the part of those affected to uphold these rules and regulations. For example, we expect the eurozone countries to uphold the Stability Pact, and their populations to have confidence in the ability of their governments to do so; just as the legitimacy of a local school board depends on its proper discharge of duties and the confidence of teachers, parents and students in the organisation.
- ***Efficacy*** is the capacity of those in power and leadership positions in the relevant organisations and regulatory agencies of governance systems to find solutions to the public problems identified, both strategically as well as in the short to medium term. In this sense, we expect the eurozone governments and central banks to find a solution to the euro

crisis, just as the efficacy of the California legislature rests on finding a proposal for a balanced budget by not raising direct taxes.
- **Effectiveness** is the capacity of those charged with second order governance to implement the strategies, policies and measures formulated, and with legitimate means yielding desired results. For example, even if the California Senate finds a proposal to balance the budget and not raise direct taxes, can the administration actually implement the plan, and deliver on its promise in efficient and effective ways without violating some other laws or agreements? Can proposals to safeguard the oceans that most actors regard as efficacious actually be implemented efficiently to yield effective results?
- **Performance** is the 'dependent variable' in terms of good governance, defined as the capacity of the governance system to meet set goals, or at least attain a level of performance seen as satisfactory by key stakeholders to maintain stability over time. Bad governance, in turn, would be systems that underperform and reveal instabilities.

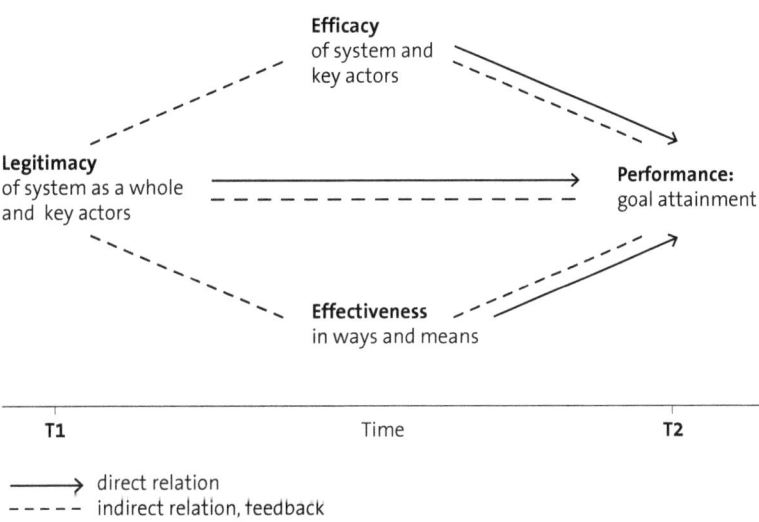

Figure 1.1 **A model of governance performance**

Thus, the performance of a governance system depends on three crucial aspects and their interrelationships: legitimacy (are trusted actors playing by the rules, and is the system as a whole to be trusted?), efficacy (do they know what they are doing?), and effectiveness (do they achieve acceptable results with reasonable means?). The legitimacy of the governance system in place becomes a positive and negative reinforcer that magnifies the effects of efficacy and effectiveness on performance and vice versa. Governance becomes a process[8].

Indeed, as Chapter 3 argues for financial regulation, ill-performing governance systems are unable to solve trade-offs that then affect the legitimacy of key actors, their plans and performance. Inabilities to address trade-offs such as liquidity vs. moral hazard or accountability vs. effectiveness cause financial governance systems to enter a downward spiral that can only be halted and potentially solved politically as first order decisions rather than through technical fixes to improve efficacy.

Chapter 2 introduces the notion of governance readiness, defined as the degree to which intended policy outcomes are actually achieved. It offers a complementary view to the model proposed in Figure 2 above, and addresses a number of key dimensions that refer to i) the improvements or modifications of existing governance systems; and ii) the incremental and more fundamental innovations needed when incompatibilities arise. Activities to improve and modify governance systems are frequent, yet fall short of meeting requirements once conditions change in more profound ways. The latter are rarer, yet of a more fundamental nature as they require thinking beyond the status quo and may involve greater uncertainty. In other words, good governance demands not only performance of a given system to secure legitimacy, but also the anticipation of, and reaction to, changing conditions.

Innovation

How, then, does good governance come about and how is it maintained? How can an overall fit between the functioning of governance systems and the governance requirements of policy fields be achieved and maintained? Governance systems are rarely designed from first principles and from some kind of tabula rasa; rather, they evolve from existing systems and through creative tensions between governance requirements, performance and legitimacy (Figure 1.1).

As explained in greater depth in Chapter 4, there are two perspectives on how such evolution occurs: one emphasising the discontinuous (Christensen 1997), the other the continuous process of governance innovation (Moore 2005). In the first view, governance systems are assumed to pass through relatively long periods of stability, building up inertia and thereby reducing their fitness over time. Unexpected bursts of fundamental changes are then triggered in response to threats, uncertainty, or crisis. The second perspective emphasises gradual changes in governance systems. In this view, new elements are introduced into an existing governance system (recombination), or a governance system relocates or expands into new contexts, policy fields or jurisdictions (refunctionality). Together, the two processes shape the system's evolution as they improve efficacy and effectiveness, with positive impacts on performance and legitimacy.

Clearly, both perspectives are useful for understanding governance changes, and the processes they imply are rarely mutually exclusive. Punctuated equilibriums and more gradual developments can be present at the same time, and indeed the former can create opportunities for the latter: the change in global power relations set in motion after 1989, the rise of the emerging markets, similar epochal events like climate change or the Internet will take time to sort themselves out, not in the least because they imply serious challenges to conventional notions of national sovereignty. Hence, design innovations and policy reforms are dearly needed.

In this Report we describe and even suggest a number of governance innovations that reflect both of these perspectives and touch on many levels, actors and policy fields. In general, these innovations suggest that there are no larger ideologies or visions of and for governance being developed–let alone debated–that in scale and ambition rival the organising and mobilising power of neo-liberalism or social democracy (Judt 2010). They are about making systems more efficacious and effective, and they are not about some new overall attack on root causes of some systemic ill or another. This finding resonates with Chapter 2, and the finding that governments are better at maintaining and improving often entrenched governance systems, even if they are increasingly incompatible with governance requirements, than pursuing more fundamental reforms, especially at the global level.

Indicators

The conceptual frameworks for governance performance and readiness presented in this Report serve one important function: they help identify the kinds of indicators and information needed to measure how well governance systems perform, and how ready they are to meet today's and future challenges. While attempts to quantify governance have grown in scale and scope, they tend to focus on the administrative capacity and efficiency as well as ills such as corruption or regulatory failures, and have addressed at most indirectly policy outcomes and the overall fit between governance requirements and the systems in place.

This, however, is what this Report attempts to do: lay the foundations for a conceptually grounded system of governance indicators that can be developed over time. As Chapter 5 will present in more detail, such a system measures indicators for three essential components: governance readiness in relation to governance requirements to gauge the gap between what is in place currently and what would be required given current and future governance conditions; governance performance in relation to policy outcomes and welfare effects, as seen in the interplay between legitimacy, efficacy and effectiveness; and innovativeness to assess the degree to which actors generate new ideas and approaches for governance.

Conclusion

As noted at the outset, this Report is about the state of governance today, with its changing conditions. It represents the analysis of a team of interdisciplinary experts assembled by the Hertie School of Governance, with each chapter examining governance challenges, opportunities and solutions at different levels and from different perspectives.

The next chapter explores the question of why we are today facing an apparently lengthening list of global challenges and why many of these challenges remain unresolved although they entail high costs, including, in some cases, potentially disastrous and irreversible consequences. The starting hypothesis is that the reason for today's crisis-proneness–or, put differently, today's apparent governance un-readiness–is that: (1) the present governance systems, nationally and internationally, are not geared to address such challenges; and (2) the required governance reform steps lack political support. The chapter tests this conjecture in three steps. First, it examines today's global challenges through the analytical lens of global public goods in order to better understand the types of governance requirements they pose. Second, the chapter scans various global policy fields in order to spot the types of policy responses with which global challenges have been met and whether these match, or deviate from, the identified governance requirements. In a third step, the chapter suggests factors that could help explain the observed response pattern.

Chapter 3 is about financial and fiscal governance–the governance challenge in focus for this Governance Report. The first part considers the politics of global finance and presents a series of trade-offs that confront policymakers when they think about the design of global financial governance–liquidity vs. moral hazard, accountability vs. effectiveness, and domestic politics vs. international commitments. To make these trade-offs concrete and to consider the practical issues of supranational institution-building and supranational cooperation, the next section discusses the evolution of financial regulation in Europe. The final section then thinks about how capital flow imbalances are part of more general macroeconomic imbalances, and it considers the politics of adjustment in both surplus countries (like Germany) and deficit countries (like Greece).

Chapter 4 offers conceptual guidance for understanding governance innovation. It then presents a set of governance innovations, describing the governance challenge that is addressed, how it is addressed, and the mechanisms affecting the innovation's potential success in fostering significant improvements. This section will remain an integral part of future editions of the Governance Report. Over time, it aims to become a central repository that not only features contemporary examples of governance innovation, but also keeps track of and evaluates the progress of previously presented innovations.

Chapter 5 on governance indicators reflects the multi-level and multi-actor approach to governance that the Report adopts, and presents the initial contours of a future three-pronged indicator system with three components: readiness, performance, and innovativeness. In a second step, the chapter presents select sets of indicators to explore and indeed underscore the usefulness and feasibility of such an indicator system.

A concluding chapter presents the major implications that follow from the Report and spells out concrete policy recommendations, addressing them, to the extent possible, to specific actors and decision makers.

The Governance Report 2013 is the first in a series of annual reports. Future editions will both present new analyses and track the development of the challenges, innovations and data presented here, and especially, review the fate of the recommendations made.

Endnotes

1 http://www.apromiserenewed.org
2 On public budgeting in Brazil, for example, see Bräutigam (2004) and Wood and Murray (2007).
3 A good overview of the acquis can be found at: http://ec.europa.eu/enlargement/enlargement_process/accession_process/how_does_a_country_join_the_eu/negotiations_croatia_turkey/index_en.htm.
4 For example, the Health Impact Fund (http://healthimpactfund.org/).
5 See the websites of the Truth Commission (http://www.truthcommission.org/) and the International Criminal Court (http://www.icc-cpi.int/). See also Glasius (2006).
6 See Scharpf (1999), Zürn (1998, 2000), Worldwide Governance Indicators (http://info.worldbank.org/governance/wgi/index.asp), as well as the Bertelsmann Foundation's Sustainable Governance Indicators (http://www.sgi-network.org/).
7 The field of governance indicators, reviewed in Chapter 5 of this Report, is essentially about how to link first and second order governance characteristics to output and outcome performance, and, ultimately legitimacy.
8 The governance performance model based on Linz and Stepan's original approach serves as a conceptual framework primarily against which to examine the role of actors across policy fields and levels, and to guide the selection and development of governance indicators (see Chapter 5). The model incorporates approaches that distinguish between input legitimacy (modes of political participation by those affected by certain policies), output legitimacy (problem-solving capacity and impact of policies) and throughput legitimacy (procedural fairness and accountability). It goes beyond conventional input-output thinking by emphasising feedback loops and over-time performance in achieving results and maintaining stability.

II. Meeting Global Challenges
Assessing Governance Readiness

by INGE KAUL

The world is facing a lengthening list of global challenges–excessive volatility in international financial markets; global climate change; the 'end of oil', and hence, the need to develop new alternative energy sources; the spectres of land and water scarcity; ever-fiercer competition for market shares, investment and job opportunities; illicit trade and the accompanying rise in crime and violence; as well as growing global inequity and civil uprisings, not to mention security challenges like the persisting problem of nuclear proliferation or the risks of cyberwar.

According to the *Global Risks 2011* report of the World Economic Forum (WEF 2011), the prospect of contagion between these challenges is rapidly growing. Should such risk-clustering occur, disastrous impacts could result, leading the authors of the WEF report to conclude that the world can neither afford any further major challenge nor allow the present challenges to linger unresolved for much longer.

> *What does the lengthening list of global risks tell us about the world's state of readiness to govern global challenges?*

Yet, a major political breakthrough does not appear to be imminent in any of the above-mentioned global-issue areas. Why is this? And, more fundamentally, what does the lengthening list of global risks tell us about the world's state of readiness to govern global challenges?

The purpose of this chapter is to explore these two interrelated questions. The first section draws on the definitions of the concepts of governance and governance readiness introduced in Chapter 1 and suggests that the reasons for today's lengthening list of global risks could be that: (1) the present governance systems, nationally and internationally, are not geared to address such challenges; and (2) the required governance reforms lack the necessary political support.

The remainder of the chapter tests this conjecture in three steps. First, drawing on the theory of public goods and global public goods (GPGs), the next section discusses what it would take in terms of governance to provide a decisive, corrective policy response to global challenges. Second, scanning various policy fields for recent governance innovations, the following section shows that change along the identified lines is happening, albeit slowly and hesitantly. Third, in explaining the hesitant response pattern, the subsequent section refers to a number of factors that give rise to the sovereignty paradox: States, notably their governments, are losing policymaking sovereignty, because they hold on to conventional strategies of realizing sovereignty, which make them shy away from international cooperation. But, in policy fields marked by GPG-type challenges and interdependence, such behaviour actually undermines rather than strengthens states' policymaking capacity.

But, how could we escape from the policy trap in which the world appears to be caught at present? The concluding section suggests, as a possible way out, exploring strategies that would allow states and governments to better combine openness and policymaking sovereignty. If retreat from globalisation is an infeasible option, a more promising alternative would be if all nations agreed to exercise their sovereignty so that it would be fully respectful of the sovereignty of other nations, what is called here 'responsible sovereignty'. In more detail, the argument is as follows.

Governance Readiness: Conceptual Considerations and a Conjecture

As Chapter 1 of this volume shows, the literature on governance offers a bewildering array of definitions. Yet, in whatever guise governance appears, it tends to be a complex process of actions through which an actor or multiple actor groups–all with potentially varying preferences– seek to generate a certain policy outcome. In this chapter we are especially interested in governance processes that aim at generating public policy outcomes or public goods, that is, things and conditions that exist in the public domain and are there for all, for better or worse–like the global challenges whose governance requirements we seek to understand.

For the most part, governance occurs within a more or less firmly established institutional framework composed of principles and norms about the modalities of governance; expectations about which are appropriate and legitimate roles of various actors; and the organisational set-up through which actors seek to accomplish their policy purposes. These features may vary over time and space, depending on factors such as socio-cultural traditions or the level of economic and political development that a particular community or polity has attained; and they may vary over issue areas. To illustrate, governing an issue like nuclear non-proliferation would not only have different actors and stakeholders around the table than, say, the issue of controlling HIV/AIDS in Africa. Together with the actors and interest groups would, also, vary such aspects as negotiation strategies, implementation mechanisms, and compliance and effectiveness monitoring.

Therefore, it is important to discuss governance in respect to the outcomes they are intended to help generate. Governance systems are tools of policymaking; the ends are the goals to be achieved; and in the interest of governance readiness the former should fit the latter. Accordingly, a sign and measure of governance readiness would be the degree to which intended policy outcomes are actually achieved.

Yet, as governance conditions including policy goals as well as power structures and political ideologies are likely to change continuously, perhaps even swinging back and forth, governance readiness in many cases is likely to be a moving target: It might exist today but be gone again tomorrow if, for example, new knowledge, new technologies or new financial resources become available, prompting a shift in policy priorities, preferred policy instruments and patterns of governance. Importantly, as institutional economists have shown (see, among others, North 1990), institutions tend to be slow in adjusting to changed realities so that, sometimes even for prolonged periods of time, mismatches can occur between the governance requirements that policy challenges entail and the structure and functioning of the present governance systems.

Types of governance requirements and their implications for governance readiness

In light of the above, it could thus be useful to distinguish between governance requirements that are essentially compatible with the existing institutional governance framework and the given political and socio-economic constellations and governance requirements that do not fit into existing governance contexts. The latter could either call for innovations that change the basic features of a particular governance system like the governance arrangement existing within a particular country, or involve governance transformations that go to the core of the present world order as a whole.

An example of foundational governance change within only one particular country or group of countries is the Arab Spring, the overthrow of the autocratic regimes that we recently witnessed in several countries of the Arab region. The promotion of economic openness during the 1980s/1990s, on the other hand, illustrates a change process of world-order quality, as it stands in sharp contrast to the Westphalian world order and its basic principles of inviolability of national borders and non-intervention.

System-compatible governance requirements might include those listed as categories 1 to 3 in Box 2.1, that is, governance processes that aim at the maintenance, improvement or modification of well-entrenched governance functions within existing governance parameters. Governance requirements with system incompatibility are categories 4 and 5, with category 4 initiatives pertaining only to one country or one set of countries and category 5 initiatives involving transformations that touch the core elements of the present world order and, thus, the basic relations among states as well as, possibly, those between state and nonstate actors, including market actors.

From the viewpoint of analysing governance readiness, the category 4 and category 5 type governance requirements are of special interest. In their case more so than in the others, 'governance reform' itself becomes a policy

> **Box 2.1 A Functional Categorisation of Governance Requirements**
>
> The governance requirements that policy issues might entail can be grouped into the following functional categories:
>
> 1. *Maintaining* established governance systems and processes aimed at generating agreed-upon policy outcomes;
> 2. *Improving* particular aspects of existing governance routines in terms of their effectiveness, efficiency and, perhaps, also equity, without altering their basic structure and functioning;
> 3. *Introducing innovations* without, however, altering the basic structure and functioning of the existing systems and processes;
> 4. *Promoting transformative change* in the basic structure and functioning of a particular existing system and related processes; and
> 5. *Promoting transformative change* in the core elements of the world order.

purpose that requires governance.[1] In other words, lagging adjustment of a governance system to the overall context in which it has to function could be a major cause for policy issues to become stalemated.

A possible conjecture

The foregoing analysis suggests that today's lingering, unresolved global challenges could, among other things, entail governance requirements of the category 5 type–that is, governance reforms that call for a reshaping of some of the basic features of the present world order. This seems plausible, because such challenges have arisen in several issue areas, which could mean that they have a common, cross-cutting cause.

Thus, it can be conjectured that the reasons for today's apparent unreadiness in terms of meeting global challenges is that: (1) the present systems of governance, nationally and internationally, are not yet geared to addressing global challenges; and (2) the required governance reforms lack, at least for the time being, the necessary political support.

In order to substantiate this conjecture further, the next section looks more closely at the governance requirements that global policy challenges tend to entail.

Identifying the Governance Requirements of Global Policy Challenges

Global policy challenges are challenges that cut across national borders, potentially–and often, also actually–affecting the populations of many, if not all countries, for better or worse. This shared characteristic signals that global challenges belong to the category of goods that economists call 'public goods'. In fact, they often constitute global, i.e. border-transgressing, interdependent, public goods (GPGs). (See Box 2.2

As the following discussion shows, it is important to take the global public good nature of global challenges into account in order to fully understand the governance requirements they pose and how to respond to them. In fact, the analysis highlights six governance requirements (GRs) that need to be fulfilled, if the challenges are to be met. They include:

- *GR1:* Averting the risk of dual actor–market *and* state–failure from which GPGs tend to suffer
- *GR2:* Fostering the fairness of international cooperation as a means of stimulating willingness to cooperate
- *GR3:* Enhancing the management of cross-border spillover effects
- *GR4:* Promoting result- and issue-orientation, and to this end, the bridging of the conventional foreign/domestic divide
- *GR5:* Recognising the global public domain as a policy space that, too, requires strategic leadership
- *GR6:* Recognising policy interdependence and the fact that in GPG-type policy areas international cooperation, often, is the best way of realising national interests.

As the discussion below shows, basic governance reforms are needed, if globalisation is to be better managed.

Reducing the risk of dual actor–market and state–failure

As empirical studies have shown and the theory of public economics predicts, public goods are at a risk of being underprovided because the very fact of their being public and available for all might tempt individual actors into free-riding. Individual actors–be they persons, firms or state entities–may not reveal their true preference and demand for a public good, lest they be asked to contribute to its provision. They avoid indicating interest in the hope that others will step forward and provide the good, which they will then, once it is available, also be able to use and benefit from–free of charge. This is why under-investment occurs and public goods tend to be underprovided.

A similar problem arises in the case of spillover effects (or externalities) generated by individual consumption and production activities. Examples are the noise that a radio or lawnmower may produce, disturbing the peace and quiet of neighbours or the polluting substances that a firm releases into a river. Another–positive–example would be the sharing of new knowledge

---

Box 2.2 Introducing Public Goods and Global Public Goods

Standard economic theory distinguishes between two main categories of goods: private goods and public goods.

- *Private goods* are goods that can be parcelled out and made excludable, so that clear property rights can be attached to them.
- *Public goods*, by contrast, are goods that are nonexcludable, meaning that the goods' effects (benefits or costs) are there for all.

If a good is nonexcludable and nonrival in consumption so that one person's use of the good or one person's being affected by it does not diminish its availability for others, the good is said to be pure public. Examples are peace and security. If a good possesses only one of these properties it is impure public. The atmosphere, for example, is nonexcludable but rival in consumption, because unrestricted pollution can change its gas composition and contribute to global warming. Patented pharmaceutical knowledge illustrates a nonrival good, whose use has, at least for a limited period of time, been made excludable. So, it, too, falls into the category of an impure public good.

The public effects of a good can be of different geographic—local, national, regional or worldwide—reach; and they can span across one generation or several generations.

Global public goods are goods whose benefits or costs are of nearly universal reach or potentially affecting anyone anywhere. Together with regional public goods they constitute the category of transnational public goods.

It is important to emphasise that, in the present context, the term 'good' has no value connotation. It is used as a short form for the goods or products, as well as services and conditions that exist in the public domain.

Also, in most cases, publicness and privateness are not innate properties of a good but the result of a social or political choice. Therefore, it is important to distinguish between the potential and de facto publicness of a good. For example, land can be freely accessible to all; or it can be fenced in, and be made excludable.

Globalness is a special form of publicness; and in most cases, it, too, results from a policy choice, e.g. a decision to promote free trade or financial liberalisation. Thus, while some global public goods are naturally global and public like sunlight, many others are human-made, including the international communication and transportation systems or the goods of communicable disease control, financial stability, or peace and security.

Source: This box draws on Kaul and Mendoza (2003). The interested reader may also wish to consult Barrett (2007); and Sandler (2004).

or information that contributes to an improved general understanding, for example, of a particular health challenge. Externalities such as these are public effects that individual actors do not take into account when making their consumption or production choices. As a result, negative externalities are often over-produced, undermining the availability of certain public goods like 'peace and quiet' for others. Conversely, positive externalities may be underprovided, but also lead to an underprovision of public goods like 'good public health conditions'.

Economic theory refers to public goods and externalities also as cases of market failure. Nationally the state is expected to step in and encourage or, if necessary, even coerce us as individual actors to contribute our share to the provision of desired public goods. Yet, internationally, the institution of the state has no full equivalent. Only a few international organisations, among them the United Nations Security Council and the World Trade Organisation (WTO) have been endowed by their member states with limited coercive powers.[2] For the most part, however, international cooperation among states has to happen voluntarily.

Yet, when appearing internationally, states are also individual and, hence, quasi-private actors, because they tend to pursue their national interests that may not necessarily be in line with global exigencies and goals or with the priorities and preferences of other nations. And they, too, tend to free-ride.

As a result, GPGs face a dual risk of free-riding, namely free-riding on the part of both markets and states, and are, therefore, even more likely to suffer from underprovision than purely national public goods.[3] An important governance requirement of GPGs, thus, is that measures are in place to discourage the free-riding of states and encourage their willingness to cooperate, including, for example, their willingness to cooperate in institutionally embedding globalising markets.

Fostering fair and just international negotiations

Not all reluctance to engage in international cooperation necessarily reflects a collective action problem like free-riding on the part of states. Rather, in a world that is marked by wide disparities and differences, the same GPG might generate different utility for different groups of people, including countries, depending on their state of income and development, their geographic location, or socio-cultural and political conditions. Thus, an international agreement that generates net benefits for some could, potentially, entail net costs for others, and might, thus, be viewed as unfair by them.

Yet, as international relations scholars (see e.g. Axelrod 1984) have emphasised for many years, clear and significant net benefits are important for international cooperation to work because it has to happen voluntarily; therefore, it needs to be incentive compatible: All parties must be genuinely motivated to support, and act on, what was jointly decided.

Strengthening national-level management of cross-border spillover effects

In part, GPGs are the drivers of globalisation. Without concerted, transborder harmonisation of formerly more nationally shaped public goods like property rights or trade and investment regimes, the integration of markets would hardly have been possible. But, in part, GPGs are also the result of globalisation. To the extent that borders were opened up not only did intended cross-border activity increase but also unintended activity–spillover effects (or externalities) from abroad–affected the availability of public goods in and, thus, the welfare of, other nations.

So, if states were to be more watchful about the effects that their national policy actions and their consumption and production choices have on other countries, fewer global challenges would exist. As the literature on subsidiarity suggests, encouraging such a bottom-up approach to dealing with global challenges might, in many cases, have important advantages over a more centralized approach in terms of efficiency and equity, and thus, also effectiveness, as it might allow states to pursue context-specific policy approaches.

In fact, given that many, if not most, GPGs emerge from a summation process, i.e. from concerted national-level policy action like the harmonisation of property rights or trade laws that fosters market integration, national-level externality management is often not merely a desirable policy option but, as the next point shows, a technical compulsion that must be met in order to get to the good.

Promoting issue-focus and result-orientation

As the national availability of globalised public goods often depends on policy actions taken elsewhere, the provision status of global public goods can, in many cases, not be altered by unilateral action alone. Rather, it may require inputs from different actor groups, including perhaps nations worldwide, and, thus, constitutes a case of policy interdependence. Moreover, the provision path of a good is likely to be highly issue-specific.

Therefore, a further important governance requirement is to add 'issue focus' to today's set of organisational criteria and to think in terms of issue management in order to ensure that all required inputs fall in place and the desired GPG actually emerges.

Such issue management would, at the same time, be an important step towards a strengthened result-orientation, i.e. a focus on resolving a given challenge in a decisive manner and in full so that the to-be-corrected problem of underprovision actually gets resolved and ceases to roam the global public domain.

Providing strategic leadership for the global public domain

Globalisation and the growing importance of GPGs have been an incremental process to which myriad actors have contributed, at different points in time and with different interests in mind. It is then not surprising that synergy as well as conflict exists among GPGs. For example, global policy regimes like the Trade-related Intellectual Property Rights (TRIPS) are aimed at fostering innovation and dynamic efficiency. Yet, as they may lead to more costly pharmaceutical or medical products and services, they could run counter to the global goal of fighting communicable diseases and reducing world poverty.

In order to reduce the likelihood of such conflicts and, wherever possible promote synergy among GPGs, it would thus be important to keep the overall composition of the global public domain in mind and encourage world leaders to provide strategic leadership to ensure its balanced composition. This kind of leadership would also entail spotting early on signs of likely future provision problems like emerging land and water scarcity to which many global risk analyses have begun to draw attention. It would also involve an open, joint deliberation on the question of which goods to globalise and which to keep within the regional or national policy domains. After all, globalness is–just like any other form of publicness–not an innate property of the good. In most instances, it reflects a policy choice. Put differently, the global public policy domain would need to be recognised as a distinct policy space that also needs political attention and design.

Pursuing positive-sum strategies of international cooperation

In order for many of the foregoing reforms to make political sense for national policymakers and their constituencies, a full understanding of the implications of policy interdependence that GPG-type challenges entail would be a further basic prerequisite. Under conditions of openness and policy interdependence, international cooperation is, in many cases, no longer merely a policy option but rather a compulsion that states can ignore only at their peril. This requires a fundamental rethinking of international cooperation rationales and strategies. Importantly, if policymakers are to rebuild their policy-shaping capacity, they need to think in terms of exercising what Nye (2010) called 'smart power', i.e. power not exercised over, but with others in order to more effectively achieve desired policy outcomes.

Power politics or moral and ethical considerations will, no doubt, continue to shape international relations. But, in policy areas involving GPG provision and, hence, policy interdependence, they need to be complemented by positive-sum strategies, i.e. mutually beneficial bargains that make all concerned parties of an international agreement want to 'crowd in' rather than 'crowd out' and actually to help produce the desired GPG.

In sum: The key governance challenge is building an effective system of global governance

Thus, addressing GPG-type policy challenges in an effective way would entail overcoming the foreign/domestic divide that is typical of the present Westphalian world order and, to this end, international cooperation at the national level, e.g. in the form of strengthened externality management, as well as at international, regional and worldwide levels, e.g. in the form of more inclusive and coherent global governance. Important would be that the national and international levels become more closely linked so that the reach of governance and policymaking matches the span of the policy challenges to be addressed.

This finding corroborates point (1) of our starting hypothesis: It shows that the present governance systems require major reforms, including transformations that touch on key features of the present world order. But, to what extent are these requirements being recognised and acted upon? This is the question to which the following section turns.

Current Practices of Governing Global Challenges: Select Evidence of Governance Reforms Underway

Even a cursory look at governance practices in global issue areas today reveals that many measures have recently been taken or are being debated that appear to be heading in the direction of the reform steps described above. However, change along these lines is still spotty, and assessments of the world's governance of global challenges tend to lean more towards 'unready' than 'ready'.

Table 2.1 presents, for each of the six governance requirements discussed in the previous section, an overview of the main types of reform trends underway. Select empirical evidence for each trend is provided below.

Measures aimed at averting the risk of dual–market and state–failure

In the immediate aftermath of the 2008 financial crisis, the G-20 leaders promised to engage in more effective international cooperation in order to ensure a better institutional embedding of financial markets. However, this resolve weakened when the crisis began to ease. More recently, G-20 communiqués shifted their focus from global regulation towards mutual monitoring and assessment, employing instruments such as the Mutual Assessment Plan or the Los Cabos Accountability Assessment Framework.[4]

Table 2.1 **Meeting the governance requirements of global challenges: Select policy responses**

Governance Requirement (GR)	Examples of Fitting Policy Responses Underway
GR1: Averting the risk of dual—market and state—failure	Added emphasis on measures like: • Accountability and reporting requirements • Compliance monitoring, rating and ranking • Use of positive and negative incentives (e.g. financial compensation and sanctions) • Consultative, transparent decision-making • Binding decisions
GR2: Correcting the fairness deficit in international cooperation	Added emphasis on measures like: • More participatory decision-making • Principles stipulating states' common but differentiated responsibility for meeting global challenges • Regionalism
GR3: Strengthened national-level externality management	Added emphasis on measures like: • Formulation of national strategies and preparation of national progress reports • Reporting and monitoring, rating and ranking • Conditionality attached to foreign aid and loans
GR4: Promoting issue-focus and result-orientation	Added emphasis on measures like: • Single-issue mechanisms for the delivery of international cooperation • Public-private partnerships • Development of new mechanisms to facilitate more adequate project finance • Establishment of targets • Cost/benefit studies • Creation of 'global affairs' units in national ministries and departments • Appointment of issue-ambassadors • Special issue representatives of the UN Secretary-General
GR5: Recognising the global public policy domain as a policy space that requires strategic leadership and management	Added emphasis on measures like: • Issue-linkage studies • Establishment of global leadership bodies
GR6: Accepting policy interdependence and the changed rationale for international cooperation, i.e. cooperation in one's own enlightened self-interest	Added emphasis on: • The importance of global, multilateral approaches to global challenges—at the level of rhetoric • Pledges of new and additional resources to meet new and as yet unaccomplished challenges

This trend of governments keeping each other in check through more mutual monitoring of national-level compliance with international agreements can be discerned in more and more global issue areas, ranging from progress towards achieving the Millennium Development Goals (MDGs) to international terrorism control, respect for human rights and the curbing of greenhouse gas emissions.[5]

In addition to such mutual monitoring approaches, states are also increasingly subject to monitoring, review and ranking by various other actors, including multilateral organisations, private firms (including rating agencies), and civil society organisations (CSOs). As Figure 2.1 shows, indicators and indices of governance performance have seen explosive growth in recent years, including indicators and indices that assess countries' and governments' performance in respect to issues like the realisation of human rights, norms of 'good governance', environmental sustainability, global energy security, or competitiveness (Bandura forthcoming).

Government activities are increasingly being drawn into the open, the public sphere, so that governments may find it harder to make international policy commitments and then renege on follow-up action. They can, now, be found out.

Also, intergovernmental negotiations have increasingly been opened up to the participation of nonstate actors. This, too, creates enhanced transparency and may place stronger pressure on states not to free-ride–in terms of making international commitments and in terms of following up on those at the national level.

Thus, it can also be shown that international agreements, increasingly, find an echo in national policy. As Biersteker (2002: 163) notes: 'There has been a general progression, direction or ratcheting up of intrusion into the domestic affairs of states'. I (Kaul 2006) have even suggested that the role of the state has already changed: States today act more as intermediaries

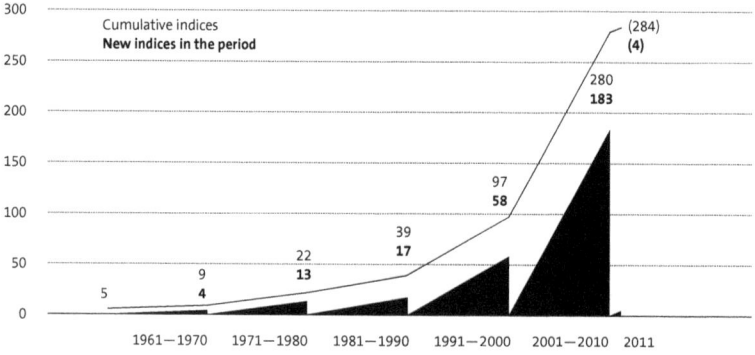

Figure 2.1 **Increase in indices measuring and ranking the performance of states in select issue areas.** Source: Bandura (forthcoming)

between external policy requirements–like international agreements or the various assessments and rankings to which they are subject–and domestic policy preferences.

But in one area, governments continue to free-ride as always, viz. in respect to the financing of international cooperation (see, also Zürn 2011). Most issue areas suffer from finance shortfalls even in high-risk areas like climate change, as can be seen from the shortfalls in promised 'fast-track' funding as well as from the protracted negotiations on the Green Climate Fund.[6] This situation is unlikely to improve now that the debt burden of industrial countries has risen as a result of the recent financial and economic crises. So, despite all problems that arose with public-private partnering and with private finance for development in the past, governments still 'bank' in a major way on private finance in order to meet, for example, climate-related investments in developing countries (UN 2010).

Measures to foster process fairness

As noted above, in terms of outreach and consultation international cooperation has undoubtedly become more open and inclusive. Just think of the thousands of participants that in recent years attended the conferences on climate change and the 2012 RIO+20 Conference on Sustainable Development.

However, international decision-making patterns have, so far, changed only moderately. In the International Monetary Fund (IMF), developing countries were, in 2010, granted a quota increase of about six percent that, in the IMF's own assessment, appears to be inadequate and requires further revision in order to better reflect members' relative positions in the global economy (IMF 2012b; Woods 2010). And after years of having had to participate in G-8 meetings on the sidelines, the developing countries, at least the major emerging market economies among them, have now found a seat at the G-20 table. This happened not only because the developing countries expected to have such a seat, but also because the industrial countries realised that without the participation of these countries key global challenges like the restructuring of the international financial architecture could not be resolved.

However, while some international cooperation venues have become more open and participatory, opposite trends can also be observed. In fact, the G-20, too, is an interesting case in this respect. True, it is more participatory than the G-8 but less participatory than, for example, IMF meetings.

In fact, there seems to be a more general trend among industrial powers towards shifting negotiations out of larger, universal venues towards more informal, smaller groupings (Foot, MacFarlane and Mastanduno 2003; Skidmore 2012). Bilateralism, too, is reported to be on the rise (Heydon and Woolcock 2009; WTO 2011).

Domestically, most countries now observe the principle of matching the circle of stakeholders and decision-makers–letting, for reasons of efficiency, equity, and effectiveness, local issues be decided locally and national issues nationally. Why should this principle cease to apply beyond national borders, when regional or global issues are at stake?

In part, the continuing fairness deficit in multilateral negotiations may be compensated for by the growing trend towards regionalisation that is discernible in the South. As more and more developing countries strengthen their governance capacity, including their capacity for regional integration, regional public goods, increasingly, become stepping stones towards global public goods, with the effect that more countries have a say in matters that concern them and global governance takes on a more open shape.[7]

Process fairness indeed appears to matter in terms of output fairness. Even the modest progress achieved in terms of process fairness to date appears to confirm that. For example, within the World Intellectual Property Organisation (WIPO), developing countries have been instrumental in initiating a debate on how one could better achieve the twin goal of technological innovation and technology transfer in such critical areas like health, climate change and energy, while, of course, also honouring TRIPS obligations.

In the climate change area, too, developing country interventions at the Copenhagen conference in 2010 were decisive for fostering a breakthrough on the issue of financial support for developing countries to assist them in mitigation and adaption efforts. It was at this conference that it was decided to establish the Green Climate Fund, a decision that played a critical role in allowing climate change negotiations to move forward. So, also in this case, did more participatory, harder but fairer bargaining actually lead to a win-win outcome.

Efforts aimed at enhancing national-level externality management

Many corrective steps have been undertaken by state and nonstate actors to limit cross-border spillovers. For example, new global principles have been introduced, including among others, the 'polluter pays' principle set forth in the Declaration of the Earth Summit held in Rio de Janeiro in 1992.[8] In preparation for the 2012 Rio+20 Summit on Sustainable Development, civil society organisations proposed that a principle similar to that of 'polluter pays' also be applied to externality problems outside of the environmental area, notably to the finance area in order to prevent 'toxic' finance products from entering international financial markets and foster enhanced investor protection.[9] Also, a wide variety of international courts and tribunals have developed, especially since the 1990s; and, in many instances, there exists no longer impunity in respect to crimes against humanity (Buergenthal 2001; ICISS 2001; Weiss and Thakur 2010). In the finance area, IMF country surveillance has broadened its focus, now assessing not only whether domestic policies have negative implications for a member state's own stability but also whether it might adversely affect international financial stability (IMF 2012a, 2012c).

Yet, while more and more global norms now require states to reign in cross-border spillovers and while government behaviour in this respect is subject to closer scrutiny, binding global regulation is still limited and, for the most part, non-attainment of set objectives still remains without any major consequence. It may just lead to new resolutions reconfirming the international community's intent to continue addressing the often long-standing but still unresolved global issues.

States still seem to have a strong preference for undertaking corrective steps nationally–to the extent that such steps are also in line with national policy objectives, e.g. with reducing local air pollution or promoting new 'sunrise industries' in 'green growth' areas that could offer national firms new business opportunities and generate for workers new job and income opportunities. Innumerous efforts along this private-good and market-based route to enhanced environmental sustainability are underway.[10] They make important contributions to meeting global challenges like mitigating climate change or promoting global energy security. Yet, uncertain is whether, without firm complementary global regulation, they will ever add up to reach the global goal, e.g. to limit global warming to 2 degrees Centigrade and to do so within the remaining window of opportunity.

Steps fostering issue-focus and result-orientation

The number of international single-issue mechanisms for international cooperation has grown exponentially since 1990, since the end of the Cold War made it possible for international organisations actually to deal with national-level issues–including globalising national public goods (Conceição 2006). The political and economic competition between 'East' and 'West' had formerly severely constrained such debates.

In line with the strengthened issue orientation, countries have appointed more 'issue ambassadors', that is, diplomats not assigned to countries but to such topics as HIV/AIDS, climate change, energy, multilateral trade, or human rights. Similarly, the UN Secretary-General appointed a growing number of eminent personalities as his Special Representatives to issues of global concern.

Some analysts have criticised this trend as a fragmentation of international cooperation (see, for example, Reisen 2010). Yet, they often look at these new developments through the eyes of foreign aid experts. Of course, foreign aid is in large measure a relation between poorer and richer countries and should therefore have a country focus. But, international cooperation now is also about GPG provision and, at times, even about addressing a particular sub-aspect of a GPG like the development of a new vaccine to fight a communicable disease like HIV/AIDS. Such efforts, especially when they are organised as public-private partnerships, require a clear issue-focus and result-orientation.

Nevertheless, critics of the present approach to more issue-focused international cooperation are also right, especially when they point out that the links between the international mechanisms and corresponding national-level initiatives are often still weak and that the financing of GPG provision is, often, taken out of the donor countries' aid budgets, siphoning off resources from the as yet unmet agenda of global poverty reduction.

Another oft-touted problem of issue management is that international organisations tend to have partially overlapping mandates with the effect that several entities deal with the same or similar issues and do so not necessarily in a coordinated manner. This point has, for example, been made in respect to global finance (Davies 2010), energy (Dubash and Florini 2011), climate change (Simon 2011), and global health (Fidler 2010). Yet again, the critics are right and wrong. No doubt, the current mandate situation is still somewhat messy. However, this is so because we are in the midst of a transition from a primarily sector-based organisation of economic activity to an organisational arrangement that will also include an issue focus. For example, 'health' will, in future, most probably be no longer just a health-sector concern but also a focus in trade, water, and energy. Therefore, what van Asselt and Fariborz (2012) argue in respect to climate change governance may, in effect, hold for other issue areas, too, viz. that the pertinent issue for now is not so much whether a centralised or a polycentric governance architecture will be more effective, efficient, and equitable but rather how to sensibly link the different institutional elements that exist.

Considering that the introduction of a strengthened issue-focus remains in a trial-and-error state, it is no wonder that developing countries, too, watch this trend with considerable scepticism. Some even feel that the international mechanisms reflect donor priorities rather than their (the developing countries') priorities and that they are a new form of conditionality. This tells us that the various governance requirements of the global challenges are interlinked. A strengthened issue-focus and result-orientation might need to be accompanied by enhanced process fairness and justice. Thus, the national and the international level remain quite separate; and a genuinely global approach to global challenges does not yet appear to be in sight.

Arrangements for strategic global leadership and management of the global public domain

Due perhaps to the dominance of neo-liberal thinking in recent decades and its emphasis on markets, the notion of public goods as well as that of the public domain have receded into the background. This also holds for GPGs and the global public domain, with two main implications. First, the global growth and development potential of creating new, additional GPGs is often being overlooked; and second, the global public policy domain as a whole suffers from a lack of strategic leadership.

As regards the 'invention' of new GPGs, issues of military security and defence have traditionally been the 'high' diplomacy areas to which the most senior foreign affairs officers were assigned. By now, however, energy and other natural resource issues also fall into this category of high diplomacy because they are increasingly scarce yet critically important for countries' competitiveness, economic growth, and well-being.

The risks of a race to the bottom in the emerging scarcity areas have been recognised. New norms and standards are being formulated in order to prevent, for example, the exploration of ever-more precarious oil sources (TERI-KAS 2011). Nevertheless, countries brace themselves for fierce competition and prepare their military forces for the prevention of attacks on pipelines and ships. Similarly, emerging water and food shortages are driving 'land grabbing' in Africa and other developing regions (HLPE 2011; United Nations Human Rights Council 2010; Vidal 2010).

More and more the realisation is dawning that such races to the bottom do not provide a longer-term, sustainable solution to the emerging scarcity problems. Rather, what is required is a switch from the present zero-sum strategies towards positive-sum strategies. And this switch brings into focus global public goods, notably non-rival goods like knowledge and technology. Hence, we can see a strengthened emphasis on R&D in several of the scarcity areas–a search for developing new knowledge and new technology that could help overcome the current scarcities. Besides new energy technologies, also new drought resistant crop varieties are, for example, being explored.[11]

In the same vein, many governments, academia and think tanks, CSOs, private business, and hybrid venues like the World Economic Forum (WEF) have begun exploring alternative growth and development paradigms, aimed at exploring a decoupling of growth from natural resource use (OECD 2011; von Weizsäcker et al. 2009). Based on the Stiglitz/Sen/Fitoussi report (2010) on the measurement of economic performance and social progress, several countries are now also reviewing their own concepts and measures of growth and development. Of course, a new vision of sustainable global growth also constitutes a global public good–in fact, a good that wants, by design, to be global and public–so that all can benefit from a more sustainable world.

Turning to the second aspect, i.e. leadership for the global public domain, due to varying policy preferences over time and space, many goods have ended up in the global public domain but are not necessarily compatible with each other. For example, on the one hand, the international community would like to achieve progress in global health, including the health of the poor; on the other hand, various elements of TRIPS mitigate against an affordable availability of medical and pharmaceutical products for the poor.[12]

Thus, although the global challenges require an issue-specific approach, their underprovision can, so it appears, not be adequately resolved on an issue-by-issue basis alone. A more comprehensive, synergistic approach is required in order to avoid the emergence of risk interactions. The world needs–but still lacks–a global governance body that could, with full legitimacy, exercise strategic leadership and foster a balanced, dynamic evolution of the global public domain–with the necessary sense of urgency that more and more issues require.

The G-20 is, at times, being referred to as the 'premier forum for international economic cooperation'. But, it is an informal body; its legitimacy is still being queried by some (Subacchi and Pickford 2011); and assessments of its performance point to a checkered record (Vestergaard and Wade 2012).

Steps signalling acceptance of policy interdependence

Whether from a major power or a least developed country, policymakers today recognise the new reality of interdependence at the level of rhetoric. Yet, at the practical-political level, many still seem to avoid accepting the consequences of interdependence, especially in not-so-good economic times.

Not surprisingly, thus, the outcomes of recent international conferences and meetings have often been assessed as disappointing–by some with regret and a call for strengthened multilateralism (Lamy 2012); and by others with a call to forget about the 'big', universal multilateralism and to promote, instead, more mini-multilateralism and more G-type arrangements (Carin 2012). And yet others (Khanna 2011) even suggest letting the powerful just do what they are willing to do.

Yet, although the industrial countries are, at present, living through relatively difficult economic times, international cooperation financing remains a constraint, and the costs of delayed corrective action are rising in a number of issue areas. The economics of GPG provision receive only limited, if any, attention in all these debates on whether more or less multilateralism should exist.[13] No doubt, many states are likely to base their negotiating position on national economic calculations; and firms, notably insurance companies, certainly have realised what especially inaction in the area of mitigating climate change costs them. Yet, global cost/benefit estimates as well as studies on whether mutually advantageous bargains are in the medium and longer run not only more effective but also more efficient are still rare. At least, considerations along these lines do not figure prominently in international debates.

In sum: 'Gearing up', but not yet ready

Thus, while the awareness of interdependence has certainly been growing and the presence of global challenges has unleashed a flurry of response activities, most initiatives seem to stay within the existing governance moulds, and largely address the first three governance requirements (Table 2.1). Indeed, among the requirements concerned with maintenance, improvement and modification of existing governance systems, reforms appear to have advanced most in respect to national-level externality management. In terms of system incompatibilities, the record is stronger on the introduction of issue-focus as an added organisational criterion. The initiatives appear to have been particularly slow as regards the recognition of the global public domain as a new, added policy space and the pursuit of positive-sum strategies, i.e. the acceptance of interdependence, as a guiding policy principle.

Of course, the evidence of governance readiness provided here is selective, as the main purpose of this chapter is to suggest a possible analytical framework. Chapter 5 will take on the initial development of a methodology and explore the data needed for the quantitative measurement of governance readiness not only at the global level, but also at other levels of governance–a task that will become a mainstay of this Report.

From a conceptual perspective, Figure 2.2 shows what such an assessment of governance readiness to address global challenges could look like, assuming that indicators showing the level of fulfilment of the six governance requirements can be found. A value of 100 would indicate full readiness. A value above 50 would signal that two trends are discernible, viz. a high volume of reform efforts and a shifting of governance gears, i.e. an acceptance of policy interdependence. A value of 50 or lower indicates that a certain volume of reform efforts is in evidence, but not yet a shifting of governance gears beyond the level of rhetoric. As actors or systems tend to have a better track record on one governance requirement or another, the resulting readiness space would be irregular.

If we were to attempt to turn the impressions collected here into scores along each dimension, i.e. the extent to which each governance requirement

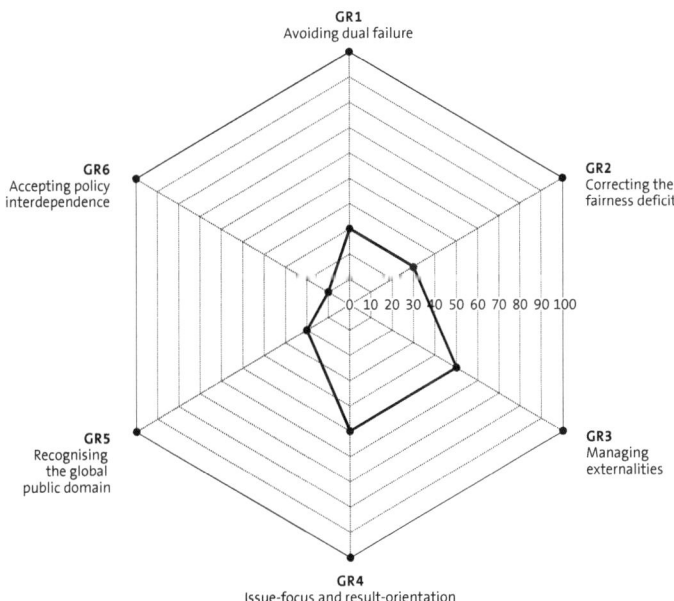

Figure 2.2 **A possible way of assessing the world's readiness to govern global challenges**

has been or is being met, the hypothetical example in Figure 2.2 would suggest an overall governance readiness score of about 35, if equal weight is being assigned to each of the governance requirements discussed here. This would be in line with our assessment of 'gearing up' but hardly ready, an assessment that other studies appear to share (see, for example, Altinay 2012).

Now that we have examined the extent to which changes are being made in the direction of governance readiness—and found that there is still some way to go in terms of addressing global challenges—the next section will trace some of the factors that might help explain why a full-fledged global policy approach to global challenges has not yet emerged.

Why the Half-hearted Responses?

A major reason for much of the policy stalemate we are witnessing appears to lie in the changing global power constellations among states as well as between states and market actors. But, states' self-interest and conceptual blinders also matter. Taken together, these factors give rise to what is called here the sovereignty paradox.

Changing state-state relations

However unsatisfactory the development of developing countries has been during the past several decades, a fact is that it has led to the emergence of new economic and political powers and set in motion the shift from the world of 'Northern', notably western-industrial-country dominance to a multipolar world (OECD 2010a; World Bank 2011). The conventionally powerful states are trying to stem this tide by retreating from the larger multilateral organisations and relying more on bilateral negotiations or taking issues that are important to them to smaller, informal venues like the G-20.

Yet, under conditions of openness and policy interdependence such mini-multilateralism simply does not work in many issue areas, because a problem may have many sources and require, for its resolution, the cooperation of many states. Where such conditions of policy interdependence exist, even the most powerful countries may depend on less powerful ones for corrective action and for their being able to enjoy a particular GPG like good health.

At the same time, however, developing countries have also become more organized. They, too, have now leadership bodies like the summit meetings of the BRICS (Brazil, Russia, India, China and South Africa) or IBSA (India, Brazil and South Africa).

These shifts in the power relations among states have blurred the conventional lines between policy- and rule-setting countries, including mainly the major industrial countries, and policy- and rule-taking nations, including mainly the developing nations. The former, notably the US, are, under the now prevailing conditions, no longer prepared to shoulder the costs of a global leadership role (Jones, Pasqual and Stedman 2009). And the newly emerging powers are not yet fully prepared to step into the resultant global governance vacuum. As a result, international cooperation stutters, especially in issue areas like climate change that entail high adjustment costs for all or any one group of nations.

Changing state-market relations

Faced with the growing trend towards multipolarity and all the uncertainties that this entails, states may, in fact, often find it convenient–and not just because of pressure from private business lobbyists–to rely more on markets and private-good innovations in meeting global challenges. Certainly, markets have a lot to contribute. Private-good innovations like the development of 'green' building materials and cars are critically important, for example, for the world's transition towards a low-carbon economy. However, even the best of private efforts may not allow the world to reach its global goal of limiting global warming to 2 degrees Centigrade. This is likely to require more than what countries are willing to do, if motivated only by their private or national interests.

An added reason for states often shying away from global regulation and matching incentive policies is that policies aimed at reducing tax rates and government expenditures have been a major ingredient of the economic liberalisation and privatisation strategies that have been pursued in recent decades. This has increased states' dependence on financial markets and weakened their capacity to regulate markets, especially global financial markets (see Chapter 3).

States' self-interest and conceptual blinders

As the *Global Risks 2012* report (WEF 2012) notes, especially at a time when multilateralism and concerted state action are needed most, states appear to be particularly weak and reluctant to undertake the necessary policy reform steps. The argument advanced by states to justify this positioning is that they want to guard national policymaking sovereignty. But, as the current policy landscape shows, just the opposite is the case. States are being tossed around by market forces and threatened by environmental crises, like the looming spectre of natural resource scarcity, and by persisting global inequity that gives rise to problems of poor governance, global crime and violence as well as health threats, and importantly, growing global political discontent.

So, why, despite all experiences to the contrary, do states nevertheless hold on to conventional notions of sovereignty and shy away from more decisive international cooperation?

One reason might be that policymakers and parties depend for their staying in power on national constituencies. So, they may prefer to spend as much of the limited public resources they have on 'pure' national purposes and on visible purposes, e.g. on local clean-up efforts after flood or storm events that might be related to global warming.

In addition, policymakers may take for granted a globalisation narrative that can be found in many academic studies and journalistic reports, namely that international cooperation implies delegating policymaking sovereignty that was hitherto held in national hands to international levels, mainly international organisations. However, as the analysis in this chapter has shown, this 'storyline' ignores how global challenges are actually resolved, especially, that many emerge from a summation process of national reform measures.

In sum: Global governance trapped in the sovereignty paradox

Thus, today's often-lamented loss of policymaking sovereignty is, in part, self-inflicted by states. Their shying away from effective international cooperation tips the market-state power balance further in favour of the market actors, while governments find that the harder they try to be sovereign, the more they fail in meeting global challenges, the more they lose the trust and confidence of their electorates–and the less sovereign they are.

So, how to escape from this policy trap?

Conclusion: More Multilateralism– More Sovereignty

An important step forward would be to dispel the prevalent notion that international cooperation necessarily means losing policymaking sovereignty and to make the case for more multilateralism, demonstrating that under conditions of policy interdependence more multilateralism helps states to regain and maintain their policymaking sovereignty. It could, for example, be useful to emphasise that policymaking sovereignty is a special type of freedom–the freedom to choose one's own policy priorities and the paths to achieve those. Freedom is usually seen as based on mutual respect for each other's freedom: If all persons accept to exercise their freedom in a way that the freedom of others is not being jeopardised, all will gain, because their own freedom also stands a better chance not to be undermined by others.

Similarly, the policymaking sovereignty of all states would be enhanced, if all states would agree to exercise their sovereignty in a considerate, respectful, and responsible manner, so that their policies do not adversely impact the sovereignty of others.[14]

Also, a parallel could perhaps be drawn between safeguarding a nation's territorial security and its policymaking sovereignty. In the former case, the international community recognised that a pooling of efforts by all to defend the territorial security of any other sovereign nation provides enhanced border security for all. In the same way, a pooling of policymaking efforts in order to defend countries against undue spill-ins from abroad might have a reinforcing effect on all countries' sovereignty, as it would significantly reduce the probability of their being 'attacked' or, should a major spill-in occur, being left alone to ward it off.

Put differently, it would be important for states and other actor groups to realize that the norm of sovereignty is a GPG itself: it is a good that no one nation can generate alone, because, in order to exist, a nation's sovereignty

---

Box 2.3 **Combining Openness and Sovereignty: Exercising Responsible Sovereignty**

Globalisation is often seen as undermining states' policymaking sovereignty. However, it is not, or at least not just, globalisation that causes states to lose control. An important factor is that states' strategies of international cooperation have not yet been fully adjusted to today's policymaking realities.

In order for states to regain or maintain their policymaking sovereignty under the present conditions of greater economic openness and deepening policy interdependence, they would need to pursue a strategy of more and more effective multilateralism, composed of three core elements.

- Commitment to voluntarily strengthen their national-level management of cross-border spillovers in order to avoid infringing on the sovereignty of other nations and reducing the need for more centralized interventions that might be more complex and difficult to arrange;
- Commitment to stand ready to contribute their fair share to international collective efforts to protect any state's sovereignty that comes under attack, including from the new types of security challenges like financial contagion, 'travelling' viruses, illicit trade or attacks against cyber-security; and
- Commitment to cooperate in meeting global systemic risks like global climate change, excessive current account imbalances, rising global inequity, or the growing threats of natural resource scarcity.

Thus, sovereignty and openness can be combined, if states are willing to deepen their commitment to international cooperation. However, for that to happen, a further condition would need to be met: Fairness and justice in international negotiations would need to be strengthened so that deepening policy interdependence and commitment to cooperate are matched by enhanced mutuality of benefit, persuading all parties that a strategy of mutually supportive, responsible sovereignty actually pays.

has to be granted and respected by all other nations. It is a collectively provided good that can be enjoyed by all; and the larger the number of states that are committed to this norm, the more entrenched it will be; and the more all states can be sure that also their sovereignty will be respected.

It seems the GPG characteristics of sovereignty have been somewhat forgotten in recent decades. Sovereignty is sometimes perceived more as a private or national good: a license for states to pursue whatever policies they wish within their jurisdictions and to join collective endeavours only to the extent that they overlap with national interests that were to be pursued in any case. However, the world now stands at a critical juncture: a choice must be made about how better to combine openness and policymaking sovereignty (see Box 2.3).

One option would be a return to reclose national borders. However, considering today's state of technology and interconnectedness as well as the advances that have been achieved in terms of social, economic and political freedoms, it is hardly conceivable that such an approach could be feasible.

Another, preferable option might, thus, be to forge global consensus around a notion of responsible sovereignty, expecting states to exercise their sovereignty in a way that is fully respectful of the sovereignty of other nations. In fact, as the growing trend towards enhanced externality management shows, states are already moving in this direction. Only, what would need to be strengthened further is the recognition that the world as a whole is not necessarily on a sustainable growth and development path, even if all nations are successful in meeting their national goals. Global systemic risks and limits have to be taken into account, e.g. the 2 degree Centigrade limit of global warming, global financial imbalances that could nourish new financial crises, or excessive global inequality that could destroy the global social and political fabric.

National policy formulation needs to be embedded into the global context in order to reduce the risk of global crises that would, ultimately, also undermine the welfare and well-being of nations that might have tried to retreat from globalisation and reclose their national borders in order to go their own way. By implication, states would need to strengthen their role as an intermediary between the national and the international context, driving the global policy loop by taking national policy priorities to the international level for negotiation and bringing international agreements back down for implementation at the national level.

But why would one assume that global consensus on such a notion of responsible sovereignty could emerge, when the other required reforms of global governance that we have examined in the previous sections are meeting with relatively frail and wavering political support?

The difference between those measures and the notion of responsible sovereignty is that the latter offers a new governance paradigm. It allows policymakers to make sense of the various other steps. As long as governance reforms like those that global challenges require are being viewed from the perspective of the conventional notion of sovereignty, they do not make much sense and are, therefore, being avoided, ignored and opposed. And as long as they do not make sense, the perennial problem of lack of financing is also likely to persist, a problem that again and again has caused international negotiations to falter and agreements to suffer from non-compliance.

But for the notion of responsible sovereignty to be persuasive, it would also be important to develop a systematic theory of global public policy to which policymakers could turn for advice, notably in order to determine when and where international cooperation 'pays'. Today, while, for example, the standard theory of public economics has a national-level focus, international relations theories mainly study international-level phenomena. Of course, a large number of studies address particular global issues. However, many focus on technical aspects; and most of this literature exists in specialised professional journals so that policymakers may hardly be familiar with it. What is still missing is a theory that synthesises all these contributions into a new standard theory of global public policy and, in particular, a theory that helps us better to understand the current problem of dual–market and state–failure in the presence of GPG-type global challenges and how to correct it. We should not, one day, have to repeat saying what many analysts, notably economists, had to say when faced with the 2008 international financial crisis: 'How could we be so wrong?'

So, if there is one further international high-level commission that the UN Secretary-General should consider establishing, it should be a small but fully representative commission charged with the mandate to develop a concept of responsible sovereignty and to submit its report thereon to the UN General Assembly for further deliberation, and possibly, adoption.

Endnotes

1 This challenge of governing a change in governance is sometimes also referred to as meta-governance. See, for example, Jessop (2011).
2 In the case of the UN, for example, only few decisions are of a binding nature, namely those taken by the UN Security Council under Chapter VII of the UN Charter (Malone 2007). Another exception to the generally non-binding nature of international agreements is the Dispute Settlement System of the World Trade Organisation.
3 The type of state failure identified here is not to be confounded with the types of government failure that public choice scholars tend to focus on, namely the self-interested behavior of individual politicians and bureaucrats. Rather the state failure referred to here has its roots in the fact that the present world order is composed of individual sovereign states.
4 See on the issue of responses to the recent financial and economic crises, among others, Eichengreen and Park (2012), Elson (2012), Véron (2012) as well as Chapter 3 in this volume.
5 For more details see the following websites: www.un.org/en/sc/ctc/; http://www.ohchr.org/; www.un.org/millenniumgoals; and http://unfccc.int/.
6 For details, see http://gcfund.net.

7   See, ADB 2011 and IDB's Initiative for the Promotion of Regional Public Goods at http://www.iadb.org/en/topics/regional-integration/what-is-the-regional-public-goods-program,2803.html and Volz (2011).

8   This principle stipulates that national authorities should endeavour to promote the internalisation of environmental costs, taking into account that the polluter should, in principle, bear the costs of pollution.

9   See, http://www.reflectiongroup.org/stuff/input-rio-2012/.

10 For accounts on such national-level initiatives to reduce environmental externalities, see, for example, DB Climate Change Advisors (2011); IEA (2011); REN21 (2011); Weischer et al. (2011); and Wijen et al. (2012).

11 See http://www.cgiar.org/.

12 See, for examples from the health and other issue areas, www.ip-watch.org/.

13 For examples of studies that attempt to assess the costs and benefits of inaction and action on global challenges, see Conceição and Mendoza (2006), Nkonya et al. (2011), and Stern (2007). For a discussion on the methodological issues involved in undertaking such assessments, see, among others, Touffut (2009).

14 It should perhaps be noted that the notion of responsible sovereignty suggested here differs in important respects from the notion of sovereignty as responsibility set forth, among others, by Deng et al. (1996), ICISS (2001) and Jones, Pasqual and Stedman (2009). Sovereignty as responsibility refers to the duty of states towards their citizens, especially their duty to ensure respect for basic human rights. If a state fails in this duty, the international community is seen to have a responsibility to intervene and protect people against unconscionable human deprivation. Thus, sovereignty as responsibility refers mainly to weaker developing nations, failing and failed states and to cases of human rights violation.

The notion of responsible sovereignty, however, refers to all states, rich and poor, developed and developing, and to states' national as well as international responsibilities in all issue areas that the international community might decide to require multilateral cooperation in order to avoid undue infringements of sovereignty.

III. Challenge in Focus
Financial and Fiscal Governance

by WILLIAM ROBERTS CLARK, MARK COPELOVITCH, MARK HALLERBERG, LUCIA QUAGLIA, *and* STEFANIE WALTER

Over the past four years the world has experienced a series of crises. The takeover of Merrill Lynch in March 2008 and the collapse of Lehman Brothers six months later touched off a financial crisis that spread to many parts of the world. Trade dropped precipitously across virtually all countries, and many experienced recessions. Some small countries, first Iceland and Latvia and later Ireland, faced the complete collapse of their banking sectors. Beginning in 2010, the European periphery, including Greece, Portugal, and Ireland, entered a sovereign debt crisis that continues to put pressure on the governance of Europe's common currency. The sovereign debt problems in turn worsen the balance sheets of private sector participants, such as banks.

It would seem that there is nothing novel about this sequence of events. As Reinhart and Rogoff's well-cited 2009 book notes in their study of eight centuries of crises, the cycle that begins with a financial crisis and is followed by a sovereign debt crisis and several years of weak economic growth is one that most countries of the world have experienced at some point. One only has to go back a little more than a decade to the Asian crisis and its spread to Latin America and Russia to find recent examples that seemed to generate similar policy lessons. The then-First Deputy Managing Director of the IMF and noted economist, Anne Krueger, noted in 2004 that the Asian crisis had taught policymakers that countries need prudent monetary and fiscal policies, including the ability to control and lower debt, well-regulated financial markets, and flexible exchange rates. With the exception of the last point, these recommendations apply to Europe today.

At the same time, there are aspects of that crisis and the current one that do not fit Reinhart and Rogoff's sweeping narrative. Since the collapse of the Bretton Woods system in 1973, capital mobility has increased to unprecedented levels, exceeding even the relative freedom capital owners had at the end of the 19th century. Contagion of crises, which was a worry in the Great Depression as bank failures in one country presaged imminent failures in others, happens with greater speed. The reason is that capital owners hold assets in more countries than ever before, and they can more easily move those assets. In theory, this should represent a greater diversification of risk so that a problem in one country does not hurt any investor that much. In practice, this has also left different types of assets more interconnected. It also means that 'mistakes' in business practices, such as relying unduly on one type of asset class like mortgage securities, spread more quickly. Moreover, the greater sophistication of financial products in recent years has meant that investors too often do not understand the actual riskiness of what they own.

This greater interdependence, also highlighted in Chapter 1, has implications for policies designed to address a crisis. For example, several governments during the most recent crisis decided to guarantee all deposits in their banking sectors, which in turn put pressure on other governments to do the same if they wanted to keep deposits in their countries. In Europe, the Irish were the first to do so, just two weeks after the collapse of Lehman Brothers. A few weeks later German policymakers took the same action. In a world that is not that interconnected, these decisions would not have affected economies outside their borders. But in today's world, the results are different. The Irish decision put pressure especially on the United Kingdom to follow suit, as depositors shifted assets from British to Irish banks. The European Union (EU) sharply criticised the Irish action. Once Germany took the same decision, however, efforts to coordinate bank deposit policies as a response to the crisis were essentially dead and each country went its own way. Moreover, the repercussions of Ireland's decision to guarantee its banks continue to be felt today. The country had one of the lowest debt levels in the European Union in 2007, but by 2010 the increasing costs of bailing out its banks meant that markets no longer considered the government's ability to continue to finance its debts as sustainable. The interdependence of Ireland with other countries that share a common currency led to an EU package of financial help for the country at the end of 2010.

> *The capacity to cope with governance challenges is about preventing such crises from happening and making countries less prone to them.*

This European episode provides several important lessons. Problems extend across borders more than before. At the same time, the jurisdictions for most economic policy remain national. Decisions national policymakers take create externalities for others. This suggests that coordination of policies across borders may help all countries. The EU attempted to coordinate policy in 2008-09 during the 'financial' part of the crisis, and it has put in place some new institutions meant to reduce the likelihood of future crises and to coordinate responses to crises when they occur.

We begin our focus on financial and fiscal governance with a discussion of the governance problem in international finance. Following earlier chapters' concerns about power shifts within and between actor groups and their implications for governance, we discuss several trade-offs that affect what sorts of 'solutions' to this problem exist and whether international institutions can ready themselves to deal with these problems. We then discuss financial governance both at the international and European levels. The more detailed examination of developments in financial regulation in the EU highlights the many coordination problems that arise in this field. The next section considers another part of the recent crisis, namely large balance of payments imbalances. It examines what options confront both debtor and creditor countries, and how politics shapes the responses one sees in practice.

This consideration of the political causes of crises, when combined with the causes of macroeconomic imbalances, allows us to ask under what circumstances such crises can be prevented in the first place. One lesson here is that the capacity to cope with governance challenges is about preventing such crises from happening and making countries less prone to them. At the same time, as the section on the EU illustrates, international and regional institutions need to be strengthened to address such crises when they spill over across borders. Whether those solutions can be put in practice depends upon whether the many actors involved can resolve the three trade-offs that face any such solution–liquidity vs. moral hazard, accountability vs. effectiveness, and domestic politics vs. international commitments.

The Governance Problem in International Finance

Given the severity, duration, and geographic reach of the Great Recession, one hardly needs to look far for reasons to justify pursuing reform of the international financial architecture. Nonetheless, it is useful to begin any discussion of the politics of global financial governance by acknowledging the fundamental governance problems of international finance:

- Financial markets and crises are now global and changing rapidly. Indeed, as evidenced by the multiplicity of newfangled financial instruments (e.g. collateralised debt obligations, credit default swaps, structured investment vehicles), global financial markets continue to evolve and become more complex.
- The rules and institutions governing international markets have not kept pace with these rapid and substantial changes. Although the IMF has returned to prominence and is once again playing a central role in the world economy, we still lack a true international lender of last resort in the global financial system.
- We are now entering our fifth decade of the 'post-Bretton Woods era,' which began in 1973, without a formal international monetary system, with individual countries and regions instead choosing a wide variety of exchange rate regimes ranging from free floating to monetary union.
- Financial regulation and supervision remain almost exclusively the domain of national authorities.
- Power and representation within the key international financial institutions (IFIs) are increasingly outmoded, given the rising clout of China, India, Brazil, and other emerging market countries in the world economy.

In short, the existing pieces of global financial governance are incomplete, outdated, and not well suited to addressing the fundamental problems facing the world economy in the wake of the Great Recession. At the same time, unilateral/national policies are unlikely to be successful and raise the spectre of the sort of 'beggar thy neighbour' policies that ultimately undermined the global economy in the interwar period. Thus, there is a strong case for reforming, extending, and redesigning the international financial architecture.

As the Great Recession entered its darkest hours in 2009, policymakers appeared to recognise the urgency of finding solutions to this fundamental governance problem in the global economy. At its April 2009 summit in London, the G-20 reached broad agreement on a three-pronged reform agenda that would address the most pressing problems in global finance. These included:

- Coordinating national fiscal, monetary, and trade policies in order to accelerate a global economic recovery;
- Strengthening supervision and regulation of financial institutions at both the domestic and international levels; and
- Reforming the resources, lending policies and governance of the IFIs.

However, as evident from the stark tensions at the June 2012 G-20 summit in Mexico, countries' general agreement on the need for more effective global financial governance has not been matched by consensus on the specific policies to be adopted in practice.

Difficult Trade-offs I: The Politics of Global Financial Governance

If there is widespread consensus on the broad reform agenda in global financial governance, why is cooperation so difficult and elusive? The answer is that reform presents international policymakers and national leaders with a set of difficult trade-offs. We will focus here on the three most salient for financial governance:

- **Liquidity** vs. **moral hazard**
- **Accountability** vs. **effectiveness**
- **Domestic politics** vs. **international commitments,** which is perhaps the most critical factor shaping current debates and tensions over the scope, speed, and substance of reform.

Liquidity vs. moral hazard

The trade-off between liquidity and moral hazard sits at the heart of debates about how much supranational organisations such as the IMF or the EU should lend to countries experiencing financial crises. This trade-off arises since any 'bailout' package has two simultaneous and inextricable effects. On the one hand, crisis lending directly benefits a country by providing it with the financing (liquidity) needed to service its debts. Indirectly, it may also enhance global financial stability by preventing a crisis in one country from becoming a larger systemic problem. On the other hand, such rescues also create moral hazard–incentives for borrowers and lenders to assume additional risk in the expectation of future bailouts (Crockett 1997). This trade-off presents such organisations and their co-lenders with a difficult choice: lend freely (large amounts on lenient terms) at the risk of increasing future demand for such bailouts, or limit current lending (smaller loans with more extensive conditionality) at the risk of having a country default and triggering a broader financial crisis.

From a purely economic perspective, choices over this trade-off depend on whether a borrower is insolvent or illiquid–that is, whether the country is effectively bankrupt due to bad economic policies, or whether it faces a temporary liquidity problem caused by an unforeseen macroeconomic shock or a 'financial panic' (Chang 1999). In this view, deciding the size and terms of 'bailouts' is a largely technocratic exercise: economists design loans based on country-specific macroeconomic indicators that determine a borrower's financing needs and the amount of policy adjustment necessary to ensure its long-term debt sustainability. To be sure, in the IMF's case macroeconomic factors play a large role in decision-making: past studies have found that loans are larger and contain more conditions when a country has fewer foreign exchange reserves, higher levels of external debt, and a record of past Fund borrowing. Nonetheless, the empirical record of this technocratic view of IMF lending is mixed: many key macroeconomic variables have weak or indeterminate effects on IMF lending.

To take the IMF again as an example, political factors also heavily influence the Fund's choice over the liquidity/moral hazard trade-off. In general, two competing explanations of Fund behaviour are offered. On the one hand, many argue that the IMF is the servant of the United States, which utilises its position as the Fund's largest shareholder to direct credit toward countries it deems economically or geopolitically important. On the other hand, scholars in the public choice tradition argue that bureaucratic politics, rather than powerful states' interests, is the key political factor in IMF lending (e.g., Vaubel 1991; Willett 2002; Dreher and Vaubel 2004). Drawing on principal-agent theory, studies have found that IMF lending behaviour is influenced by the Fund staff's bureaucratic incentives to engage in 'rent-seeking' and/or to exploit 'agency slack' in order to maximise its autonomy, budget, or the likelihood of program success.

As this literature highlights, choices over the liquidity/moral hazard trade-off at the heart of IMF-led crisis lending are as much about politics as economics. This fact has only been reinforced by the Fund's lending behaviour during the Great Recession: it has provided generous financing and terms to several countries (Latvia, Greece, Iceland) with strong economic and geopolitical ties to the US and EU member-states that enjoy substantial influence within the Executive Board. As illustrated by tensions over the terms of Ireland's bailout, however, even these powerful states may disagree over the terms of a Fund rescue package, and these disagreements are often driven more by domestic politics than by real disagreements over the borrower country's economic or financial need.

Accountability vs. effectiveness

A second critical tradeoff confronting policymakers weighing global responses to the Great Recession is the tension between accountability and effectiveness. This trade-off is strongly intertwined with debates about national sovereignty and the domestic political costs associated with delegating authority and resources to the IFIs. The underlying issue here is that the most effective institutions of global financial governance—in terms of maintaining financial stability or managing and resolving crises—are quite likely to be the least accountable from the standpoint of state sovereignty. For example, a 'global financial regulator with real teeth,' as Kenneth Rogoff has advocated, would probably be extremely effective in regulating and supervising international financial markets and minimising cross-border regulatory arbitrage by globally active banks (Norris 2009). Similarly, creating a WTO-style dispute settlement mechanism within the IMF to address questions of currency manipulation would also likely be very effective at resolving the global macroeconomic imbalances that have been a key contributing factor to the Great Recession.

However, creating such powerful new international organisations, or delegating further authority to existing ones, presents a direct challenge to national sovereignty and democratic accountability. This tension is also visible in the discussions of a 'banking union' in the eurozone. One regulator with the ability to investigate and shut down troubled banks would be more effective than the hodgepodge of regulation that now exists, and that we discuss in more detail below. But there remain open questions about accountability, along the lines of first order governance issues as described in Chapter 1. Who appoints the regulator? To whom does this common regulator report? Will domestic populations consider this regulator as democratically legitimate?

Domestic politics vs. international commitments

The final key trade-off shaping the politics of global financial governance is the one governments face between domestic politics and international commitments when considering whether or not to coordinate macroeconomic policies. One can readily identify many recent and historical examples of this tension between the trade, monetary, and financial policies maximising a government's domestic political support and those most conducive to international economic stability. Perhaps the most well-documented of these is the debate over adherence to the gold standard during the interwar era. As the Great Depression wore on during the interwar era, governments faced severe domestic pressure to engage in 'beggar thy neighbour' policies–including competitive devaluations, capital controls, and protectionist trade policies–that directly contradicted their international monetary commitments to fixed exchange rates under the revived post-WWI gold standard.

In the current crisis, governments are wrestling with similar tensions. Calls for the use of trade protection have increased, and a growing number of countries have begun to actively manipulate their exchange rates in order to alter the terms of trade and enhance domestic producers' competitiveness in global markets. In 2010, the Japanese government intervened in foreign exchange markets for the first time since 2004, spending approximately $20 billion in an effort to drive down the yen's value from its 15-year highs against the dollar in order to bolster the country's export competitiveness (Whipp and Garnham 2010). Other countries, including South Korea and Taiwan, followed suit in their own efforts to enhance export competitiveness. European and American policymakers decried these unilateral attempts at currency depreciation, and some observers spoke of the need for an international agreement to prevent competitive devaluations and address exchange rate imbalances through international coordination (Beattie 2010). Even Brazil–whose Finance Minister, Guido Mantega, was the first to warn of an impending 'currency war' in the global economy–imposed capital controls and threatened direct intervention in order to suppress further appreciation of the real (Wheatley 2010).

Prospects for Global Financial Regulation

While the G-20 and IMF have dominated recent discussions about global financial governance, some of the most important changes have taken place behind the scenes. Since the 1980s, a web of international financial regulatory bodies has coalesced around the Bank for International Settlements (BIS) in Basel, Switzerland. The BIS, established in 1930 to administer German war reparations from World War I, has long been a forum for central bank cooperation. Its membership now includes 59 countries plus the European Central Bank, and the BIS hosts the secretariats for a number of important committees that bring together financial regulators from the world's leading economies. These include the Basel Committee on Banking Supervision (bank regulation), the Committee on Payment and Settlement Systems (payments and clearing), and the Committee on the

Global Financial System (market stresses and systemic stability). In addition, the BIS also hosts the secretariat for the Financial Stability Forum (FSF), an umbrella organisation formed, like the G-20, following the Asian financial crisis to bring together regulatory and financial authorities in major economies with representatives of the IFIs and the aforementioned BIS-hosted committees. The FSF has been the main institution linking this growing list of regulatory bodies, and it has spearheaded technical work on several key issues (e.g. offshore financial centres, deposit insurance systems, and highly leveraged institutions) of importance in recent crises.

Together, these regulatory bodies have made substantial progress in developing numerous international financial standards and harmonising financial regulation across the world's major markets. As with the G-7 and the IMF, however, these institutions have, until recently, been comprised only of representatives from the advanced industrialised economies. This changed at the April 2009 G-20 summit in London, where the FSF was elevated in status to the Financial Stability Board (FSB) and membership was extended to the entire G-20, along with Spain and the European Commission. In the ensuing months, talks accelerated among the FSB's participants on a number of key topics, including enhancing regulators' ability to 'unwind' large cross-border financial institutions in the event of failure, strengthening adherence to international financial standards, and the imposition of a potential global levy on internationally-active banks. These are important, if less visible, developments in global financial governance, since the central bankers and regulators involved in the FSB and the other Basel-based institutions meet regularly and have the direct ability to implement policies at the national level.

Nonetheless, we should not overestimate these institutions' role and effectiveness, for several reasons arising from the trade-offs and political variables emphasised above. First, given the market power of the US, UK/EU, and Japan in the global financial system, it is still the case that these countries' national policies–rather than internationally-negotiated standards–have the greatest impact on the activities of internationally-active financial institutions.

Second, the lack of enforcement power in the FSB and the BIS-related committees makes implementation of new financial regulation difficult at the global level, even if G-20 officials can reach agreement on the substance of reform. For global regulatory rules and standards to be effective, national regulators and central bankers must enforce them, and this raises difficult problems of credibility, particularly in some large emerging market economies (Russia, China) where the independence of central bankers and regulatory officials is less clear and institutionalised than in the advanced industrial democracies.

Third, the expansion of these global regulatory bodies to include the full G-20 membership plus additional 'guests' once again raises the problem of global collective action. Although this enlargement makes sense from the standpoint of bringing all of the key borrower and creditor countries in the global financial system to the table, it makes agreement on global standards on new regulations substantially more difficult to achieve. This collective action problem is further exacerbated by the fact most members of the FSB have multiple representatives at the table, depending on how regulatory responsibility is divided among their respective domestic agencies. For example, the US government is represented at the FSB by officials from the Federal Reserve, the Securities and Exchange Commission (SEC), and the Department of the Treasury, while the German government is represented by the Bundesbank, BAFIN (the Federal Financial Supervisory Authority), and the Finance Ministry. In contrast, some countries (e.g. South Africa, Indonesia, Singapore) send only a single finance ministry or central bank official, given that this domestic agency holds consolidated national authority over regulation.

Finally, questions about the evolution of international financial regulation cannot be discussed without also considering cross-national variation in ideas and ideology. In particular, as evidenced by the very different national responses to the banking crises of the Great Recession, there is substantial diversity in national governments' perspectives about the appropriate balance between states and markets, as well as about the legitimacy and efficacy of Keynesian economic ideas concerning countercyclical demand management and economic stimulus packages. For example, while the British government effectively nationalised most of its banking sector at the height of the crisis and the Irish government rapidly moved in to guarantee the debts of its largest banks, the US opted for an alternative series of proposals (e.g. TARP, the 'Geithner plan') aimed at avoiding a banking collapse without full nationalisation or assumption of private debts by the government. At the same time, we have also seen how economic ideologies have contributed to global tensions over the content of regulation, with French and German officials decrying the 'freewheeling Anglo-Saxon' model of capitalism and calling for more extensive regulation of the hedge fund and 'shadow banking' sectors than their American and British counterparts (Le Guernigou 2009). Indeed, such tensions over ideas have also emerged in intra-European debates over the merits of fiscal austerity, as well as whether (and on what terms) the EU should provide bailouts to troubled member states.

The Crisis Response and Financial Regulation in Europe

Instead of thinking on the global level to analyse these issues, one can also consider the regional level, namely the issues that have confronted the European Union (EU). Of paramount importance in the EU is, or should be, cooperation among national governments, central banks and financial supervisors in crisis situations. The bases for such cooperation prior to the crisis were bilateral and multilateral memoranda of understanding as well as the Economics and Finance Minister (ECOFIN) Council conclusions, in both cases non-binding. It is fair to say that, before the financial turmoil, there were no specific EU rules for crisis management and the sharing of the financial costs of public intervention in a crisis situation.

Given this background, the immediate crisis management of the EU to the global financial crisis worked rather well. During the first outbreak of the turmoil in the summer of 2007, the ECB intervened in a timely way and repeatedly in the market, injecting emergency liquidity into the eurozone's financial system. At the national level, liquidity interventions also took place in 2007 under the aegis of the national central banks. For example, in Germany, where public banks were amongst the most exposed to the credit squeeze and liquidity crunch in Europe, the Bundesbank provided liquidity to illiquid financial entities, and together with the German financial supervisory authority orchestrated rescue operations of two banks.

Following the failure of Lehman Brothers in the US in September 2008, the unsecured interbank money market froze in the EU and worldwide. In the eurozone, banks became increasingly dependent on ECB liquidity operations and overnight borrowing. This triggered the height of the credit crunch, and the ECB decided to ease the procedures for the provision of liquidity for as long as this was deemed necessary.

Given its relatively good performance, one could say that the EU must have been 'ready' for the crisis. But there were also significant problems of coordination. While the ECOFIN discussed a coordinated response to the financial crisis, relating in particular to support for systemic financial institutions and the definition of common principles for action, more specific measures were not adopted. Moreover, as discussed earlier, the unilateral declarations of state guarantees on all bank deposits in Ireland and Germany had adverse effects on other EU member-states.

The main institutional innovations at the European Union level were as follows. First, the Union established the European Systemic Risk Board (ESRB)–perhaps the most noteworthy of the innovative solutions–which monitors macroprudential risk, or risk to the system that occurs through the collective behaviour of individual firms like banks. Second, the Union agreed to transform the so-called level-three Lamfalussy committees of national regulators into independent authorities with legal personality, and to give them an increased budget and enhanced powers beyond merely advisory ones. The newly created bodies, namely the European Banking Authority, the European Insurance and Occupational Pension Authority, and the European Securities Markets Authority, were charged with the tasks of coordinating the application of supervisory standards and promoting stronger cooperation between national supervisors.

Nonetheless, the architecture for financial supervision and crisis management was not fundamentally changed, despite its evident shortcomings. Some important issues, such as financial institutions too big or interconnected to fail or cross-border banking failures have been left unaddressed, even though the Commission is working on these dossiers.

Given the current set-up, the EU does not appear to be 'governance-ready' to deal with future financial crises, despite its relatively good performance during the most recent crisis. The public good of financial stability remains underprovided in the EU because its provision would require institutional changes (potentially with fiscal implications) that go to the core of national sovereignty. This indicates an inherent tension between the ambition of providing EU-level financial stability and the reality of member states' reluctance to renounce national competences in this field. Member states' attitudes depend upon how they view the above-noted trade-off with international cooperation, given that they are primarily accountable to their national electorates if something goes wrong.

Indeed, there are at least six problems that the crisis illustrated that still need to be addressed if Europe is to be 'governance-ready' in the future (see Box 3.1).

The first problem is the disjuncture between globalised financial markets, financial market integration in the EU, and national systems of supervision. This fragmentation of powers and responsibilities, i.e. first order governance, severely constrains public authorities' ability to regulate and supervise financial markets and financial entities active in their jurisdictions, i.e. second order governance.

The second problem is posed by ailing cross-border financial institutions. A key issue is the distribution of burden sharing (i.e. the costs of rescue plans) between the home and host countries and across the several host jurisdictions in which cross-border financial institutions operate. This came to the fore when one of the largest continental banks, Fortis, had to be rescued by the Benelux authorities, generating a heated political debate about who should bear the cost. Furthermore, sometimes financial institutions are

---

Box 3.1 **Six Problems to be Addressed if Europe is to be 'Governance-ready' in the Future**

- Disjuncture between globalised financial markets, financial market integration in the EU, and national systems of supervision
- Ailing cross-border financial institutions
- Disjuncture between a common monetary policy and national financial supervision and crisis management
- Separation of central banking functions from supervisory functions

- Lack of attention to macroprudential or systemic supervision to safeguard the stability of the entire financial system and to the interconnection between micro and macro financial supervision
- Lack of awareness of the interconnection among monetary policy, macroeconomic imbalances, and financial stability

too big to be rescued by their home countries, as was the case of the Icelandic banks operating cross-border in the EU. This is a challenge not only for small countries, but also for large ones that are home countries of very big financial entities.

The third problem is the disjuncture between a common monetary policy, which in the eurozone is conducted by the ECB, and national financial supervision and crisis management, including arrangements for emergency liquidity assistance. In the early years of the eurozone there was an intense debate on the allocation of the responsibility of lender of last resort, in particular whether the ECB should (or not) perform this function. One critical argument was that the responsibilities for managing a banking or financial crisis were not clearly assigned (or openly disclosed), and that the large number of authorities potentially involved hampered the provision of emergency liquidity. During the global financial crisis, the IMF's assessment of ECB liquidity provision was overall positive. This assuaged some of the early concerns raised about ECB's performance in crisis situations and shifted the location of related problems from the national to the eurozone level. Nevertheless, the issue has not been definitively resolved.

The fourth problem is the separation of central banking functions from supervisory functions. This in turn raises the issue of which authorities should be responsible for macro-stability (i.e. stability of the system), micro-stability (i.e. solvency of individual financial entities) and consumer protection.[1] It also feeds into the ongoing debate concerning the establishment of a single financial services authority responsible for the oversight of all financial services, as an alternative model to the allocation of supervisory functions to a variety of sectoral authorities. The sketch of a 'banking union' agreed to at the European Council meeting in June 2012 presupposes that the ECB will house the EU banking regulator. Will the ECB worry more about the health of the financial sector than about its goal of maintaining price stability? Copelovitch and Singer (2008) suggest that countries where the banking regulatory power resides in the central bank have higher inflation than countries where the regulatory body and the central bank are separate institutions.

Fifth, the global financial crisis drew attention to macroprudential (or, systemic) supervision designed to safeguard the stability of the entire financial system and to the interconnection between micro and macro financial supervision. Prior to the global financial crisis, some policymakers, including senior officials at the BIS, had repeatedly singled out the need to 'marry' the micro- and macroprudential dimensions of financial stability. At the time, though, attention had very much focused on microprudential supervision designed to maintain the solvency of individual financial institutions. The global financial crisis demonstrated that this narrow focus was not enough to ensure financial stability. It also emphasised the need to regulate and supervise adequately all systemic institutions, i.e. the financial institutions whose failure might endanger the stability of the system.

Sixth, the global financial crisis brought into sharp relief the interconnection among monetary policy, macroeconomic imbalances and financial stability. Several authors have pointed out the effects of macroeconomic imbalances, such as the permanent deficits in the US balance of payments and of relatively accommodating monetary policies in the US, but also to some extent in the EU, in fuelling the global financial crisis. In the following section, we explore what governments can do about macroeconomic imbalances.

Difficult Trade-offs II: The Domestic Politics of Global Financial Governance

The global financial and economic crisis and the euro-crisis in particular demonstrate unmistakably that external imbalances can pose significant fiscal challenges. Although the nature of these challenges differs between deficit and surplus countries, they can be serious for both sets of countries. These differences also affect the types of 'policy efforts' to respond to governance challenges, as described in Chapter 2.

To understand the problem, one must understand how 'balance of payments' works. The balance of payments (BoP) summarises all transactions between domestic residents and foreigners. It has two components: the current account, which is defined as the difference between domestic savings and investments and records all nonfinancial transactions between domestic and foreign residents, and the capital account, which denotes the difference between capital outflows and capital inflows. By definition, the balance of payments is always balanced: deficits in the current account are matched by surpluses in the capital account, and vice versa. What is meant by external or balance of payments imbalances are large deficits or surpluses in the current and capital account.

Such imbalances come in two flavours. BoP imbalances in *deficit countries* are characterised by a deficit in the current account and a related capital account surplus. In these countries, domestic savings (both public and private) are smaller than public and private investments. Current account deficits are often associated with an accumulation of debts owed to foreigners held either by the private or the public sector. In most cases current account deficits also imply a trade deficit, which means that the country is importing more goods and services than it exports. Examples of deficit countries are the US, which has exhibited a current account deficit since 1982; Greece, whose current account deficit peaked at almost 15 percent of GDP in 2008; and Portugal, which had double-digit deficits as a percent of GDP during the years 2005 to 2009 (OECD 2012: 283).

In contrast to deficit countries, *surplus countries* exhibit a current account surplus (typically driven by a trade surplus) coupled with a capital account deficit. In these countries, domestic savings are larger than investments. Surplus countries are therefore usually home to creditors who have lent money to foreign firms, banks, or public entities. China, Japan, and Germany are currently the biggest surplus countries in the world, but Switzerland, Norway and the Netherlands are also in this situation. For example, Germany's current account surplus averaged 4.4 percent of GDP (or 138,7 billion US$) over the last 10 years, while China's current account surplus averaged 5.5 percent of GDP (or 186,7 billion US$) over the same period (IMF 2011). As a result, these countries have accumulated large claims against deficit countries.

A considerable debate exists about when current account deficits become unsustainable in industrialised countries, and under what circumstances they can be sustained for very long periods of time (e.g. Freund 2005). What is undisputed, however, is that in order to address balance of payments imbalances, domestic and foreign prices need to be realigned. In deficit countries, this realignment comes in the form of a reduction in real prices, which increases the international competitiveness of domestic vis-à-vis foreign products and hence reduces the current account deficit, while the opposite is required in surplus countries.

In order to achieve such a realignment of relative prices, governments need to adjust economic policies. For this purpose, they can choose between two ideal types of adjustment strategies: internal adjustment strategies (involving public spending, taxes, wages, monetary policy, and structural reform) and external adjustment strategies (mainly involving depreciation or appreciation of the exchange rate). Of course, countries can also pursue more mixed strategies, which involve exchange rate adjustments and adjustments in the domestic price level, but for analytical purposes, we focus here on the two ideal adjustment strategy types because they best highlight the trade-offs and choices policymakers face.

The politics of responding to balance of payments imbalances

The types of adjustment strategies countries choose vary significantly across time and space. During the 2007–12 global financial and economic crisis, governments in deficit countries responded quite differently to the problems associated with their current account deficits. Countries like Latvia addressed the emerging problems by significantly raising interest rates and slashing government spending, while keeping the exchange rate firmly pegged to the euro. These measures induced a severe recession in which the Latvian GDP shrank by almost 20% and unemployment tripled. Other countries, such as Poland and Iceland, adjusted externally and let their exchange rates depreciate substantially. Still others, like Hungary, opted for a mixed strategy, in which domestic economic tightening was coupled with a moderate adjustment of the exchange rate.

What explains this variation? Existing research in economics has identified several factors, including country characteristics such as size, openness or labour market flexibility (Mundell 1961; McKinnon 1963) and the types of international capital inflows into an economy (Frankel and Wei 2004), which influence the relative cost of external and internal adjustment strategies and therefore contribute to this variation. Despite these insights, one of the main conclusions of this research is that policymakers' macroeconomic policy choices are not predetermined solely by economic considerations.

Instead, the choice between external and internal adjustment strategies is thoroughly politicised. This is not surprising if one considers that macroeconomic policy decisions have distributional consequences. The distributional conflicts and related political choices are discussed in the next section.

Distributional conflicts in deficit countries: Internal vs. external adjustment

Let's begin with internal adjustment. To achieve the goal of internal adjustment, policymakers in deficit countries need to contract fiscal policy by cutting public expenditure and/or increasing taxes. Moreover, internal adjustment usually also involves a tightening of monetary conditions through a rise in interest rates and structural reforms designed to increase the economy's international competitiveness.

Usually, most individuals in the country are directly and negatively affected by such measures. It is, however, impossible to identify general groups of voters who will be hurt or helped by contractionary fiscal policies because the effect of these policies depends on the specific measures chosen. Not only can fiscal contraction and a rebalancing of the budget deficit be achieved by budget cuts or tax increases (or both), which tend to affect different groups of citizens, but the specific effects also depend on which taxes are increased and which budget items are cut.

The possibility to distribute the costs of internal adjustment in a variety of ways makes almost unavoidable strong political conflict about who is to bear the main burden of adjustment and significantly complicates the speedy implementation of such reform. The violent protests against the recent attempts by the Greek government to reduce the twin budget and current account deficits, which brought about the balance-of-payments crisis that began in 2010, and the political stalemate which surrounded the resignation of Prime Minister Papandreou, are but two examples of the political difficulties facing policymakers embarking on a path of internal adjustment. Because of these difficulties and the large costs the median voter has to bear during phases of internal adjustment, the dominant view in political economy research to date has been that internal adjustment is particularly difficult to achieve in democratic deficit countries (Simmons 1994; Eichengreen 1996; Bearce and Hallerberg 2011). When faced with the choice between internal and external adjustment, many industrial countries in the past have therefore chosen exchange-rate adjustment over monetary and fiscal tightening.

The notion that depreciation (and hence external adjustment) is less painful than internal adjustment originates in the argument that depreciation stimulates output in the tradable sector. This creates a positive effect, which can then spill over into the general economy with expansionary effects on output and employment, despite the fact that non-tradable producers are hurt by the loss in the currency's value. Exporters gain because a depreciation of the currency lowers the price of the exported goods abroad and thus boosts exporters' international competitiveness.

Unfortunately, it is by now well established that in contrast to this textbook view, devaluations of the currency can also have significant contractionary effects. First of all, depreciations reduce consumers' purchasing power and therefore tend to have contractionary effects on aggregate demand. This is unpopular politically, evidenced by the fact that devaluations and depreciations exhibit a clear association with the electoral cycle: they are significantly less likely shortly before and significantly more likely shortly after elections (Stein and Streb 2004). Second, despite the positive effect on relative prices for tradable products, they can also depress aggregate supply by increasing production costs through more costly imported inputs and intermediate goods or by making borrowing capital more expensive.

The biggest concern related to external adjustment is, however, related to the increasing borrowing and investment activities on foreign financial markets in which individuals, firms, and public entities have increasingly become active as financial globalisation has deepened. This has had profound effects on their balance sheets, which now often contain not

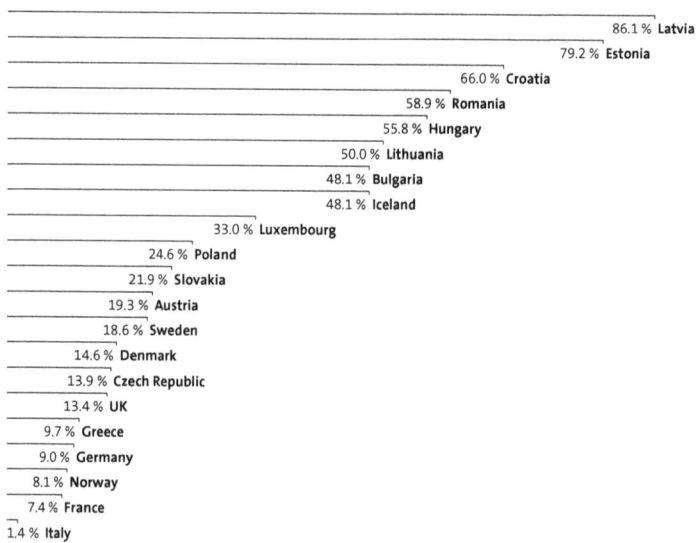

Figure 3.1 **Share of foreign currency loans to non-bank clients relative to all loans in 2007, selected European countries.**
Source: Brown, Peter and Wehrmüller (2009: tables 1 and 2), own calculations

only assets and liabilities denominated in domestic currency, but foreign-currency denominated positions as well. As a result, in many countries large proportions of the debt owed by the private and public sector is now denominated in foreign currency. Figure 3.1 shows the proportion of privately held, foreign currency-denominated debt relative to total private debt for selected European countries. In some, such as Latvia or Estonia, over 70% of all private debt is denominated in foreign currency, mostly euro and Swiss francs (Brown, Peter and Wehrmüller 2009). In such a setting, a devaluation or depreciation of the currency can easily bankrupt a debtor holding unhedged, foreign-currency denominated debt because the debt burden increases significantly when the domestic currency loses its value. This equally holds for the public sector: External adjustment can have a direct and negative effect on the fiscal position when large portions of public debt are unhedged and denominated in foreign currency, so that a depreciation of a country's currency substantially increases the public debt burden.

The politics of responses in deficit countries

The strong distributional effects associated with external and internal adjustment in deficit countries influence democratic policymakers' decisions about how and when to respond to current account deficits in their balance of payments. In general, governments whose voters are on average less vulnerable to a depreciation of the exchange rate than an internal devaluation of relative prices, both directly and indirectly through the effects of adjustment on their employers, government finances, and the general economic climate, are more likely to opt for external adjustment over internal adjustment.

Unfortunately, governments often face an electorate highly vulnerable to both external and internal adjustment. These governments are likely to meet significant opposition to plans involving any type of adjustment. The distributional consequences of adjustment can therefore create strong political incentives for policymakers to implement only minimal reform, or at least to delay necessary macroeconomic adjustment (Cooper 1971; Frankel 2005). Although this strategy typically allows the existing problems to deteriorate, the expectation of significant short-term political costs associated with adjustment creates strong incentives for policymakers to delay significant adjustment in these political settings.

Such a course of action is possible because both internal and external adjustment can be avoided as long as the government finds ways to finance the current account and fiscal deficits. Thus, as long as foreign capital flows freely into the country, the pressure to adjust is low. But even when capital inflows dry up, the government can avoid adjustment by financing the deficit through sterilised sales of the country's foreign currency reserves. When these reserves run out, a further delay of necessary adjustment is only possible when new sources of funds materialise–usually in the form of support from external sources such as the EU, the IMF, or other governments.

The more the international community worries about a potential default or currency crisis in the deficit country, the easier it will be for the country to acquire such funds.

Although these funds usually come attached to conditions designed to invoke an adjustment of the current account and a rebalancing of the budget, they can also be used to avoid a harsh adjustment of macroeconomic conditions. The funds channelled to Greece, Portugal, and Ireland through the EU and the IMF in the form of bailout packages are an example for such measures. Similarly, the ECB's purchases of these countries' sovereign bonds or the accumulation of target liabilities in these countries' national central banks' balance sheets can be viewed as efforts to avoid or delay harsh adjustment in these countries (Sinn and Wollmershäuser 2011).

Sometimes not adjusting is the appropriate policy response to current account deficits, especially when the BoP imbalance has emerged in response to a temporary shock, such as a sudden and temporary change in the world market price of an important tradable good or a natural disaster that temporarily disrupts a country's productive capacity. When the imbalance results from more fundamental problems, however, financing the deficit usually only serves to allow the imbalance to deteriorate further so that the strategy of delaying adjustment fails in the long run. Indeed, the amount of adjustment required at a later point in time tends to increase as a result of this strategy. This explains why phases of delayed adjustment often end with either a major crash of the currency or a serious recession. Surprisingly, policymakers frequently try to avoid macroeconomic adjustment. On average, they wait between six and thirteen months after the beginning of serious problems (especially a turn-around of capital flows) before genuine macroeconomic adjustment occurs (Frankel and Wei 2004).

The politics of responses in surplus countries

The question of whether and how to adjust balance of payments imbalances can emerge in surplus countries as well. These countries usually face less pressure from financial markets to adjust because current account surpluses indicate a high level of international competitiveness. Moreover, as capital exporters, surplus countries are less dependent on the fickleness of financial markets. Rather than adjust, they can build up foreign currency reserves or engage in other types of financing their current account surplus and hence are less likely to fall prey to speculative pressure. Nonetheless, when the issue of adjustment becomes salient, distributional conflict is likely to characterise macroeconomic decision-making in these countries as well.

Adjustment in surplus countries requires an increase in the real price level, either through exchange rate appreciation/revaluation or through an internal revaluation of prices, usually in the form of higher rates of inflation. The increase in domestic prices leads to a loss in international competitiveness, slows export growth and hence lowers the current account surplus.

As in deficit countries, both of these external and internal adjustment strategies create winners and losers.

External adjustment (i.e. exchange rate appreciation) tends to benefit consumers and domestically-oriented industries through an increase in purchasing power. However it can substantially hurt export-oriented industries. Exporters therefore usually put up a lot of resistance against a revaluation of the currency. For example, although the Chinese government, which presides over one of the largest current account surpluses in the world, has been under severe international pressure to revalue its currency, it has largely resisted this pressure because Chinese exporters have actively lobbied against such a policy of external adjustment. Exporters' vulnerability to an appreciating currency is highest when they are characterised by a low level of internationalisation, so that their ability to engage in 'operational hedging' is limited (Kinderman 2008), or when their ability to hedge against currency appreciation through financial derivatives is limited.

The financial turmoil associated with external adjustment is particularly large when it is associated with the break-up of a formerly fixed exchange rate regime. The current fears associated with a potential break-up of the euro illustrate this point in its extreme. Such a break-up would likely lead to a substantial currency appreciation in surplus countries and a substantial depreciation in deficit countries, with potentially fatal consequences for the banking systems in both types of countries. Such a development would also constitute a significant challenge for exporters in countries with appreciating currencies.

The alternative to external adjustment in surplus countries is an internal revaluation of prices. This strategy usually involves a fiscal expansion in the form of tax cuts and higher public spending, as well as a loosening of monetary policy. These measures serve to boost domestic demand, lower domestic savings and increase domestic investment, all of which decrease the current account surplus. The increase in domestic economic activity typically leads to higher real wages and hence benefits workers, especially those employed in the nontradables sector. This is likely to be particularly welcomed by workers in surplus countries in which the high level of international competitiveness has been the result of real wage compression. At the same time, however, such increases tend to benefit those in secure employment, but may hurt workers employed in tradables industries which face a stiffer wind on international export markets.

Moreover, the internal revaluation associated with internal adjustment also usually implies higher rates of inflation. Note that, as Chapter 1 foreshadowed and we alluded to earlier, there remain battles of ideas about the appropriate level of inflation in an economy. In practice the state of the 'conventional wisdom' varies across countries, as does the level of inflation aversion among domestic populations. Nevertheless, some groups are harder hit by high rates of inflation than others. Most notably, asset holders tend to be hardest hit by inflation, because it depreciates the value of their investments. In contrast, debtors tend to benefit from high rates of inflation.

Overall, macroeconomic adjustment in surplus countries can lead to distributional conflict between the winners and losers of this process. As in deficit countries, policymakers can therefore have strong incentives not to adjust, but to maintain the current account surplus. This strategy tends to be facilitated by the fact that surplus countries need not attract foreign funds to sustain the imbalance in their current account, but can finance the surplus by either accumulating foreign reserves (a strategy pursued by many Asian countries in recent years) or by re-channelling the proceeds generated by the trade surplus back to deficit countries via financial investments by the private sector (a strategy pursued for example by Germany before the onset of the euro crisis).

An additional option–currently pursued by the surplus countries in the eurozone–is to finance deficit countries through public guarantees and loans. The funds necessary for financing such deficits can be huge. For example, in response to the ongoing crisis in the eurozone, the euro area member states created the European Financial Stability Facility (EFSF) in May 2010. The facility's mandate is to safeguard financial stability in Europe by providing financial assistance to euro area member states through loans to countries in financial difficulties or interventions in the debt primary and secondary markets. As of November 2011, the guarantee commitments from euro area member states for the EFSF and its successor the ESM are disproportionally borne by surplus countries.

Improving governance readiness for adjustment

In terms of balance of payment imbalances, distributional concerns can provide powerful incentives to deviate from economically efficient outcomes. Rather than adjusting economic policies quickly to address emerging imbalances and the macroeconomic problems associated with such imbalances early on, the fear of hurting voters directly or indirectly–and feeling the impact at election time–can induce governments to delay such adjustment as long as possible. Since this strategy often leads to a worsening of the economic problems, such delays often result in financial crises, with potentially destructive effects not only for the affected countries but the entire global financial system, as the current crisis in the eurozone vividly demonstrates. In light of the significant economic and political costs associated with severe balance of payments problems and with the measures required to reduce these imbalances, pressing questions include what countries can do to increase their readiness to address potential problems associated with imbalances in countries' current and capital accounts early on and how the emergence of unsustainable imbalances can be prevented in the first place.

The best way for governments to avoid that current account deficits turn into major threats for the country's public finances is to forestall the emergence of unsustainable current account deficits. In this regard, the country's fiscal policy is directly under governments' control. Since current account deficits often emerge in response to fiscal expansion, a balanced budget reduces the risk of running up unsustainable 'twin deficits'. Such deficits are particularly problematic for countries with a high degree of 'debt intolerance' (Reinhart and Rogoff 2009), which characterises countries with a history of serial default and high rates of inflation. These countries are likely to experience extreme duress and speculative pressure at comparatively low debt levels.

Of course, as we have shown above, implementing prudent fiscal policies is not always easy politically. The incentives for expansionary fiscal policy tend to be particularly significant in financially open countries with fixed exchange rates, because in such settings fiscal policy is particularly effective (Fleming 1962; Mundell 1963; for a recent discussion see Chiu et al. 2012).[2] This has significant consequences for macroeconomic discipline. For example, electorally motivated fiscal spending cycles have been found to be particularly prevalent in such settings (Clark and Hallerberg 2000).

What can be done to dampen governments' temptation to overspend in such situations? One option is to implement institutional constraints, such as fiscal rules (Hallerberg 2004; Hallerberg, Strauch and von Hagen 2007). Such rules can help policymakers to pursue prudent fiscal policies despite heightened political incentives to forego fiscal discipline. The European Stability and Growth Pact and the Swiss and German 'debt brake' (see Chapter 4 on Governance Innovations) are examples of such constraints, although the former also demonstrates that in order to provide fiscal discipline and prevent the emergence of significant balance of payments imbalances, such institutions need to be credible. Another option is to focus on the type of public expenditure. A widening of the current account deficit driven by expansionary fiscal policy tends to be more problematic when the increase in public spending is channelled into consumption rather than productive investment. By encouraging the latter, policymakers can hence reduce the risk of a future crisis.

Governments can also increase their readiness to confront potential problems associated with current account deficits by building up financial firepower. A unilateral approach involves the accumulation of foreign currency reserves so that if a current account deficit cannot be matched by sufficient capital inflows, the authorities can draw upon these funds. Moreover, large foreign currency reserves are likely to deter speculative attacks on countries' currencies (Eichengreen 2004). A second strategy of increasing financial firepower relies on multilateral action. It involves large pools of money, which can be provided to countries experiencing speculative pressure although their economic fundamentals and policies are fairly strong. This strategy builds on the insight that financial crises are often characterised by herding behaviour and contagion and can therefore even affect countries with comparatively low levels of vulnerability to crisis. Examples of such multilateral strategies are the IMF's precautionary lending facilities or the ESFS's precautionary programme.[3]

Finally, governments can increase their readiness to deal with imbalances by focusing on the financial root causes of many of the vulnerabilities to internal and external adjustment in the private sector. As we have seen, many of these factors are related to imbalances in the capital account, creating vulnerabilities both on the side of debtor and creditor countries (Reinhart and Reinhart 2008; Reinhart and Rogoff 2009; Chinn and Frieden 2011).

Conclusion

This chapter considered the governance challenges that arise in the realm of financial and fiscal governance. The focus has been especially on financial crises, both on how they arise and what steps countries take to address them. We discussed what makes some countries more prone to crisis than others. A key issue is the extent of macroeconomic imbalances: countries with large macroeconomic deficits are more likely to fall into crisis, and to be affected by crises that may begin in other countries. There are both systemic and domestic reasons why such crises arise.

At the same time, the politics of responding to the imbalances depends upon whether one is in a deficit or surplus country. One would be tempted to say that the problems are in deficit countries only–they are the ones that fall into difficulties first because in many cases they have trouble repaying money they have borrowed from surplus countries–but there are two sides to the same coin, and we indicated that surplus countries must also adjust.

This chapter also reviewed the coordination problems that the European Union has confronted in dealing with the financial crisis. It found that the EU institutions performed reasonably well in the initial period after the crisis hit in 2008. But it suggested that the institutional configurations to deal with a more serious crisis that caused more spillovers across borders would cause significant problems. The institutional structures to deal with such issues at the EU level are not yet present.

Finally, we considered the trade-offs inherent in any international coordination on financial matters. As earlier chapters have noted, the effectiveness of international coordination is important if it is to address crises as they develop. At the same time, we argued that accountability and legitimacy issues may get in the way of more effective coordination.

We also noted that innovations tend to come when there is real pressure. In the European Union example, we found that the European Systemic Risk Board as well as the emphasis on macroprudential risk arose only in the immediate aftermath of the crisis. Chapter 4 will consider in more detail where innovations come from as well as some specific innovations in the financial realm.

Finally, the goal of this chapter was to explain the nature of trade-offs actors face and the dilemmas that exist if international coordination in financial and fiscal governance is to succeed. To understand where actors will come down on the trade-offs and whether they will coordinate, we need information on their ability to develop and implement innovative policies. Chapter 5 will discuss both how to measure these attributes and provide initial data.

Endnotes

1. This point was made in several reports issued in the wake of the financial crisis, such as the reports by the De Larosière Group (2009) and the Group of Thirty (2009).
2. In contrast, monetary policy is more effective when capital is mobile and exchange rates are flexible.
3. These programs offer credit lines to countries with sound policies and fundamentals, which nonetheless experience temporary external shocks or financial stress. By imposing strict eligibility criteria, these programs are intended to signal the strength of qualifying countries' fundamentals and policies and to provide liquidity to these countries as a form of insurance designed to prevent or resolve crises before they deteriorate.

IV. Governance Innovations

by HELMUT K ANHEIER *and* SABRINA KORRECK

The conditions of governance have changed–so a first basic premise triggering this Report. A second premise is the subject of this chapter: the cacophony of approaches of many kinds that emerge in response to the pressure put on existing governance systems. As the previous chapters have shown, many new ideas and practices are being put forth by different actors and at various levels. How are we to make sense of them; how can we assess their potential for improvement, especially in terms of policy outcomes? This chapter offers conceptual guidance for understanding governance innovation, and, based on a broad scan and systematic vetting, presents a series of cases that seem to harbour significant potential.

What Governance Innovations Are

The term innovation is frequently used by business managers, policymakers and experts alike–but rarely with precision. Available definitions, usually from corporate management perspectives, are rather broad. A widely accepted definition, proposed by Kanter (1983: 20) in her research on changes in corporations, sees innovation as the 'generation, acceptance, and implementation of new ideas, processes, products, or services.'

Governance innovations are novel rules, regulations, and approaches that seek to address a public problem in more efficacious and effective ways, to achieve better policy outcomes and to enhance legitimacy.

Unlike innovations around private goods, the kinds of problems and issues of public goods, as discussed in Chapter 2, are such that they are rarely driven by incentives to maximise the utility of one actor alone; it is not primarily a limited group of shareholders but a broader set of stakeholders, even the public at large, that should benefit from governance innovations. Such innovations require some form of collective action among actors and across policy fields, and in response to signals that may be weaker and less incentive-bound than in market situations.

We understand governance innovation as novel rules, regulations, and approaches that, compared to the current state of affairs, seek to address a public problem in more efficacious and effective ways, to achieve better policy outcomes, and, ultimately, to enhance legitimacy.[1]

While governance innovations involve something new, they do not occur in isolation as one-off acts of enlightened policymaking. For their eventual success and adaptation, they require adequate structures and processes in terms of institutional and organisational design.

Thus, in contrast to invention, which is the creation of a novelty *hic et nunc*, the concept of innovation presupposes a certain evolutionary process, whereby new ideas are elaborated, adopted and changed, improved and implemented and eventually popularised. Innovation requires at least some integration into conventional policy for wider adaption to take place and a strategic opening of what Kingdon (1995) described as policy windows that allow a particular agenda to receive favourable attention by policymakers. For this to gather momentum, governance innovations require some early form of uptake by several stakeholders when the idea first arises, and throughout the process of implementation, adaptation and diffusion.

Yet the 'publicness' of governance innovations is not the only way in which they differ from the kinds of innovations in the corporate world. There, innovation connotes market advantages and potentially higher profits; and competition is primarily viewed as a zero-sum game. In what Schumpeter (1950) calls 'creative destruction,' market producers have incentives to innovate for better market positions, and thereby trigger changes that are good for some, but bad for others. While private good innovation can be zero-sum games for competing corporations, the great majority of consumers and the population at large can benefit and be better off.

How does innovation in the public sector compare? The central competitive element of markets is missing, owing to the nature of public goods, even though key players, including governments, can see competition rather than cooperation as the preferred option. An over-emphasis on competition for public goods is ill-guided, as Chapter 2 argues, and cooperation strategies, which can certainly contain competitive elements, are better and more beneficial to society at large. The challenge, then, becomes to devise innovative solutions to public problems that invite cooperation towards 'positive-sum' policy outcomes for at least a majority of stakeholders involved.

The public sector is a major–if not the major–part of governance systems. Hence, any look at governance innovation has to start with the public sector's innovative potential. While market dynamics make incentives for innovation in private firms self-evident, incentives in public agencies are different. Of course, there are electoral pressures, yet they can be anticipated and prepared for; they typically affect the great majority of public sector employees indirectly at most, as agencies and their staff are usually protected by civil service regulations and the like. Not surprisingly, the public management literature posits that it is easier for the public sector not to innovate than to do so.

Weaker signals demanding innovation reach public agencies from the outside, and weaker incentives for innovations operate within them. As a result, agencies have a greater tendency to build up inertia, which, in turn, affects their ability to respond adequately to changes. In response to alleged public sector sluggishness and change resistance, the paradigm of New Public Management has for nearly 25 years sought to foster 'a performance-oriented culture in a less centralized public sector' by introducing market elements whenever possible to allow for stronger signals and incentives, and with a quest to become more innovative–albeit with rather mixed results (OECD 1995: 8; see also Hood 1995; Parsons 2006).

How, then, does public sector innovation come about? The answer seems sobering at first (Borins 2000: 55–6): changes happen if strong demands are put forth by politics, be it as a result of elections or some legislative pressure, preferably coinciding with new leadership; changes also happen in response to publicly visible crises or failures, as well as internal dysfunctions not publicly visible; and changes result from new opportunities either created by new technologies (e.g., e-governance) or otherwise (e.g., EU expansion).

These highly contingent factors suggest that innovation is rather exceptional and rarely regular practice in public agencies. Although some governments have introduced internal change and innovation agencies,[2] few public sector agencies have the equivalents of R&D or marketing departments incentivised to read and react to market signals. The exceptional nature of governance innovations highlights the role of 'windows of opportunity' to initiate change processes in the public sector. Unlike Lindblom's (1959) conclusion that public agencies are prone to incrementalism and muddling-through, Kingdon (1995: 80) notes that agenda change is usually a sudden process, which 'hits', 'catches on' and 'takes off'.

Next to corporations and public agencies, civil society organisations are key actors in both governance and governance innovation. The role of social movement organisations and advocacy nonprofits to protect and further agendas of many kinds has long been highlighted in national contexts (Anheier 2005; Salamon 1995; Jenkins 2006), including the role of endowed foundations to prepare and advance agendas (Minkoff and Agnone 2010; Anheier and Daly 2007).

Archibugi and Iammarino (2002) suggest that the relevance of civil society in innovation is increasing, and indeed, the cases reviewed below reveal a significant role of civil society actors in initiating and seeing through innovation in governance. The change potential of civil society stems from its structural location: close to the grassroots and the local level, civil society actors are usually the first to become aware of social problems of many kinds. Their ability is also based on the lower transaction costs required for mobilising public opinion and for capturing popular sentiments in favour of one policy or another. What is more, advances in communication technologies and lower costs made it much easier for groups to mobilise and organise across borders. Finally, not beholden to the ballot box and market expectations, civil society actors enjoy a degree of independence neither public agencies nor corporations may have.

That civil society actors have become more visible policy actors at local, national and global levels is without doubt. But have they become successful innovators as well? Clearly many important agendas, from human rights to the environment, from freedom of information to social justice were pushed by civil society. Some like Zelner, Henisz and Holburn (2009) are cautious and point out that 'global victories' of agendas pushed by civil society actors may not guarantee better policy outcomes, as governments and corporations can engage in subsequent stalling without repealing old policies, with the Kyoto Agreement as a case in point (see chapter 5).

What is more, civil society has many voices expressing many different interests and preferences. This is a great strength of civil society, and one that generates and percolates many new ideas and approaches on how to improve a wide range of public problems. Yet it is also a weakness when it comes to finding out whose voices count, whose ideas are worthwhile, and for whom.

Change and Innovation

It seems that corporations are good at innovations, but less so for the kinds needed for public problems. The literature on public sector innovation is long on reasons why innovation does not happen and short on remedies for improvement, yet points to the importance of windows of opportunities for change to come about. As regards civil society, it seems that many innovations do come up yet fail to find take-up and to connect to institutional structures, especially when linking local, national and international agendas. Each actor comes with distinct advantages and disadvantages. So how does governance innovation come about?

There are two perspectives from which to approach that question, one emphasising the discontinuous process of governance innovations, as suggested by Kingdon (1995), the other the continuous and incremental, more in line with Kanter's (1983) vision of 'change masters' continuously recreating the modern organisation, and, indeed, Lindblom's (1959) idea of muddling-through.

The discontinuity view assumes that governance systems pass through relatively long periods of stability in terms of structure and activity. While aligned with the demands of their policy environments, systems tend to build up inertia as well as certain 'blindness' for small changes especially, thereby reducing their fitness over time. Such stability can be punctuated by seemingly unexpected bursts of fundamental changes that come about when two types of disruptions occur simultaneously: internal inertia or bad decisions that create misalignments, and external changes like new competitors, pronounced free-riding or spill-ins that threaten the system's overall stability. In response, some but not all institutions and actors in governance systems seek to adapt by introducing changes in terms of strategy, structure, incentive and control systems as well as power relations that are more far-reaching than would have been the case without the pressures resulting from the crisis.

Organisational theory (e.g., Gersick 1991; Romanelli and Tushman 1985, 1994; Tushman and O'Reilly 2002) suggests that periods of greater uncertainty are also times of greater innovation as organisations break with the inertia of embedded routines in order to survive by gaining in performance and, ultimately, maintain legitimacy. Such periods of profound uncertainty may affect the 'deep structure' of institutions and organisations, i.e., a set of fundamental, interdependent assumptions and choices about rationales, objectives and activities. They may also lead to the creation of new approaches to governance based on what could be called first principle, i.e., the search for a formula with the dual ability to capture the underlying problem and propose a solution.

These first principle innovations can apply to both first and second order governance decisions and need not be complex and complicated. Examples of first order decisions that involved first principles include the notion of dual sovereignty between the federal government and the various states that allowed for the US system of government and governance to emerge, including the principle of checks and balances.[3] The German principle of subsidiarity formed the basis for the development of a modern welfare state after World War II. It established a division of labour between state, community and civil society organisations by giving private actors preference over public providers (Anheier and Seibel 2001).

> *It may well be that the current period presents this 'rare' combination of external and internal disruptions to the deep structure of existing governance systems.*

The basic insight of Jean Monet that cooperation was preferable to competition in the coal and steel markets in 1950s Europe is another example where fundamental innovations in the way of framing both problem and solution pointed the way forward–and paved the way for what became the European Union (Brinkley and Hackett 1991). For second order decisions, such innovations have many implications and require follow-up innovations in institutional and organisational design, with the current debate about 'fixing' the Euro as a case in point.

Indeed, it may well be that the current period presents this 'rare' combination of external and internal disruptions to the deep structure of existing governance systems. The Westphalian notion of sovereignty–the very principle that equates sovereignty with the nation state–as well as the UN system and other international institutions may have come to a point of rapture that requires more fundamental redesign of institutions and corresponding organisations based on some kind of new understanding of assumptions, principles, objectives and outcomes–first principles.

A second perspective emphasises the gradual evolution of governance systems, with limited, targeted innovations that help the overall system evolve over time. As governance systems tend to be less complex than the policy fields they are designed for, they may be unable to manage all demands and contingencies generated. Organisational theory suggests that two major change processes are more or less continuously at work in governance systems: recombination and refunctionality (Romanelli 1991). Together, they shape the systems' evolution, as they can improve efficacy and effectiveness, with subsequent positive impacts on performance and legitimacy.

Recombination is essentially about copying from others,[4] and involves the introduction of 'borrowed' elements into an existing governance system: using financial risk management in public sector service delivery (which is the case for the social impact bonds reviewed below); or introducing corporate social responsibility programs in mining corporations (as exemplified by the Extractive Industry Transparency Initiative).

Whereas recombination is about borrowing, refunctionality is the relocation and expansion of a proven principle, product or service into new contexts, policy fields or jurisdictions. In this case, governance institutions and organisations migrate and expand. Examples include the gradual extension of the Monet 'coal and steel' first principle into a wider range of policy fields at national and regional levels of member states as manifest in the Maastricht, Nice and Lisbon treaties; or the migration of rating agencies to look at an ever broader number of organisations and fields.

These processes are rarely mutually exclusive. Punctuated equilibriums and more gradual developments can be present at the same time, and indeed the former can create opportunities for the latter. The concept of responsible sovereignty proposed in Chapter 2, if developed, tested and advanced properly, harbours the potential for becoming a governance innovation of first principle. However, its institutional design remains to be worked out. By contrast, the regional monetary cooperation among Asian economies (Chiang Mai Initiative Multilateralisation) reviewed below constitutes a case where the institutional innovation has been established, but it remains unclear if a new principle of regional monetary governance has been found.

Institutional design innovations are behind many national and international organisations. These institutions came into being in response to significant but not necessarily systemic public problems. Such innovations can involve first principles and first order decisions, with the UN or the EU as cases in point, and the Chiang Mai Initiative Multilateralisation reviewed below for a second order case (Table 4.1). The Organisation of African Union and the North American Free Trade Agreement are essentially refunctionalities based on the UN as a model in the first and the European free trade agreements in the second case.

Table 4.1 also lists some of the innovations reviewed below, such as the Norwegian Government Pension Fund Global where different elements are (re)combined to bring about a new institution, and the charter cities case and others for innovations based on refunctionalities. However, Table 4.1 anticipates an important finding of the search for innovations leading to the chapter: first order decisions involving first principles are rather rare, and second order decisions involving either refunctionality or recombination are more frequent.

Table 4.1 **Governance orders and innovations**

Innovation \ Order	First Order Governance Decisions	Second Order Governance Decisions
First Principle	Rare, and often result of punctuated equilibrium with serious multiple governance failures of systemic proportion *Established examples:* • United Nations • European Union • Subsidiarity *On agenda today:* • Euro settlement involving greater political, fiscal union	Somewhat more frequent, and often result of limited punctuated equilibrium and multiple governance failures *Example reviewed in this chapter:* • Potentially: Chiang Mai Initiative Multilateralisation *Example proposed in Report (Chapter 2):* • Notion of responsible sovereignty
Refunctionality	More frequent, based on specific governance failures/requirements and/or limited combinations thereof *Established examples:* • Organisation of African Union • NAFTA *Example proposed in Report (Chapter 3):* • Solving financial policy tradeoffs based on political solutions	Rather frequent, based on specific governance failures/requirements *Examples reviewed in Report:* • Charter Cities • mySociety • Transition Initiatives • Ushahidi
Recombination	More frequent, based on specific governance failures/requirement and/or limited combinations thereof *Established Examples:* • Town Twinning as a form of reconciliation based on soft diplomacy model • Truth Commission in South Africa *Example proposed in Report:* • Solving trade-offs based on political solutions	Rather frequent, based on specific governance failures/requirements *Examples from past:* • Extractive Industry Transparency Initiative • Environmental Protection Agency in US *Examples reviewed in Report:* • Norwegian Government Pension Fund Global • Debt Brake • Open Government Partnership • Social Impact Bonds

Table 4.2 **Overview of governance innovations (in order presented)**

Case	GR	Challenge	Basic Proposition	Type of Innovation	Key Insight
Chiang Mai Initiative Multilateralisation	GR1 GR3 GR5 GR6	Providing 'financial firepower' to prevent financial contagion	Creating regional fund and ensuring surveillance via link to IMF	First principle	Two-tiered financial architecture to create nested institution to solve tradeoff between liquidity and moral hazard
Hybrid Organisations: The L3C business entity	GR1	Stabilising co-producing, hybrid organisations that seek to combine social and economic returns	Providing a forprofit form with internal non-profit governance structure	Primarily recombination but inviting refunctionality	Allow for diversity of incentives but create checks and balances to avoid goal displacement
Norwegian Government Pension Fund Global	GR1 GR5	Assuming active responsibility as a socially responsible investor	Using CSR investment guidelines for public fund	Recombination	Scale of funds not only requires ethical responsibility but can help create it
Debt Brake	GR1 GR4	Finding more effective ways and means for sustainable public finances	Recreating legal requirements and disincentives	Recombination	Effective ex post control mechanisms via compensation accounts to take away incentives to overspend
Charter Cities	GR1 GR4	Building capable institutions needed for growing cities in the Global South	Creating governance systems in context of special reform zone	Refunctionality	New systems with new rules enforced in cooperation with trusted partner have greater chances of success than reforming entrenched systems
Social Impact Bonds	GR1	Finding new finance mechanism for social services	New risk allocation by creating a social investment market	Recombination	Reform low-performing systems by realigning, enforcing and adding new incentives demanding outcome performance

Case	GR	Challenge	Basic Proposition	Type of Innovation	Key Insight
Transition Initiatives	GR1 GR4 GR5	Reducing oil dependence and responding to climate change in policy agendas	Civil society mobilisation to develop joined up policy thinking	Refunctionality	Aggregation of many small-scale projects can impact global problems
Ushahidi	GR1	Coordinating more effectively through information management	Using citizen-based information to help manage responses	Refunctionality	Crowd-sourcing saves time and resources, and improves outcomes
Open Government Partnership	GR1 GR2	Providing a basis for more transparent, participatory and collaborative public policy-making	Collaboration platforms for engagement between politicians and civil society	Recombination	Openness, dialogue and exchange lead to better informed, more accepted and effective policies
mySociety	GR1 GR2	Promoting greater citizen engagement	Citizen-led creation and use of public websites	Refunctionality	Increasing transparency on how public sector deals with 'everyday problems' reduces citizen-government gap

We see innovations not as an end in themselves but as responses to the governance requirements, as introduced in Chapter 2 for addressing global challenges, but adapted here to address public policy challenges at all levels. These are:

- **GR1:** Averting the risk of dual–market and state–failure
- **GR2:** Correcting fairness deficits
- **GR3:** Strengthening externality management
- **GR4:** Promoting issue-focus and result-orientation
- **GR5:** Recognising and promoting synergies, requiring leadership
- **GR6:** Taking account of policy interdependence

Each edition of the Report will showcase recent and significant governance innovations and review the development of cases presented previously.[5] Table 4.2 summarises the ten cases selected for this edition.

Governance Innovations: Ten Cases

How could we identify in a timely and methodologically-sound manner recent governance innovations occurring in different regions and fields and among different actors? We monitored the relevant organisations and the media in fields where governance innovations are likely to occur, but this search proved logistically demanding. We complemented it by inviting over 280 governance scholars and practitioners to participate in an online survey in late 2011 and report developments in their area of expertise. We benefited from the advice of an international steering group.

We identified a large pool of innovative practices, arrangements and ideas and, after an initial vetting based on available print and web-based sources, analysed some 50 cases in more detail, using a set of criteria according to which the proposed governance innovations had to:

- Have occurred within the past ten years.
- Have been applied in at least one instance or context.
- Comprise something significantly new to solve a particular governance challenge.
- Show scalability and replicability.
- Hold a promise of leading to better policy outcomes and higher levels of public welfare.
- Clearly address governance of a public problem.

What is more, we looked for innovations addressing the governance requirements noted here and in Chapter 2 and sought coverage of different actors (governments, corporations, civil society), fields (finance, social services, disaster management), and types of innovation (first principle, refunctionality, recombination). In the end, we arrived at ten innovations and, in their presentation below, addressed a sequence of questions:

- What is the particular governance challenge or problem?
- What is the innovative solution?
- What is the potential impact?

Chiang Mai Initiative Multilateralisation

Challenge. Current account imbalances can turn into serious threats to financial stability. In this respect, one lesson learned from Chapter 3 is that it is best to prevent crises from happening by making countries less prone to difficulties associated with current account deficits. For example, 'financial firepower' built up by accumulating large stocks of foreign currency reserves can be used by authorities to service debt and stabilise their currency, thus averting speculative attacks and preventing initial problems from turning into larger systemic problems or spilling over across borders.

The 1997 Asian financial crisis illustrates what can happen if speculative attacks are not offset by sufficient foreign currency reserves. The financial crisis, which was partly caused by significant current account deficits, began after Thailand was forced to let its national currency (baht) float once authorities had depleted foreign currency reserves used to maintain the peg to the US dollar. The effects extended throughout the East Asian region, and in the course of the crisis, several countries appealed to the IMF for help. IMF bailouts came with tough conditionality. In the aftermath, many in the region felt that the crisis could have been resolved less painfully if the region had had more voice in developing the bailout packages (Sussangkarn 2010). These experiences led the East Asian countries to seek mechanisms to protect against future crises and to realise that, to this end, regional cooperation was indispensable.

Innovative Solution. Already in September 1997, the Japanese Ministry of Finance proposed creating an 'Asian Monetary Fund' that would fulfil these ambitions independent of the IMF. That first proposal received little support in the region and strong opposition from the IMF. Twelve years later, an effort that incorporates this original vision emerged: the 13 countries comprising ASEAN+3[6] agreed to pool their resources in a common fund, known as the Chiang Mai Initiative Multilateralisation (CMIM). The CMIM was set up '(i) to address balance of payments and short-term liquidity difficulties in the region, and (ii) to supplement the existing international financial arrangements' (Grimes 2011: 94). Member countries can draw from a foreign currency pool worth US $240 billion (in 2012). However, an 'IMF-link' remains in place, meaning that borrowing countries must be in negotiations with the IMF for a stand-by agreement if they want to access more than 30% of their maximum credit.

The CMIM replaces a network of bilateral currency swap agreements among ASEAN+3 countries, the Chiang Mai Initiative (CMI), which had been in place since 2000. Although a roadmap to merging the bilateral agreements into a single contractual framework was developed in 2005, its institutionalisation was delayed primarily by political rivalry between China and Japan resolved only when they agreed to contribute equal amounts to the pool.

The multilateralisation not only standardised countries' earlier CMI agreements around a single contract, but also introduced a weighted voting system, with contributions determining vote shares, and established its own surveillance mechanism, conducted by the ASEAN+3 Macroeconomic Research Office (AMRO). AMRO's functions include monitoring and macroeconomic analysis, and most importantly, support for decision-making regarding the activation of funds from the common foreign currency pool.

Potential Impact. The Chiang Mai Initiative Multilateralisation as a financial architectural innovation must be analysed against the background of the liquidity vs. moral hazard trade-off, described in Chapter 3. On one hand, the emergency liquidity provided via the CMIM common fund facili-

Box 4.1 **Other Hybrid Business Models**

An early forerunner:
Social cooperatives
In 1991, the legal framework for social cooperatives in Italy was finally made consistent with decades of practice and sentiment. Such cooperatives focus on delivering health, social or educational services for general community benefit or promoting social integration through employment and other services. The statues allow any profits to be distributed to members under certain conditions, though these profits and any assets may not be distributed upon dissolution. Social cooperatives also enjoy special tax benefits and preferential treatment in contracting. Today, 60% of social services in Italy are supplied through social cooperatives. Many other countries in Europe have incorporated the Italian model into their own legislation.

Benefit Corporations (B Corps)
Unlike L3C, 'B Corp' is a designation—not a legal corporate structure—under which business entities must consider the environment, community, employees' and suppliers' interests in its decision-making and report publicly on their performance. This allows directors to legally consider social goals without violating fiduciary duties to the owners and investors. Unlike with the L3C, however, the social goals of the benefit corporation do not necessarily have to outweigh the profit motive. In the US, legislation to support B Corps had been enacted in eleven states as of 2012. According to a third party B Lab website, there are currently 552 certified B Corps across 60 industries, totalling $3.11 billion in revenues.

Community Interest Companies (CICs)
Introduced in Britain in 2005, CICs are essentially LLCs that have a dual focus of commercial profit and social or community benefit, like L3Cs. Unlike L3Cs, however, they are restricted in the distribution of profits and assets, though some may pay dividends. Like B Corps, CICs publish annual reports under the UK Department of Business, Innovation and Skills. According to the 2011/2012 Report, there are nearly 5,000 CICs operating in industries such as sports, the arts, real estate, education, health, and social work.

tates economic recovery and enhances financial stability in the borrowing country and within the region. On the other hand, it creates moral hazard: If large amounts of liquidity are provided based on easy terms, borrowing countries may be encouraged to assume too much risk, thereby increasing the likelihood of higher future demand for crisis lending. Thus, the question of whether CMIM is an effective crisis lending arrangement depends on how well it balances the need to limit moral hazard, while providing sufficient liquidity to prevent defaults or contagion.

Moral hazard is prevented by either imposing conditions when a loan is made or refusing to bail out an economy that has not met accepted standards of economic management. However, enforcement of such conditions is a politically charged issue, and decision-making needs to be delegated and carried out on the basis of clear criteria. In principle, this is AMRO's job, but, in its relatively early development stage, the surveillance mechanism is not yet able to fashion appropriate policy conditions for balance-of-payments lending (Henning 2009; Sussangkarn 2010). Until AMRO is fully functional, the CMIM resolves the liquidity vs. moral hazard trade-off by relying on the above-mentioned IMF-link. Enforcement of conditionality is outsourced to the IMF, which possesses appropriate analytical capacity and maintains a neutral position in relation to political rivals China and Japan.

The IMF-link, however, is heavily criticised. Proponents of greater CMIM independence argue that members are unlikely to use the CMIM unless it is de-linked from the IMF (Sussangkarn 2010). Moreover, it has been noted that financial regionalism was not the reason that East Asian economies were never seriously threatened during the 2008 financial crisis. The fact that these economies had protected themselves through their own policies, particularly by building up their own foreign exchange reserves, could indicate a lack of confidence in regional solutions such as the CMI (Grimes 2011). Nevertheless, ASEAN+3 countries continued to push for the creation of the CMIM, which represents a step towards a more independent alternative to the IMF as envisioned in the original Asian Monetary Fund proposal. While the CMIM remains–perhaps reluctantly–nested in a global institution for now, the intent to continue the de-linking process is apparent (Henning 2009).

The L3C

Challenge. In gaps where market mechanisms, central allocation by state actors, and the best efforts of nonprofits fail to provide public goods, organisations have emerged that operate between and across sectoral boundaries. Such hybrid organisations pursue a double bottom line, seeking to further a social goal while maintaining a businesslike manner and generating modest financial returns. By doing so, they provide solutions to meet citizens' needs.

Despite the benefits they potentially produce for society, hybrid organisations do not operate under ideal conditions. On one hand, tension between social and economic goals exists as long as hybrid organisations are subject to traditional corporate law. It implies a constant danger of mission drift, i.e. the organisation could prioritise the economic goal at the expense of the social goal. On the other hand, hybrid organisations often face barriers to attracting capital needed to start, develop and scale up their operations. More adequate frameworks of governance for these organisations are clearly needed.

Innovative Solution. Such a framework is offered by a new form of business entity, first introduced in 2008 in Vermont, USA. The low-profit, limited liability company (L3C) builds on the same structure as a for-profit company, namely the limited liability company (LLC). The new legal form combines the flexibility of a traditional business with the pursuit of social purposes as the entity's explicit primary organisational goal, thus mitigating the tension that could lead to mission drift.

Another innovation within the L3C form is its translation of the requirements for a particular financing tool used by some US foundations, i.e., the programme-related investment (PRI)[7], directly into the statute. With a PRI, a foundation invests its own capital in an organisation or activity that furthers the foundation's charitable purposes. Many foundations have been reluctant to use this tool because of the relatively high cost of making sure that specific requirements are met. By writing these requirements into the statutes governing L3Cs, proponents expect to reduce those transaction costs and encourage foundations to use the PRI tool.

Potential Impact. The new form is not without controversy. Some critical voices have pointed to the lack of a clear definition about what qualifies as a 'socially beneficial purpose'. Others have criticised insufficient reporting mechanisms and hence, an apparent lack of accountability. Despite these shortcomings, there are convincing reasons for optimism that the L3C business format could become successful over the longer term.

First, such hybrid organisations are capable of addressing many problems that have not been resolved via market mechanisms or government programs. This is so largely because they bring together the best attributes of the traditional sectors, enjoying the flexibility of a forprofit business, while primarily pursuing a social purpose. New legal frameworks for hybrid organisations, such as the L3C and other forms (Box 4.1), provide a more adequate structure for their operations because they recognise and protect these multiple characteristics.

Hybrid organisations operate in a low-profit environment, i.e., their underlying business ideas are, in principle, financially sustainable and can generate modest returns. However, they face difficulties in attracting capital because traditional investors have little incentive to participate in a low-profit, potentially high-risk venture. The L3C's flexible ownership structure allows for tailoring shares according to combinations of reward and risk as preferred by different groups of investors. Thus, a foundation (through the PRI mechanism) or other social investor, concerned more with social than financial returns, can become involved at an early stage, paving the way for more traditional investors to come in once the enterprise has proven results. In that sense, this multiple-tier investment structure enables hybrid organisations to set up, expand and scale their operations.

The Norwegian Government Pension Fund Global

Challenge. Since investment strategies generally tend to focus only on financial returns, conflicts between profit-making and social goals could arise, for instance, if funds are invested in companies that produce harmful products or engage in ethically questionable activities. By contrast, investments could be an important tool to promote sustainable development since ownership can create possibilities to shape private business behaviour.

Typical characteristics of sovereign wealth funds imply that they have good reason to pay attention to this issue as they determine their investment strategies. On one hand, most sovereign wealth funds seek to maximise returns over the long term, which is dependent on sustainable development in not only the economic, but also environmental and social sense. On the other hand, sovereign wealth funds are state-owned, i.e., the owner and ultimate beneficiary is the general populace, implying that its support for the Fund's investment strategy is crucial. Thus, it is no surprise that socially responsible investment, which involves assessing extra-financial risks in investment decisions, is of increasing interest among reserve funds (Yermo 2008).

Innovative Solution. One of the most interesting examples in this regard is the Norwegian Government Pension Fund Global (GPFG), which manages its assets in conformity with the 'Ethical Guidelines for Responsible Investment Practice' first introduced in November 2004[8]. The GPFG[9] was set up in 1990 to support government savings to finance the National Insurance Scheme's pension expenditures and to manage Norway's petroleum revenues over the long term. By early 2011, the fund controlled some NOK 3,100 billion in assets. Its primary objective is to achieve the highest possible international purchasing power for the Fund's capital over time, subject to a moderate risk (Norwegian Ministry of Finance 2011).

Acknowledging the importance of political support from the Norwegian public and the connection between social factors and achieving a good return over time, the GPFG's investment strategy emphasises its role as a responsible investor. Introduced in the wake of a public debate triggered by the discovery of investments in weapon-producing companies, the GPFG's ethical guidelines stipulate that companies shall be excluded from the Fund's investment portfolio if they manufacture certain products (e.g., weapons that violate humanitarian principles in their normal use, tobacco) or if they are deemed to contribute to, or are responsible for, grossly unethical conduct (e.g., human rights violations, environmental damage, corruption) (Norwegian Ministry of Finance 2011). Since 2010, companies can also be placed under observation, allowing the Fund to express concern while holding up the possibility of change.

Decisions regarding exclusion or observation and the direction of investment policy more generally are taken by the Ministry of Finance, which acts as the GPFG's central governing body. Responsibility for operational management and for ensuring that assets are managed in accordance with the ethical guidelines is delegated to the Norges Bank Investment Management, a subsidiary of the Central Bank. An independent Council of Ethics, composed of five members appointed by the Ministry of Finance with its own secretariat, is responsible for evaluating whether companies' business behaviour complies with the Fund's ethical guidelines.

Potential Impact. The Norwegian Government Pension Fund Global's investment strategy is innovative as it brings ideas from socially-responsible investing into the public sector (recombination); the Fund admits its responsibility–on behalf of the Norwegian public–for the products produced by and the conduct of companies in which it owns shares. The Fund's sheer weight as one of the world's largest state-owned investment funds is testimony to its potential for influence. The threat of divestment, which would follow exclusion, or even observation–and the negative publicity likely associated with it–should create incentives for companies to pursue more ethical, sustainable avenues for profitmaking.

Among the critical arguments are that such responsible investing may not contribute to return maximisation (at least in the short-term) and that it is not possible to identify all misbehaviour and thus to exclude all companies which violate the criteria. Moreover, the environmental NGO Bellona suggests that the Fund still helps to maintain 'business as usual' by investing in resource-intensive companies, thereby allegedly becoming a de-facto supporter of global warming[10]. Despite these criticisms, GPFG's ethical guidelines can still be an important tool for responsible investment, especially if its impact is supplemented by, for example, active exercise of ownership (through voting) or promotion of good corporate governance or cooperation.

The Norwegian Fund seems to have become a model of socially-responsible investing for sovereign wealth funds in other countries, including Canada, France, Ireland, Sweden and New Zealand, which have specifically incorporated such criteria into their investment policy or engaged part of their portfolio in this manner (Yermo 2008).

Debt brake

Challenge. As described in Chapter 3, the global financial and economic crisis and the sovereign debt crisis in Europe have highlighted how external imbalances can turn into major threats for a country's public finances. When current account deficits become unsustainable, a government has to choose an adjustment strategy to realign domestic and foreign prices. Both external and internal adjustment strategies entail significant economic and political costs, making the best alternative the prevention of such deficits in the first place. Since current account deficits often emerge in response to fiscal expansion, governments should subject themselves to stricter budgetary discipline to limit excessive growth of public debt. In this regard, institutional constraints such as fiscal rules may offer a tool to restrain government spending behaviour. However, fiscal rules are effective only as long as governments comply with them.

Innovative Solution. In the 1990s, public debt in Switzerland increased even despite the existence of a constitutionally anchored principle requiring that expenditure and revenue be in balance. Finally, following much debate and a referendum approving amendment of the Swiss constitution in 2001, a new type of fiscal rule, namely the 'debt brake', went into effect in 2003, though because of initial difficulties, its full effectiveness was shifted to 2007 (Feld and Kirchgässner 2006).

In essence, the debt brake stipulates a structurally balanced federal budget, i.e. current expenditure has to be covered by current revenue without additional borrowing. To this end, a binding expenditure ceiling is specified one year in advance for the subsequent budget period. The expenditure ceiling allows for cyclical fluctuations, i.e. government may borrow more during a recession, but includes an obligation to offset the deficit with surplus revenue in times of economic upswing. Thus, cyclically induced deficits have to cancel out over a multiple-year period.

In this regard, a separate 'compensation' account where all unanticipated deviations from the expenditure ceiling are registered, i.e. an ex post control mechanism, represents the debt brake's main innovation over other fiscal rules. Any negative balance on this account must be eliminated, though no time horizon is specified; however, if the negative balance exceeds 6% of the expenditure of the preceding year, it has to be balanced within the next three years (Danninger 2002). Exceptions from the rigid rule are possible (in case of, for instance, natural disasters) but tied to strict conditions. The fiscal rule stipulates that all extraordinary expenditures that deviate from the calculated expenditure ceiling by more than 0.5% require the approval of the qualified majority of members in both chambers of the federal parliament and must be repaid in subsequent years.

Potential Impact. Fiscal rules, no matter how well designed they are from an economic point of view, may be ineffective if governments find easy ways to get around them (Drazen 2002). The decisive question is why the debt brake–in contrast to many previous rules–manages to effectively restore fiscal discipline?

First, the debt brake is anchored in the constitution, increasing the likelihood that a government does indeed act in accordance with its commitment. This alone, however, does not suffice. The debt brake adds an effective ex post control mechanism, a compensation account, which allows monitoring deficits, which in turn have to be considered in the computation of the ceiling[11] in subsequent years. Thus, government has no incentive to spend more in a current budget year, as its financial scope in later budget years would be limited. In that sense, the compensation account effectively forestalls excessive accumulation of debt by incorporating past deviations into calculations of future expenditures (Danninger 2002).

As shown in Figure 4.1, Switzerland's rate of central government public debt relative to GDP has declined since the debt brake became fully effective in 2007. Convinced by the rule's ex post control mechanism and this early evidence that it works, several jurisdictions have taken the Swiss debt brake as a role model. In particular, Germany adopted such a model in 2009 and was a proponent of European-level reforms stipulating that the eurozone countries insert debt brakes into their national constitutions. Moreover, proposals to implement similar fiscal rules in the US (Mitchell 2012) and on a global level (Dolls, Peichl and Zimmermann 2011) have also been put on the table.

However, critics point out that the rigid nature of the debt brake and similar rules puts fiscal policy in a straitjacket. Such is the case in the US state of California where balanced budget requirements are accompanied by restrictions against raising taxes (see Box 1.2 in Chapter 1). Furthermore, it does not sufficiently acknowledge borrowing as a means to facilitate economic recovery, and efforts to comply with the rule possibly force stagnation if cyclical downturns persist longer than upturns.

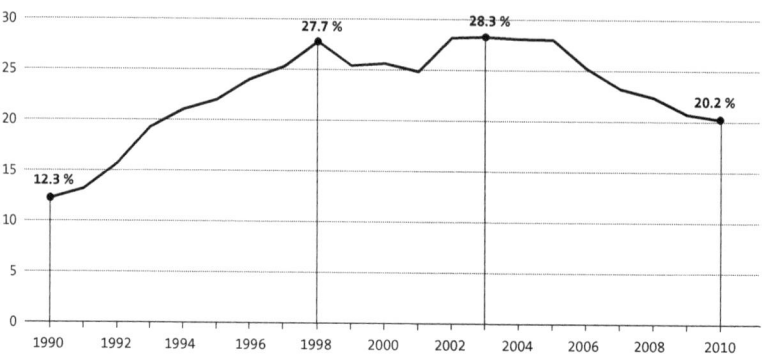

Figure 4.1 **Development of Switzerland's total central government debt as % of GDP, 1990—2011.**
Source: Based on OECD Statistics, http://stats.oecd.org/ (accessed 1 May 2012).

Charter cities

Challenge. Many developing countries are stuck in poverty, and what matters is to enact rules that set incentives to encourage adoption of more advanced technologies and institutions, thereby promoting progress. However, transitioning from existing rules to more conducive ones is a difficult process, due to rigid patterns of behaviour and political roadblocks. As a consequence, closer attention needs to be drawn to questions of how to accelerate changes so that better rules will more easily be adopted. To this end, meta-rules, i.e. superordinate rules that determine how rules are changed, are important. Usually, people associate meta-rules with standard political systems, which require some form of voting (i.e. democracy) or approval of an executive (i.e. authoritarian decision-making), but more open-mindedness may be needed (Romer, 2010: 7).

Innovative Solution. A new meta-rule lies at the base of 'Charter Cities', i.e. new entities that are established within the territory of developing countries but governed by their own administrative systems and set of rules. According to this concept, changes in rules are driven by migration of people who voluntarily opt in and out of the entity ('voting with their feet') as they search for better living conditions. The concept was introduced in 2008 by Paul Romer, an economics professor and President of the non-profit organisation Charter Cities, which offers advice for countries where this concept may be applied.

More precisely, to establish such an entity, a government must provide an uninhabited piece of land suitable for locating a large new city. This location is then designated as a special reform zone, making it relatively autonomous from the rest of the country. Charter Cities are governed by a charter that specifies their own, new set of rules that are designed to be more conducive to growth. Most importantly, enforcement is ensured through cooperation of authorities with trusted guarantor governments. The charter guarantees that all rules apply equally to all residents and that people can voluntarily enter and exit at any time. Thus, the logic behind the Charter Cities concept is that improved governance will attract investments, and as companies start producing, newly created job opportunities will incentivise people to opt in. Revenue from land leases to investors finances public goods, while investors provide public infrastructure, financed via collection of fees for services. Finally, theory predicts that over time Charter Cities will grow and become engines of growth, leading to significant improvements within the whole region.

The first place where Romer's ideas are being put into practice, though not completely ('Hong Kong in Honduras' 2011), is Honduras. A window of opportunity arose in the wake of the 2009 political crisis in the form of a broad consensus about the need for a new path. In 2011 the Honduran National Congress passed a constitutional amendment and later a constitutional statute, that together enable and guide the creation of 'Special Development Zones' (abbreviated RED after 'Regiones Especiales de Desarrollo' in Spanish). According to these measures, a governor assumes responsibility for executive functions and is accountable to a Transparency Commission of five international experts, appointed by Honduran President Lobo in December 2011 'to ensure that the process governing the development of the RED remains open, honest and free of corruption'[12]. To this end, the Transparency Commission may also rely on an audit committee, which has responsibility to scrutinise finances and monitor performance of government agencies. The judiciary enjoys a high degree of independence from the rest of the country, and its judges may be drawn from jurisdictions around the world (but must be approved by the Honduran National Congress). Moreover, the RED government may also rely on cooperation with trusted foreign courts as an external court of appeal. The development of Honduran Charter Cities is still at early stages. Among the next steps are choosing the actual locations and establishing a process for evaluating proposals from potential investors.

Potential Impact. Starting from scratch implies that problems typically impeding reforms and growth are avoided. Charter Cities allow experimentation to find out which rules work in the particular context, which would not be possible under current political processes for changing rules. Moreover, rules and governance structures are designed from the beginning to create the right conditions for attracting investment, including involving trusted partner countries and anchoring governance in their strong institutions to reduce political uncertainty. To ensure long-term investor confidence, Honduras has stipulated in its constitutional provisions that a two-thirds majority of members of the National Congress and approval by residents of the RED in a referendum would be required to return to the old system. Finally, given that they can freely opt in and out, it is intuitive that people will migrate to a Charter City only if they perceive it as a more attractive place. If this is the case, they will enjoy direct benefits in the form of better living conditions, and as more and more come, the city will prosper and in theory, other cities will replicate the rules and quality in the entire country will rise.

Charter Cities are unsurprisingly a highly controversial proposition, criticised as being undemocratic and neo-colonial. Romer, however, argues that exactly this form of governance, which is neither authoritarian nor fully democratic (yet), is needed to drive changes in rules and facilitate transition to better sets of rules: 'Changing the rules for a nation as a whole using existing political mechanisms forces leaders to persuade and sometimes coerce everyone to change what they are doing. The potential for opt-in avoids the need for coercion or for consensus, and can therefore speed up experimentation with new rules' (Romer 2010: 9). Moreover, advocates reject the idea that Charter Cities are neo-colonial, arguing that legitimacy derives from the concept's voluntary basis. In any case, many uncertainties remain, and it is unclear how this theory will play out in practice.

Social impact bonds

Challenge. A nonprofit organisation has developed and proven a solution to a pressing social issue, say, preventing criminals from returning to a life of crime. However, the organisation lacks the resources to scale up the programme beyond its original core. Government agencies, typically most comfortable with addressing social issues only after they have become acute, are reluctant or unable to take the risk of financing such preventive or early intervention programmes, in part because the results become visible only after a long period of time, if at all. At the same time, many programs continue to be financed year after year without proof of their effectiveness due both to contracts that emphasise inputs over outputs and to non-existent or insufficient monitoring and evaluation. There remains a gap to be filled, not merely in terms of money, but in terms of mechanisms that restructure responsibility, risks and incentives.

Innovative Solution. Social impact bonds (SIBs) are such a mechanism. Essentially, SIBs are based on a contract between an intermediary organisation and a government agency, in which both contracting partners agree on a clearly defined target that reflects a significant social improvement. The intermediary takes on the responsibility for selecting service providers, raising operating capital by issuing SIBs to philanthropic and other social investors, and monitoring progress. The government agency commits to pay the intermediary if and only if the target is achieved.

The fundamental concept for such bonds was outlined at a meeting of the UK's Council of Social Action in 2007, and, shortly afterwards, the idea was taken up by Social Finance, a UK-based organisation aiming to develop a market for social investments. Criminal justice appeared as an obvious choice for testing the proposition: Little money was spent on support for resettling prisoners after their release, so the high re-offending rates were hardly surprising. The potential for government savings seemed huge, as costs of criminal prosecution and prison maintenance would be much lower if crime was prevented. The first pilot scheme building on a six-year contract between the Ministry of Justice and Social Finance was launched at Peterborough Prison, UK in September 2010. The contractually agreed target was to reduce the re-offending rate (i.e. the rate of prisoners committing another crime within 12 months after release) among a clearly defined group of 3,000 male prisoners by 10 percent compared to a control group. According to the contract, Social Finance is responsible for selecting providers to do the rehabilitation work and overseeing their service delivery, whereas the Ministry of Justice is committed to pay if the target is met, but only then. Building on this arrangement, Social Finance raised £5m by issuing SIBs to investors, including charitable trusts and foundations. This initial cash was used as operating capital to commission service providers to support the cohort of Peterborough prisoners in finding work and appropriate housing, obtaining medical treatment and more generally, giving them confidence to reintegrate into society.

Potential Impact. Attracting capital via SIBs overcomes the gap in resources and ideas associated with the funding of prevention and early intervention services as well as other social services. At least three factors are likely to contribute to the success and future uptake of SIBs. First, they build on the growing trend toward public-private partnerships, whereby public agencies and private entities agree to share responsibility in solving public problems. In the case of SIBs, government agencies contract with an intermediary that is responsible for mobilising financial and organisational resources on the front end and for ensuring results. Other stakeholders such as service providers and social investors have specific roles as well, so that SIBs become true multi-stakeholder solutions. Second, as responsibilities and tasks are distributed or re-assigned, the risks are also redistributed. For example, the risk that the desired results are not achieved is transferred to the intermediary and, ultimately, the investor, relieving the government agency of the fear of failing to perform with taxpayer money. Finally, to attract resources despite the inherent risks, incentive systems that also ensure mutual accountability are built into the arrangements, as are rigorous evaluation systems. Most obviously, the financial reward is an incentive to investors and to the intermediary to conduct careful due diligence before engaging in the programme and close monitoring throughout in order to ensure the agreed-upon social outcome is achieved. Service providers have the incentive to deliver results, not only because of their values, but also because the intermediary can easily replace them.

SIBs are not appropriate arrangements for financing every type of social purpose, but there does seem to be a significant potential for replication. In the UK, several government departments have articulated interest, and Social Finance has identified other policy fields in which SIBs may be applicable. The concept is also popular in the US, where Barack Obama proposed pilot schemes to test what he calls 'pay-for-success-bonds' and several states and cities have begun pilots and feasibility studies. More generally, it is hoped that experimentation with SIBs will catalyse the development of other social investment options.

Transition initiatives

Challenge. World economic growth has been accompanied by high levels of energy consumption as well as high levels of greenhouse gas emissions. Such activity has contributed to climate change and brought the world closer to 'peak oil', i.e. the point at which oil extraction reaches its limit and the rate of production declines. Climate change and 'the end of oil' are among the greatest global challenges today due to their far-reaching and potentially catastrophic consequences. In order to become more independent of fossil fuels and to tackle effects of global warming, radical economic, social and behavioural changes will be required. Nevertheless, as shown in Chapter 2, global governance systems are not yet up to the task of developing and implementing adequate responses. Global challenges usually call for international cooperative action, but while nation states might agree on ideas, the translation of ideas into action remains controversial. On the other hand, while grassroots initiatives have sprung up across the globe, their impact has been rather small-scale.

Innovative Solution. The perception that it may be too late if citizens wait for governments to take adequate action and that it may be too little as long as citizens act as individuals was a driving force behind the emergence of the Transition movement. At its core is the aim to engage citizens in community-level action to prepare for a future with less oil dependence by strengthening resilience, i.e. 'the capacity of a system to absorb disturbance and to reorganise while undergoing change, so as to still retain essentially the same functions, structure, identity and feedbacks' (Hopkins 2008: 37).

The idea was initially developed by Rob Hopkins, a teacher of permaculture, who together with his colleague Naresh Giangrande launched the first Transition Town in the small town of Totnes, England in 2005/06. By 2012, the Transition model had spread to more than 400 officially registered initiatives in some 40 countries around the globe[13]. The members of each initiative organise their own activities following the model and adhering to a set of common principles (see Box 4.2 for examples). Yet, all local groups are also part of the Transition network (or movement). The Transition Network Ltd., an NGO based in Totnes, and a growing set of national and subnational hubs provide training and advice to local initiatives and facilitate collaboration both within the movement and with partners.

Potential Impact. The fact that the Transition movement appears to have expanded at viral speed suggests that it may go much beyond a small-scale impact. What is unique about the movement is that it succeeds in bringing together large numbers of volunteers, who come from different backgrounds and hold different political views. Despite their diversity, they work towards a common goal, i.e. to promote a transition towards an economy less dependent on high levels of fossil fuel consumption and greenhouse gas emissions. To achieve this goal, community members undertake a myriad of small-scale projects at the local level. While such small-scale responses

---

Box 4.2 **Examples of Transition projects**

Building

Carbon Neutral Development (Groningen, Netherlands) seeks to strengthen the bond between local food production and distribution whilst also sharing skills, knowledge and expertise. A social structure is created by arranging private homes and communities around central shared spaces, thereby offering greater combined value.

Energy

Solar Buyers Club (Presteigne, Wales) achieves an economy of scale on solar panel purchases, reducing local energy usage.

Food

Local Food (Sommen District, Sweden) creates a map of the nine boroughs in the district, showing the local food producers, the products they produce, and a series of videos of them telling their story as to the whys and hows of local food production.

Transport

Hills Electric Bike Project (Adelaide Hills, Australia) encourages people to consider cycling as a means of transport and makes it more accessible by providing the community short loans of electric bike conversion kits.

Business

Time Bank (Saratoga Springs, NY, USA) connects community members and their skills to service needs (computer help, keeping an elderly person company) without the exchange of cash, valuing everyone's contributions equally.

appear nearly irrelevant against these global challenges, the Transition model demonstrates that together their overall impact may become visible at a macro level. Thus, the Transition model builds on the principle of 'think global, act local'.

One of the keys to the Transition movement's success lies in its organisational structure. In particular, the movement functions as an umbrella, providing cohesion among hundreds of local initiatives. The Transition Network Ltd. defines and upholds the main principles of Transition, a 'common denominator' underlying all local initiatives. In addition, these movement support organisations promote collaboration between local groups and provide information and training to support individual initiatives. Participation in the network provides a certainty of being part of a wider movement, while granting freedom to individual initiatives to self-organise their activities makes it possible for local groups to take decisions independently and dedicate themselves to the projects and topics about which they are most concerned. Moreover, the Transition movement embraces an explicitly positive vision of a better life without oil that provides an incentive for people to become active.

The Transition movement appears promising. On the one hand, it does not depend on governments to at some point take adequate international action; instead, its bottom-up approach allows immediate action. On the other hand, even though individual Transition initiatives start from the local level, the contributions of all initiatives add up to a bigger response. Thus, the Transition movement starts from the bottom to bring about the behavioural changes that climate change and peak oil are likely to require. Whether the incipient movement's growth continues at its current pace will depend on its capacity to continue to mobilise people and resources and its ability to handle its own transition from upstart to a global movement. Nevertheless, these small-scale initiatives may indeed make up a global response in the end.

Ushahidi

Challenge. Information is a crucial prerequisite for proper decision-making. The less complete information is, the higher the likelihood that a wrong decision will be taken. In cases such as violent conflicts or natural disasters, even human lives can depend on the availability of timely and accurate information. Arriving rescue and relief personnel must quickly decide where to allocate their efforts, but they need to have a clear picture of the situation: What exactly happened? Where were most people killed or injured? What is the scale of destruction? However, in light of the chaos that prevails in such crisis situations, only limited information is available at the outset. Precious time is often lost until rescue teams sent by the government or relief organisations and journalists have obtained and conveyed their own picture of the situation. Furthermore, especially in the cases of disaster or armed conflict,

Table 4.3 **Other contexts in which Ushahidi platforms were used**

Date	Country	Purpose
April 2009	Worldwide	To track the dissemination of the H1N1 virus.
January 2010	Haiti	To assist rescue workers in delivering relief in the aftermath of the devastating earthquake.
February 2010	USA	To map the effects of oil refinery accidents in the state of Louisiana by encouraging citizens to document their stories and experiences.
May 2010	El Salvador	To bring 3G wireless technology to create and test a crime reporting and mapping system.
July 2010	Russia	To better coordinate information flow and relief efforts for the thousands of families who lost their homes due to the wildfires.
February 2011	Canada	To prepare for extensive flooding expected in the Red River Valley and Saskatchewan River regions.
March 2011	Japan	To map individual reports in the aftermath of the 2011 earthquake.
October 2011	Morocco	To monitor elections and promote transparency.

the sites in most need of assistance may be difficult or impossible to reach. Thus, crisis relief efforts are not always concentrated in the places where help is most urgently required.

Innovative Solution. Such conditions were the case in Kenya, where riots broke out in early 2008 after disputed elections. A blogger, Ory Okolloh, attempted to keep track of the violence, posting a request online for local people to send eyewitness reports to her email address. She was overwhelmed by the mass of incoming information and subsequently appealed to the Internet community to determine whether it was feasible to aggregate and display such data using a Google map. Her call drew the attention of two technically savvy volunteers who managed within a few days to get a platform running that assembled and presented incoming information about where violence was occurring. Thus, Ushahidi emerged out of a citizen journalism effort and was considered of inestimable value for information collection and visualisation, which ultimately helped improve the coordination of emergency responses in the Kenyan context.

Today, the term Ushahidi, which means 'testimony' in Swahili, refers to both a non-profit company as well as its product, i.e. free and open-source software that helps create online platforms to serve as a centralised information hub. It enables collection of eyewitness reports of incidents from hundreds or even thousands of citizens on the ground, which can be sent by SMS via mobile phones, communicated via email or twitter messages, or directly entered on the website. Ushahidi's additional benefit is that its software aggregates all available information and then visually documents the frequency of events on a map, which is posted on the Internet for anyone who needs the information. In addition, instructions on, for example, how individuals can respond to such events can be sent directly via SMS to anyone who has registered a phone number at Ushahidi.

Potential Impact. So why is a new software programme considered a governance innovation? By creating a novel platform for collecting, visualising and re-distributing critical information in a timely fashion, Ushahidi (the organisation) has indeed found a better way to address public problems that leads to better outcomes. For example, in the case of crisis management, Ushahidi's original application, relief workers can now receive real-time information from numerous eyewitnesses close to the scene, so that emergency personnel can be better prepared to act as they arrive. The ability to visualise events makes it easier to detect patterns and thus to allocate assistance and address problems more effectively.

In addition, Ushahidi (the software) enables every citizen with access to some kind of communication technology, including mobile phones that are widely spread even in less developed regions, to submit their eyewitness reports. More informants tend to provide a more precise overall picture of the situation. While the use of 'crowdsourcing'[14] to mobilise collective action toward a common objective is not necessarily novel (think Wikipedia), its application to solving public problems makes the Ushahidi platform a clear governance innovation. Furthermore, since Ushahidi builds on an open-source approach and the software is available free of charge, it can and has been adopted and adapted in numerous settings and policy fields and by diverse types of actors (see Table 4.3). The team at Ushahidi (the organisation), the many volunteers involved in both developing the tool and making it work by actively reporting useful information, and others have only just begun to uncover Ushahidi's (the software's) potential to democratise the collection and use of information and to put it to work to solve public problems of many kinds.

Ushahidi's future development will depend on how well it manages to overcome persistent problems. Because of the potential impact on Ushahidi's legitimacy, not the least among these issues are information reliability and the risks associated with possible manipulation or intentional misinformation.

Open Government Partnership

Challenge. Shortly after his inauguration in 2009, US President Obama introduced a memorandum stating that his administration was committed to creating an unprecedented level of openness in government[15]. Greater openness in government and administration is expected to bring about many positive changes in governance, including increased efficiency and effectiveness in the public sector as well as strengthened democracy. The call for more transparency, participation and collaboration in government and governance–at all levels and on the part of all actors–is not new. The challenge continues to be translating this demand into concerted action.

Innovative Solution. Addressing this challenge requires political leadership, technical knowledge, sustained effort and investment, and collaboration between governments and civil society[16], i.e. many of those governance requirements outlined in Chapter 2. The Open Government Partnership (OGP) was founded to provide exactly this. The multilateral, multi-stakeholder initiative was officially launched at the UN General Assembly meeting in September 2011, a year after Obama had invited concrete commitments to promote open government worldwide (see a list of participating countries in Box 4.3).

Essentially, the initiative aims to secure country commitments to their peers and their citizens to support or implement activities to promote transparency, empower citizens, ensure professional integrity, and harness new technologies to strengthen governance. In order to join the OGP, countries must first meet a verifiable set of minimum eligibility criteria relating to fiscal transparency, public access to information, disclosures related to elected and senior public officials, and citizen engagement. In the context of a public consultation process, national governments then develop a national action plan, in which they specify measures to be implemented. In preparing their plans, governments may also draw on the 'Networking Mechanism' to connect with experts and acquire know-how necessary to turn their promises into meaningful action. Finally, aspiring members must endorse the 'Open Government Declaration', a high-level political statement defining the initiative's core principles.

Box 4.3 **Members of the Open Government Partnership (as of August 12, 2012)**

Albania	Estonia	Malta	South Korea
Armenia	Georgia	*Mexico*	Spain
Brazil	Greece	Moldova	Sweden
Bulgaria	Guatemala	Montenegro	Turkey
Canada	Honduras	Netherlands	Ukraine
Chile	*Indonesia*	*Norway*	*United Kingdom*
Colombia	Israel	Paraguay	*United States*
Croatia	Italy	Peru	Uruguay
Czech Republic	Jordan	*Philippines*	
Denmark	Latvia	Romania	
Dominican Republic	Lithuania	Slovak Republic	Note: Founding
El Salvador	Macedonia	*South Africa*	members in italics.

The OGP is governed by an International Steering Committee, comprised of both government and civil society representatives, and funded by voluntary commitments from some participating governments (US, UK, Norway) and grants from corporate, private, and multilateral donors.

Potential Impact. It may well prove that the Open Government Partnership fulfils the governance requirements necessary to advance greater openness and, thus, in theory, more efficient and effective public problem-solving. Current participants include a host of leading developed, emerging market and developing countries. As long as they sustain their commitment, the initiative could exercise the political leadership necessary to effect change. Furthermore, other governments will likely see the advantages of participation, be they external support for implementing internal reforms, favourable public relations, or perhaps access to sources of foreign aid, although nowhere has this been made an explicit condition.

The Partnership also enhances access to the technological knowledge needed to make the required changes. The OGP encourages learning from each other through dialogue and offers a Networking Mechanism that connects public officials with experts from civil society and the private sector. Thus, the Partnership should promote quicker dissemination of novel ideas and best practices, while also providing support and technical assistance to governments while they develop their commitments and implement national action plans.

Once countries have made their commitment to openness, a sustained– and potentially credible–effort is ensured through a set of complementary monitoring mechanisms. First, each participating government must publish an annual report based on a self-assessment of its performance. Second, governments must also submit themselves to the scrutiny of independent assessment reports, conducted by local governance experts to determine governments' compliance with their commitments and published in both the local language and English on the OGP portal.

Still, appropriate sanction mechanisms must be in place should a country's commitments turn out to be empty promises. OGP's Articles of Governance allow Steering Committee representatives to engage with non-performing governments to address concerns. If such efforts fail, the Steering Committee may review and in the worst case suspend that country's participation. However, there are no sufficiently clear statements about how to deal with countries that fail to keep their promises.

The fourth requirement is collaboration: Many elements, e.g. civil society participation on the Steering Committee, are built into the Partnership arrangements, and participating governments commit to developing their action plans through a multi-stakeholder process, including public consultations. In many action plans, civil society organisations also take on diverse roles in implementation. Ideally, such civil society involvement will stimulate citizen engagement to ensure that their governments follow up on their promises.

As the OGP is a novel multilateral, multi-stakeholder initiative, questions and criticism abound regarding, for example, the robustness of monitoring and sanctions, measuring and comparing performance, and ensuring that country commitments are ambitious enough to make a real difference. Furthermore, it remains to be seen whether the Partnership's leadership role is maintained as political leaders change over the coming years.

mySociety

Challenge. Falling voter turnout, lower levels of public participation in civic life, public cynicism towards political institutions, and a collapse in once-strong political loyalties: such observations may indicate an estrangement between elected representatives and those they supposedly represent (Crabtree 2003). In response, many governments have asked how information and communication technologies could be harnessed to strengthen citizens' interest in public policy-making and have taken to the Internet. However, despite posing the right question, governments often came up with the wrong answer, as most mainstream e-government approaches are simply existing services put online and are largely mired in a top-down 'Government 1.0' mode, which primarily serves the needs of government itself (Millard 2010). Furthermore, assuming the flow of information increases with initiatives such as the Open Government Partnership described above, what will citizens be able to do with all that input?

Innovative Solution. Calling for 'a new agenda for e-democracy', policy analyst James Crabtree (2003) claimed that the Internet could be more helpful in promoting citizen engagement if based on a different principle, i.e. one that would cater to the needs of citizens rather than the needs of government. Tom Steinberg put these ideas into action and launched 'mySociety', a project of the UK Citizens Online Democracy (UKCOD) in 2003. An independent civil society venture funded by donations as well as profits generated from a commercial services spin-off, mySociety employs some core staff, but relies heavily on volunteers.

The innovations mySociety offers help citizens connect with and improve society through websites that provide tools to achieve offline impacts. Each website, based on open source technology, serves a single purpose, but the majority are dedicated to providing relevant information and facilitating dialogue between citizens and their political representatives. Among their most visited websites is TheyWorkForYou.com, where citizens can find usefully organised information about their representatives' voting patterns, contributions to parliamentary debates, statements on key issues, and financial interests. TheyWorkForYou.com is connected via links with WriteToThem.com and HearFromYourMP.com, two other websites that help to establish connections between the two sides. Box 4.4 provides more information on selected websites united under the umbrella of mySociety.

Potential Impact. In contrast to many governments' supply-side approach to using information and communication technologies to enhance civic engagement, mySociety seems to give a 'better' answer. This civil society-led project uses the Internet to enable citizens to engage so they can actually enjoy tangible benefits. Volunteer programmers build websites to make government data available and usable and to initiate dialogue and hence, eliminate information gaps that may hinder democratic participation. Though today more official information is published online, it is widely dispersed making it difficult to retrieve. In that sense, websites like TheyWorkForYou provide added value by gathering bits of information and compiling it in a more user-friendly structure, so that citizens can easily be informed about and monitor their representatives' activities. In addition, the websites are designed to make sure that even people with very poor computer skills can

---

Box 4.4 **Selected mySociety Websites**

FixMyStreet.com (since 2007)
FixMyStreet is a simple map-based application using crowdsourced information that allows citizens to report public infrastructure problems, e.g., broken street lamps, abandoned vehicles, or potholes. Since many citizens are unaware of where to report local problems, FixMyStreet automatically sends the complaint to the appropriate authority, based on the identified location of the reported problem. The progress of the report is further tracked and posted online, encouraging accountability between citizens and local authorities. Users can post reports from their smartphones and sign up for email or RSS alerts to receive updates on problems reported in their area, whether at home or the workplace.

HearFromYourMP.com (since 2005)
To encourage more open communication, citizens can sign up to receive messages from their local representatives. Pooling these requests, HearFromYourMP then sends a message such as, 'X number of your constituents would like to hear what you're up to'. As the number of interested constituents grows, messages will continue to be sent until that member of parliament responds. MP responses are linked on the website, posting a copy of the email with a section for comments. A related effort WriteToThem.com sent over a million messages to elected representatives between 2005 and 2012.

TheyWorkForYou.com (since 2004)
As mySociety's most visited site with roughly 3.5 million visits in 2010, TheyWorkForYou provides citizens with information about their local member of parliament and tracks public statements, speeches, voting decisions, expenses and media publicity in an effort to improve transparency and accountability through citizen monitoring. Content derives mostly from the Hansard parliamentary records and other sources of media coverage and are compiled via the parliamentary informatics project software, Public Whip.

use them. mySociety thus not only increases transparency, but also alleviates barriers for citizens to connect with their elected representatives and public officials. Furthermore, mySociety's services are essentially user-centric, focusing primarily on the everyday needs of citizens. Thus, there is much to suggest that mySociety can even reach some of those people who were not previously interested in public policy. In fact, mySociety claims that 40% of the people using WriteToThem have written to their MP for the first time[17]. In that sense, mySociety serves as a good example of how information and communication technologies can be used to foster greater citizen engagement and therefore, promote positive impacts on democracy in addition to public sector performance.

In terms of uptake, since mySociety websites are based on open source software, replication and refunctionality are easy. As with the Ushahidi programme, websites and other tools based on the mySociety approach are now being used in many countries and in many public policy fields. Some government agencies have also taken up the approach to focus on citizen demands and needs.

Conclusion

The cases analysed above suggest several key findings. For one, the larger scan revealed no larger ideologies or visions of and for governance being developed–let alone debated–that in scale and ambition rival the organising and mobilising power of neo-liberalism or social democracy (Judt 2010). If described in terms of a multi-polar world or the end of history, the current era is less ideological than previous ones. This does not mean that governance innovations are non-ideological or lack a value base, but they do tend to be more on the technocratic than normative side, and more targeted on specific issues and less part of some grander agenda, let alone design. Referring back to Table 4.1, the absence of first order and first principle innovations is striking given the threat of punctuated equilibriums.

By contrast, innovations are more frequent at the second order level of governance decisions: they are about making existing systems more efficacious and effective, like the social impact bonds in the case of pay-for-performance in social services or Ushahidi or Open Government Partnership in helping governments manage and disseminate information; they are about dealing with effects, and they are not about some new overall attack on root causes of some systemic ill or another, with the Chiang Mai Initiative Multilateralisation for currency fluctuations being at least a partial exception. In this sense, while the crises of recent years do suggest something close to a punctuated equilibrium, governance innovations are less at the system level of first order decision than they are concerned with second order improvement.

A second result is the pronounced presence and indeed involvement of civil society in the innovations reviewed. Governments themselves do not appear as generators of new governance ideas, although the Chiang Mai Initiative Multilateralisation and Norwegian Pension Fund are notable exceptions, but frequently think tanks and civil society initiatives, including social movements, are. However, it is not civil society action alone but cooperation with governmental agencies and even business that brings about change and governance innovations.

Related to the active role of civil society is the difference in levels at which governance problems are located and addressed. For example, a global challenge is addressed at a local level, as is the case for Transition initiatives, or provided on a regional level instead of relying on an international institution such as the IMF, which is the approach taken by the Chiang Mai Initiative Multilateralisation. Likewise, innovations involve changes in the types of actors involved. For example, a national government, which was primarily responsible for emergency responses, gets valuable assistance from members of civil society, who crowdsource information and support coordination of relief efforts–which is the essence of Ushahidi. What is more, instead of governments, civil society makes government data available for citizens and thus, eliminates information gaps that hinder democratic participation–the case of mySociety.

The innovations reviewed above reveal mostly recombination and refunctionality strategies, with only one case based on first principle (Table 4.2). Their dominance and the frequent presence of some form of partnership in bringing about innovations underscore the importance of understanding governance as a multi-level and multi-actor process. It seems unhelpful to assume that one particular actor is responsible for solving a certain challenge (e.g. 'government is responsible for provision of public goods'), or that a challenge has to be tackled on a specific level (e.g. 'global challenges need global-level action').

Indeed, many innovations build on cooperation from public and private sectors as well as civil society. In light of the urgency of action that today's governance challenges would require, efforts on multiple levels by different actors appear to be the current pattern on how to improve governance readiness. The set of governance innovations presented in this chapter indicates that it may be worth paying more attention to bottom-up approaches, whose individual impact may seem rather limited at first, but which impact may be leveraged, if successful models are copied in other contexts.

Finally, it is worth emphasising that the selection of governance innovations presented in this chapter may well reflect 'the tip of the iceberg' only. In view of future editions of this Report, this section will add more cases over time, and revisit ones reported. Against this background, readers are invited to share their opinions and provide suggestions via the Report's website.

Endnotes

1. We also recognise that, because of the unintended outcomes that might result from the innovation, what appears today to be a clear case of a governance innovation might not fit the definition a decade from now.
2. See US Vice President Al Gore's National Partnership for Reinventing Government during President Clinton's Administration (1993-2001) (http://govinfo.library.unt.edu/npr/whoweare/historyofnpr.html (accessed 20 August 2012)); Painter (1999) for analysis of Blair's public sector reform; Howarth (2001) and Pollitt and Bouckaert (2000) for comparative analyses of public management reforms. See also World Bank (2008) for evaluation of World Bank initiatives.
3. See for example the debate in the Federalist Papers (Madison 1788; also Hamilton 1787).
4. For further reading on neo institutionalism, see DiMaggio and Powell (1983, 1991), Drori, Meyer and Hwang (2006), Meyer and Rowan (1977), and Scott (1995).
5. For this purpose, the Report is complemented by a website where policymakers, academics as well as interested readers are invited to share their opinions, exchange ideas and discuss.
6. Member states of the Association of Southeast Asian Nations (ASEAN) are Brunei, Cambodia, Indonesia, Laos, Malaysia, Burma, Philippines, Singapore, Thailand and Vietnam. The +3 countries include the People's Republic of China (including Hong Kong), Japan and South Korea.
7. In order to qualify as a PRI, an investment 1) must further the foundation's exempt (charitable) purpose; 2) must not have production of income or appreciation of property as a significant purpose; 3) its purpose may not be to influence legislation or take part in political campaigns on behalf of candidates.
8. Revised guidelines were introduced in March 2010.
9. The Norwegian Government Pension Fund consists of two separate funds: the Government Pension Fund Global (known as Government Petroleum Fund until 2006) that exclusively invests abroad, and the Government Pension Fund Norway (previously known as National Insurance Scheme Fund, which was established in 1967) that mainly invests domestically.
10. See Bellona's Recommendations for the Ethical Guidelines of the Norwegian Pension Fund—Global; available at website of Norwegian government: http://www.regjeringen.no/upload/FIN/etikk/h_uttalelser/bellona.pdf (accessed 3 July 2012).
11. Since Switzerland has maximum tax rates set in the national constitution, policymakers cannot simply raise taxes to increase expected revenue and thereby the expenditure ceiling.
12. Website of Honduran RED: http://www.red.hn/ (accessed 24 June 2012).
13. The list of official initiatives can be found at the website of the Transition Network: http://www.transitionnetwork.org/initiatives/by-number (accessed 29 June 2012).
14. According to Jeff Howe's commonly used definition, crowdsourcing refers to "the act of taking a job traditionally performed by a designated agent (usually an employee) and outsourcing it to an undefined, generally large group of people in form of an open call." See his weblog: http://crowdsourcing.typepad.com/cs/2006/06/crowdsourcing_a.html (accessed 3 July 2012).
15. See President Obama's Memorandum for the Heads of Executive Departments and Agencies: http://www.whitehouse.gov/the_press_office/TransparencyandOpenGovernment (accessed 1 June 2012).

16 http://www.opengovpartnership.org/sites/www.opengovpartnership.org/files/page_files/OGP_Oficial_Brochure_1.pdf (accessed 3 July 2012).
17 http://www.mysociety.org/ (accessed 22 May 2012).

V. Introducing a New Generation of Governance Indicators

HELMUT K. ANHEIER, PIERO STANIG, *and* MARK KAYSER

The preceding chapters in the Report presented conceptual frameworks for governance performance and readiness, and used insights from organisational studies to approach governance innovations. Their combined purpose is to provide a foundation for developing an indicator system measuring, once fully developed: governance readiness in relation to governance requirements, and the gap between what is in place currently and what would be required given current and future governance conditions; governance performance in relation to policy outcomes and welfare effects, as seen in the interplay between legitimacy, efficacy and effectiveness; and innovativeness to assess the degree to which different actors in governance systems generate new ideas and approaches.

Attempts to quantify governance have grown in scale and scope as well as sophistication. An impressive array of indicators and measures have become available that prominently include the World Bank Institute's Worldwide Governance Indicators, Transparency International's Corruption Perceptions Index, the Revenue Watch Index, the World Economic Forum's Competitiveness Index, Bertelsmann's BTI, the Legatum Prosperity Index, and the Ibrahim Index of African Governance, among others.[1] And while we recognise the significant gains made in the brief history of governance indicators, we do nonetheless see important limitations in available indicators and their approach to measuring governance.[2]

Available indicators do not take the fundamental notion of governance as multi-sector, multi-actor systems seriously.

One basic limitation is that available indicators do not take the fundamental notion of governance as multi-sector, multi-level systems seriously. Indicators tend to suffer from what has been called methodological nationalism in that they only consider the nation state as the appropriate unit of analysis, and neglect the importance of supranational dynamics (e.g. UN system, EU) and the subnational level (e.g. cities, regions).[3] Private actors, especially the role of transnational corporations, international NGOs, and civil society organisations, generally feature at the margins, if at all.

Next, they concentrate on dimensions internal to the country in question. As a result, the interdependencies of governance that underlie much of this Report are neglected and too easily escape empirical attention. Finally, conventional governance indicators tend to focus primarily on the capacity of state administrations and public sector ills such as corruption or failures to implement some kind of regulation or another. At most indirectly do they address the overall fit between governance requirements and the governance systems in place, and, if they try to show what difference governance makes, they focus on broadly defined concepts like prosperity and development or simpler measures like economic growth. Our aim is to focus more directly on the links between legitimacy, efficacy and effectiveness, and performance.

The purpose of this chapter is not to dismiss prior efforts and question their usefulness altogether. Rather, the analysis of the state and conditions of governance presented in the preceding chapters calls for a new generation of indicators that go beyond a singular focus on seemingly self-contained nation states as the primary unit of analysis, that are grounded in conceptual models, and that stay close to the governance problématiques of our times, especially the notion of interdependence. Of course, building such a system will take time and effort, to be sure, and will require the sustained attentions of future editions of this Report. What then, is this new generation of governance indicators we propose?

Towards a Governance Indicator System

Like any indicator system, its purpose is to offer an empirical portrait of the key dimensions of the phenomenon under consideration–in this case, governance. The system has to meet three basic requirements: it has to take the fundamental notion of governance as a multi-actor and multi-level system seriously; it has to address interdependence; and it has to have an analytic and policy-oriented focus, and be more than description. In other words, the indicator system, once developed and tested, could be applied to different actors (international organisations, states, corporations, civil society organisations) and across different levels (international and regional systems, nation states, or cities) and policy fields–and show or otherwise reveal interdependencies. And, in terms of focus, the system should take account of the central governance issues that are the mainstay topics of this Report: readiness, performance, and innovativeness.

One can easily imagine the complexity of any such system, and indeed anticipate the danger that it might become unwieldy. Against this background, it is useful to keep a number of methodological 'best practices' in mind:[4]

- Parsimony, i.e. 'achieving most with least' by aiming for design simplicity;
- Significance, i.e. focusing on the truly critical aspects of governance and its relationships;
- Conceptual focus, i.e. developing a system that improves understanding and generates knowledge; and
- Policy relevance, i.e. selecting indicators useful for policy analysts and policymakers alike.

The conceptual models introduced earlier in this Report serve as central building blocks for three indicator systems: governance readiness, governance performance, and governance innovation. Specifically:

The governance requirements described in Chapter 2 can be developed into an **indicator system of governance readiness**. As its unit of analysis, the governance readiness system puts primary focus on actors, be they at supranational, international, national, regional or municipal levels. A version of the indicator system could measure the readiness of corporate and civil society actors. The system would distinguish between governance requirements that are essentially compatible with the existing institutional governance framework as well as the given political and socio-economic constellations (GR1 to GR3), aiming at the maintenance, improvement or modification of established governance functions within existing governance systems; and governance requirements that do not fit into existing governance contexts (GR4 to GR6), requiring innovations that change features of a particular governance system.

Table 5.1 offers an initial operationalisation of the six governance requirements by listing sample dimensions to guide indicator development. Recall that while Figure 2.2 in Chapter 2 presents the case of governance readiness globally, one can also think of a hypothetical country ranked by each of the six readiness indicators, where a value of 100 would indicate full readiness, and lower values increasing levels of un-readiness.

By contrast, the **governance performance model** emphasises policy fields such as education, the environment, or finance. It can also be used to assess the performance of a particular actor such as national and municipal governments as a whole, but its primary focus is the policy field.

As pointed out in Chapter 1, the performance of a governance system, as the outcome, depends on three crucial aspects and their interrelationships: legitimacy, efficacy, and effectiveness. The legitimacy of a governance system in place becomes a positive and negative reinforcer that magnifies the effects of efficacy and effectiveness on performance, and feeds back to legitimacy itself. As a result, governance systems can find themselves in downward spirals when losses in performance and legitimacy reinforce each other; it can also enter a stage where gains in either strengthen the other, thereby improving performance and fostering legitimacy to achieve greater stability.

For most applications of the performance system, the unit of analysis is the policy field, whereas the units of observation are the main actors and stakeholders operating in that field. Indicators would be measures in terms of the legitimacy actors enjoy, how efficacious and effective they are, and their contribution to policy outcomes in the sense of performance, defined as the capacity of the governance system to meet set goals, or at least attain a level of performance seen as satisfactory by key stakeholders to maintain stability over time. By contrast, bad governance is indicated by underperforming and unstable systems.

Table 5.1 **Governance Readiness Indicator System**

Governance Requirement (GR)	Sample Indicators		
	Nation state	Private corporation	International NGO
GR1: Averting the risk of dual —market and state—failure	Internal administrative capacity Accountability and transparency Regulatory implementation track record Compliance enforcement Monitoring system Knowledge generation Use of positive and negative incentives Independence, functioning of legal system Anti-corruption measures	Due diligence Conflict of interest policy Anti-corruption measures Accountability and transparency Rules governing lobbying Tax behaviour Violations of laws and regulation	Due diligence Conflict of interest policy Anti-corruption measures Accountability and transparency Rules governing lobbying Tax behaviour Violations of laws and regulations
GR2: Correcting fairness deficits	Joint consultations Monitoring and reporting Transnational agenda-setting Voting record in international bodies Participatory decision-making Creating regional partnerships	CSR and international responsibilities	Contributions to global fairness and justice
GR3: Strengthening externality management	Formulation of national strategies national progress reports Reporting and monitoring, rating and ranking Conditionality attached to foreign aid and loans	Reporting spill-ins and spill-outs caused In-house prevention and early warning system Contract regimes CSR includes externality management	Detecting and monitoring externalities, watchdog Pushing agendas

Governance Requirement (GR)	Sample Indicators		
GR4: Promoting issue-focus and result-orientation	Improving single-issue mechanisms for international cooperation Development of new mechanisms Creation of administrative and diplomatic capacity Creation of adequate regulatory capacity	Seeking improvements to above Improve national CSR	Seeking improvements to above Improve national CSR
GR5: Recognising and promoting synergies	Pointing to issue-linkages and creating mechanism, e.g. peace and development Establishment of global leadership bodies Support of global institutions and commons	International CSR	Creating and shaping debates Establishing global leadership bodies with civil society voice
GR6: Taking account of policy interdependence	Recognition in political agendas of the importance of global, multilateral approaches to global challenges Concrete proposals at national and international levels Resourcing global agenda setting, proposals Pledges of new and additional resources to meet new and as yet unaccomplished challenges	Global CSR Recognition of global responsibilities as part of corporate strategy, including investment	Creating a global civil society infrastructure and agenda Resourcing

Table 5.2 **Governance Performance Indicator System**

	Sample Indicators		
	Nation state	**City government**	**Private organisation**
Efficacy	Problem definition and framing	Problem definition and framing	Corporate strategy
	Solutions and concrete proposals	Solutions and concrete proposals	In-house planning units
	Knowledge base, policymaking capacity	Knowledge base, policymaking capacity	Knowledge management
	Resourcing	Working relations with regional and other governments	R & D
		Resourcing	Adequate oversight structures
			Role of business associations
			Resourcing
Effectiveness	Administrative capacity	Administrative capacity	Administrative capacity
	Regulatory capacity and sanctions	Regulatory capacity and sanctions	Change management capacity
	Implementation capacity	Implementation capacity	Resource management
	Resource management	Resource management	
Performance	Overall performance	Overall performance	Performance criteria (e.g. triple bottom lines)
	Attainment of set goals in policy field	Attainment of set goals in policy field	Investments
	Other relevant achievements	Other relevant achievements	
	Stability overall and in regulatory system applied to policy field	Stability overall and in regulatory system applied to policy field	
Legitimacy	Degree to which national government and its main agencies are seen as legitimate	Degree to which municipal government and its main agencies are seen as legitimate	Legitimate corporate governance
	Violations of laws, regulations	Violations of laws, regulations	Violations of laws, regulations
	Role of loyal and disloyal oppositions	Role of loyal and disloyal oppositions	Trust in corporations, confidence
	Elite capture and role of special interests and constituencies	Elite capture and role of special interests and constituencies	Stability of key corporations

Table 5.2 offers an initial operationalisation. Of course, actual indicators would have to be adapted to the requirements of the policy field under consideration, especially as the performance model has a time dimension built in. As a system based on a process model, a baseline for each of the three components (legitimacy, efficacy, and effectiveness) is needed to allow for the measurement of changes, and therefore of the direct and indirect relations involved. Figure 5.1 offers a hypothetical and stylised result of such a baseline governance performance analysis.

The third indicator system is about **governance innovation**. Here the unit of analysis is either the innovation itself or the actors involved. For the former, indicators would measure different attributes in terms of what kind of innovation, in what field, involving what actors and level as well as in terms of scalability and replicability records and potential; and for the latter, they would measure different dimensions of innovativeness and their characteristics. Most likely, some form of broad-based expert survey could yield the data required.

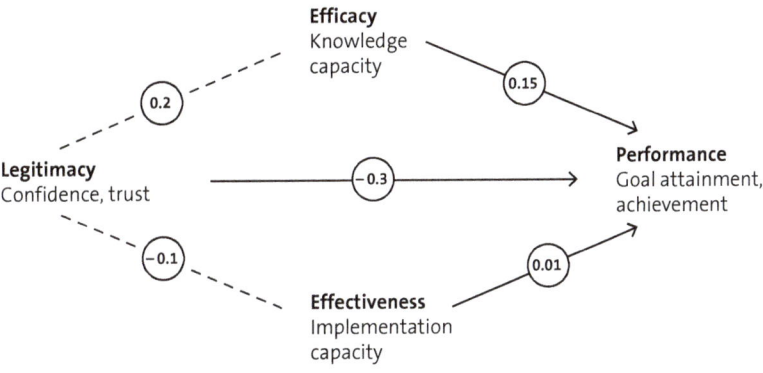

Figure 5.1: Governance performance showing baseline measurement

Of course, developing and testing any of the three systems will take time and require sustained effort. We will, in the course of these annual reports, present regular updates as the systems expand in terms of indicators and improve in data coverage. In the balance of this chapter, however, we will present initial results for some aspects of the three systems, however incomplete.[5]

Dashboards

How to present indicators? Clearly, each of the three systems goes beyond a simple listing of countries and some particular indicator, as many conventional indicator systems do. Of course, it will be of interest to learn which countries, cities, corporations or NGOs are ranked how by some indicator or another; and which country or city fares better and which ones worse when it come to governance. We will list the various indicator tables on the Report's website, with sample rankings, data quality and availability permitting.

Of greater import, however, are not the rankings per se, but the relationships among indicators. For this end, we develop sets of thematically-related indicators, called 'dashboards' or 'suites'[6] that are to serve as repositories from which the analysis of the three models can draw. In other words, the main purpose of the dashboards is to offer inputs and data for different kinds of analysis. In some instances, it will be possible to express indicator relationships using statistical analysis; in others, data limitations may invite more qualitative assessments.

We have been able to develop three dashboards (see Tables 5.3a–5.3c for sample indicators), and we hope to improve these and add others in future editions:

- The **Transnational Governance Dashboard** is about the governance behaviour of countries in the context of international organisations such as ratification of international treaties and voting behaviour in the United Nations General Assembly. We also focus specifically on the production of important global public goods: environmental protection and peacekeeping.
- The **National Governance Dashboard** relates to administrative state capacity; expertise and knowledge resources; and civil society. We estimate administrative state capacity with various measures of effectiveness (e.g., the degrees of professionalism and impartiality of the bureaucracy), efficacy (the expertise and knowledge resources available to government for governance), and the strength of civil society as a third force next to the state and business.
- The **City Governance Dashboard** focuses on large metropolitan areas, and concentrates on four central themes of city governance: social capital and trust; quality of institutions; public good provision; and corruption.

In the balance of this chapter, we draw from these dashboards to present first applications and initial results for each of the three governance indicator systems, with more material available on the Report website and in the relevant chapter (Stanig, forthcoming) of the edited volume.

Table 5.3a **Transnational Governance Dashboard—Sample Indicators**

Focal Theme/ Dimension	Main Indicators	Description
Kyoto Protocol	Actual reduction vs. target reduction of greenhouse emissions, by country	Difference between actual reduction in emissions and commitment, relative to baseline emissions
WTO	Antidumping measures enacted against country	(Log) number of antidumping measures enacted against country (dumping defendant)
	Antidumping measures enacted by country	(Log) number of antidumping measures enacted by the country (accuser)
	Openness of economy, by country	Total value of imports and exports, in US$
UN General Assembly	Voting on the Palestine question, by country and over multiple years	Ideal point estimate on latent dimension dealing with the Middle East conflict
	Voting on conventional weapons control, by country and over multiple years	Ideal point estimate on latent dimension dealing with conventional weapons control
	Voting on nuclear weapons, by country and over multiple years	Ideal point estimate on latent dimension dealing with nuclear weapons control
	Voting on international economic fairness, by country and over multiple years	Ideal point estimate on latent dimension dealing with economic fairness
UN Treaties	Ratification of treaties dealing with legal matters, by country and over multiple years	Ideal point estimate, propensity to ratify treaties that deal with legal matters
	Ratification of treaties dealing with natural resources, by country and over multiple years	Ideal point estimate, propensity to ratify treaties that deal with natural resource management
Peacekeeping	Financial contributions, by country and over multiple years	Financial contributions to peacekeeping budget as a share of country GDP
	Troop contributions, by country and over multiple years	Troop contributions, adjusted by population

Table 5.3b **National Governance Dashboard—Sample Indicators**

Focal Theme/ Dimension	Main Indicators	Description	Selected Sub-Indicators
Efficacy	Think tanks, by country	Presence and quality of organisations that contribute to policy by generating ideas	Count of existing think tanks Rating of think tanks
	Academic resources, by country	Academic infrastructure in place for generating ideas and educating for the future	Research funding as fraction of GDP Ranking of economics departments Number of policy graduate programs
Effectiveness	Weberian bureaucracy, by country	The extent to which government exercises its functions impartially and professionally	Professionalism Impartiality
	Intellectual resources, by country	Government employees with a higher education degree	
Civil Society Strength	Civic engagement of population, by country	Involvement in civil society organisations through participation and membership	Participation Membership Inequality in participation and membership
	Civil society infrastructure, by country	Number of organisations involved in peace and environmental work	
	Recruitment patterns in civil society organisations, by country	Participation and membership according to social differences	
Legitimacy	Confidence in government, by country	Population's confidence in executive, legislature, and political parties	
	Confidence in government services, by country	Population's confidence in government service provision (police, civil service, education)	

Table 5.3c **City Governance Dashboard—Sample Indicators**

Focal Theme/ Dimension	Main Indicators	Description	Selected Sub-Indicators
Social Capital, Trust, and Other Intangibles	Confidence in elites, by city population	Confidence in executive, legislature, and political parties	
	Generalised trust, by city population	Perception that 'most people can be trusted'	
	Inequality in perceptions, by city population	Difference in perceptions according to income level	Inequality in life satisfaction
			Inequality in happiness
			Inequality in generalised trust
Quality of Institutions	Confidence in government services, by city population	Confidence in police, civil service and education	
	Perception of meritocracy, by city population	Difference in responses to questions about how important to get ahead in life are education, ambition, and hard work, rather than knowing the right people, having political connections, and paying bribes	
	Perception of impartiality, by city population	Responses to questions regarding the impartiality of government and courts	Perception of impartiality (citizens)
			Perception of impartiality (business managers)
			Perception of court impartiality (business managers)

Table 5.3c **City Governance Dashboard—Sample Indicators (continued)**

Focal Theme/ Dimension	Main Indicators	Description	Selected Sub-Indicators
Public Good Provision	Crime and security, by city population	Assessment of security city provides	Expenditures for security as % of firm revenues
			Perceptions of crime as an obstacle to business
	Perceived environmental quality, by city population	Composite index of perceptions of environmental quality	Air quality
			Water quality
			Sanitation
	Public transport, by city	Performance of public transportation system	Public transit • Volume • Speed • Operating costs • Energy consumption
			Emissions due to private and public transport
	Innovation, by city	Input and output of innovation	Patent applications per 1000 inhabitants
			Private R&D investment per capita
			Public R&D investment per capita
Corruption	Corruption victimization, by city	Experiences with corruption of citizens and entrepreneurs	Proportion of citizens asked for a bribe in interactions with public officers
			Percentage of firm revenues usually spent on bribes
			Percentage of government contract value usually paid as kickback
	Culture of corruption among businesses, by city	Citizen's perception of corruption as part of normal business culture	
	Corruption as obstacle to business, by city	Entrepreneur's perception of corruption as an obstacle	

First Applications and Results

Governance Readiness System

For the governance readiness system, we are interested in responsible sovereignty as the exercise of sovereignty in a way that is fully respectful of the sovereignty of other nations. As Chapter 2 argues, GR3 (Externality management), GR5 (Recognising and promoting synergies) and GR6 (Taking account of policy interdependence) are closely related to responsible sovereignty. Therefore, we examined cases that bring these government requirements into focus, and typically in some combination:

- Kyoto Protocol–GR3 and GR6
- Trade policy at WTO–GR1 and GR3
- UN voting record–GR2 and GR5
- Ratification of treaties–GR3 and GR4
- UN Peacekeeping–GR4 and GR5

We will present each briefly in turn, and direct the reader to the Report website (www.governancereport.org) for methodological detail and more information.

The Kyoto Protocol–GR3 (Strengthening externality management) and GR6 (Taking account of policy interdependence). Under the Kyoto Protocol, 38 countries and the European Community committed to reduce or limit the increase of their greenhouse emissions by some percentage over the base year, in most cases, 1990.[7] This is called the 'quantified emission limitation or reduction commitment', and a prime example of what Chapter 2 labelled as improved controls of spill-ins and spill-outs in managing interdependencies.

Countries, however, vary in commitments made. Some, particularly Eastern European countries, committed to limiting increases of emissions only, while others, mostly advanced market economies, committed to actual reductions. According to the Kyoto Protocol, emissions over the 2008-2012 period count towards the fulfilment of the commitments. Hence, we compute the average change in greenhouse gases emission for the years 2008, 2009, and 2010, using data from UNFCCC, and compare it with commitments made.

The vertical axis in Figure 5.2 shows the difference between target and effective reduction of emissions as of 2011: countries ranked towards the top of Figure 5.2 are 'more virtuous' in terms of their commitment, emitting fewer greenhouse gases than committed, while countries located towards the bottom are less virtuous. We can see a central cluster of countries around the target mark (from Croatia, Ireland, Portugal, Belgium to the

Netherlands, France and Germany), and some virtuous countries like Estonia and Ukraine, and also the Russian Federation.

However, once we take the size of economies into account, a strong pattern emerges: were it not for a set of smaller countries in the lower left corner of Figure 5.2 unable to meet their respective targets (e.g. Iceland, Luxembourg, Slovenia, and New Zealand), there would be a relatively close correlation between the total size of the economy and target fulfilment: smaller economies (upper left) were able to behave more virtuously than larger economies (lower right).

To some extent, this pattern reflects the fact that the targets for countries outside of the core of most developed economies were set somewhat more leniently, requiring a deceleration of the increase in emissions rather than an actual reduction in emissions. More importantly, however, the upper left quadrant is dominated by countries that underwent deindustrialisation in the 1990s and may have even had stagnating if not shrinking economies well into the 2000s. In essence, therefore, Figure 5.2 suggests that most virtuous countries did so involuntarily (upper left). By contrast, the less virtu-

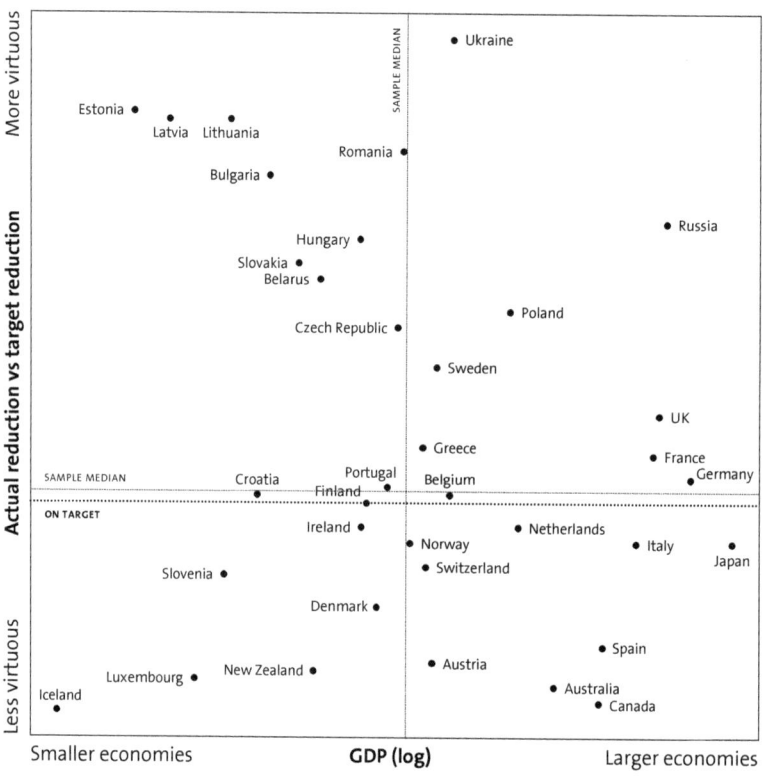

Figure 5.2 **Difference between greenhouse gas emissions and Kyoto target, and size of the economy.**

ous countries did so willingly (lower right), either by being unable to implement adequate policies called for, or by stalling.

Indeed, the considerable variation among countries with economies of approximately the same size points to a country's willingness and ability to contribute to the production of a global public good. In particular, among the largest economies signatory to the Kyoto Protocol, some (Germany, France, Sweden, and the United Kingdom) seem to behave somewhat more virtuously than others (Canada, Australia, Spain, Italy, and Japan).

What do these results suggest for the assessment of the two governance requirements involved? Looking at GR 3 (Strengthening externality management) first, hypothetically, a high rating would mean that all countries, especially developed market economies, would meet their committed targets. As Figure 5.2 shows, 21 of the 38 countries party to the Kyoto Protocol are located at or above the target line; what is more, hardly any of those that met their targets did so in reference to GR6, which would anticipate the interdependence of environmental policies with other global public goods. One indication of GR6 would have been active attempts to introduce and push proposals at follow-up meetings to Kyoto, be it at Copenhagen in 2009 or at Rio+20 in 2012. Thus, without giving precise numerical ratings, the scores would be low for both, yet lower for GR6 than GR3.

One way we could calculate the degree of meeting GR3 is the average of the difference between actual and target emissions, weighted by (log) size of the economy. This index is above 0 if more emissions are produced than the target, 0 if everyone is on target, and negative if emissions are lower than target. With the data we have on hand, the value of this index is -0.0175 meaning that the reduction (accounting for size of the economies) is on average actually more virtuous than the target, albeit not substantively by much. This result is not due only to the very good performance of Russia, one of the largest economies among the signatories. Even if Russia were excluded, the value would be -0.0151, and the substantive implication would be the same.

One can also compute the total GDP of countries that were at least on target, as a fraction of the total GDP for the countries included in Figure 5.2. The countries that fulfilled their Kyoto target (or did better than they had projected) and therefore lie below the dashed line in the figure account for 53% of the GDP of all countries involved in the Kyoto Protocol. Again excluding Russia does not change the substantive implication radically, yet the Kyoto fulfillers would account only for 48% of the GDP of the Kyoto signatories, meaning that, in a sense, the Kyoto targets were achieved on average by less than half.

The World Trade Organisation–GR1 (Averting the risk of dual–market and state–failure) and GR3 (Strengthening externality management). What could responsible sovereignty in trade policy mean in the context of the WTO/GATT? To approach this question, we look at three measures: The first indicator is about 'accusing' and measures how often a country claims some foreign firm is engaging in dumping or benefits from illegitimate export subsidisation. It does so by counting the number of Antidumping (AD) and Countervailing Duties (CVD) incidents listed in the Antidumping Database (Bown 2012a) and the Countervailing Duties Database (Bown 2012b), which are part of the Temporary Trade Barriers Database at the World Bank. The value on the vertical axis of Figure 5.3 is the (log) number of antidumping measures that a country has taken against other countries. The data are based on averages over the 2006–2010 period. However, this measure does not capture all the dumping and subsidies that might exist; nor does it mean that the target country of any AD or CVD measure is actually violating WTO provisions.

The second indicator looks at the other side of trade behaviour, i.e. rather than crying foul, it is about being accused of a trade violation. The indicator measures how often firms from a given country are alleged to engage in dumping and related activities. The vertical axis in Figure 5.4 plots the log number of antidumping measures taken against firms located in that country. The data are from the same data source and, too, are based on averages over the 2006–2010 period.

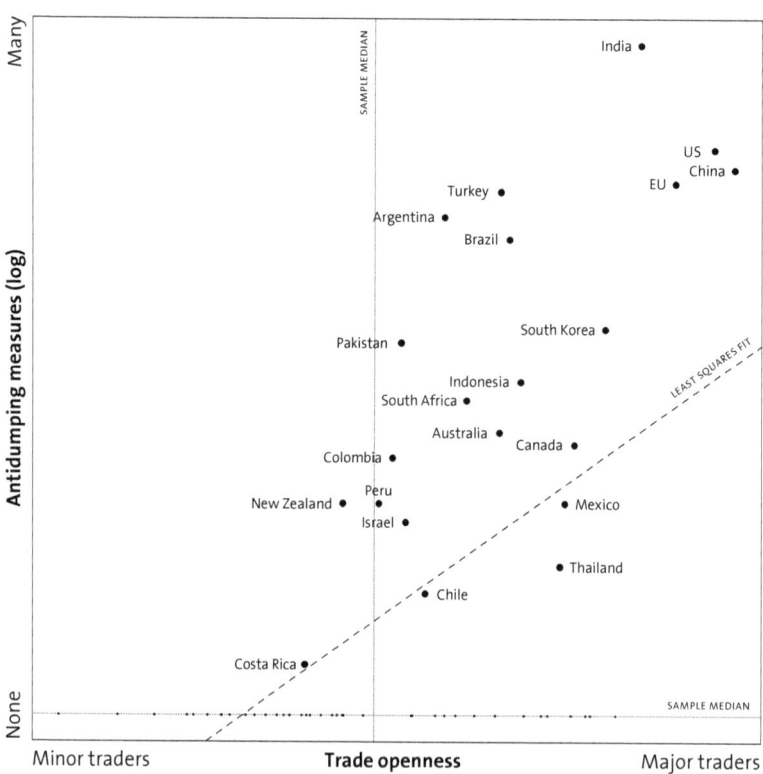

Figure 5.3 **Antidumping measures enacted by country and trade openness**

The third indicator directly addresses protectionist behaviour vs. trade openness, calculated as the sum of the real value of imports and exports of a country, and shown along the horizontal axis in Figures 5.3 and 5.4. It is therefore a measure of the weight a country has in global trade.[8]

The two figures underscore an essential premise of this Report: the more you trade, the more interdependent you become, the more likely you are to charge others with illegal trade practices such as antidumping, and the more likely you are to be charged–a typical GRI challenge. In other words, the more open economies become, the more likely are trade disputes to emerge. This applies to developed market economies like the US or South Korea as it does to the emerging economies, as the prominent positions of China, India and Brazil in Figures 5.3 and 5.4 suggest. What seems important is for countries to have a fair and open system of reaching settlements and of enforcing them.

At the same time, some countries are more often 'accuser' than 'defender', some are both, and few are neither in any pronounced way. In terms of governance requirements, more countries should fit the pattern of potential

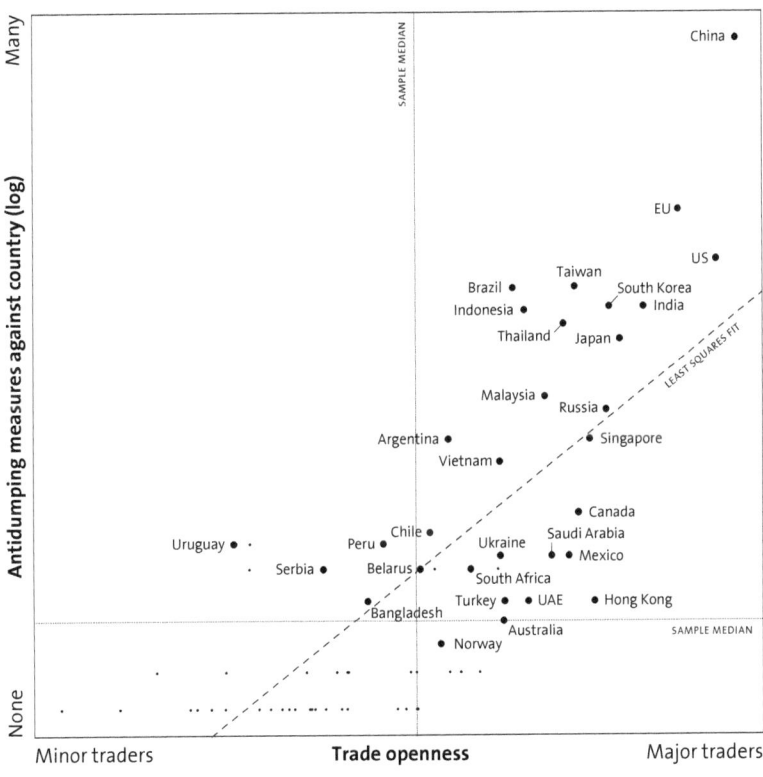

Figure 5.4 **Antidumping measures involving firms in the country and trade openness**

Table 5.4 **Charging trade violations: Accusing and being accused**

	Below Median Being Charged	Above Median Being Charged
Below Median Charging Other Countries	Passive traders n= 10 e.g. Egypt, Hong Kong, Kuwait, Norway, Philippines, Saudi Arabia, Switzerland, Ukraine, United Arab Emirates, Venezuela	Potentially regressive traders n= 5 e.g. Japan, Malaysia, Singapore, Taiwan, Vietnam
Above Median Charging Other Countries	Potential watchdog traders n= 5 e.g. Australia, Chile, Mexico, South Africa, Turkey	Potential trade bullies n= 10 e.g. Argentina, Brazil, Canada, China, EU, India, Indonesia, South Korea, Thailand, US

watchdogs: pointing to alleged trade illegalities of others, but being relatively 'clean' themselves, i.e. meeting WTO trade requirements and standards.

Given that we have data also for a large number of countries that play a relatively small role on the global trade scene, we restrict the analysis based on the four categories in Table 5.4 to the 30 countries that trade more than the median in the sample[9], which together account for around 80% of world trade. We calculate the median number of the two types of antidumping measures for these 30 countries and then allocate countries based on whether they fall above or below that median.

According to the data, only 5 of the 30 high volume trading countries fit the 'watchdog' pattern. By contrast, 10 could be classified as trade bullies. This group includes a majority of the emerging economies that are members of WTO: Brazil, China, India, and Indonesia. Only South Africa, among the BRICS, qualifies as a 'watchdog'. Among the group of passive traders are oil-exporting countries, while the 'regressive' traders are all East and Southeast Asian economies. Overall, the rating of countries in terms of GR1 and GR3 would be higher than for the Kyoto Protocol, but far from perfect.

Voting at UN General Assembly–GR2 (Correcting fairness deficits) and GR5 (Recognising and promoting synergies). The UN General Assembly (UNGA) is the highest body for all member states in which to express political preference. Through voting, member states can influence political decisions and policies of many kinds. What is the overall track record of the UNGA based on the vote calls on 517 resolutions between December 2005 and December 2011? For the world body as a whole, what do observed voting records reveal in terms of promoting fairness and synergies? We analysed these voting records (Strezhnev and Voeten, 2012–08 up to 2009; UNBISNET for recent years) and fitted a four-dimensional ideal point model summarising voting behaviour in the UNGA in the post-Cold War era.[10]

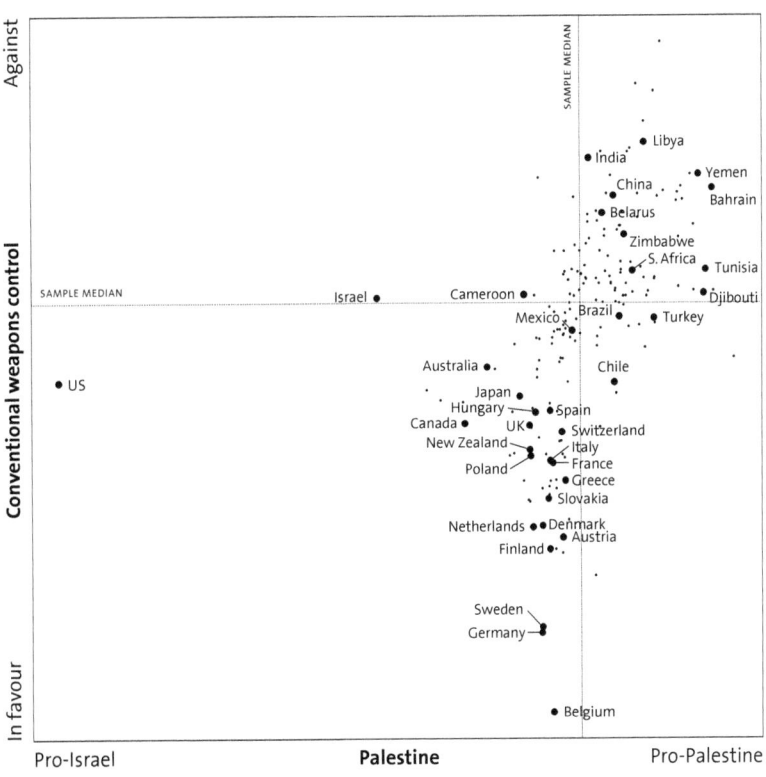

Figure 5.5a/b UN General Assembly voting behaviour: Ideal point estimates

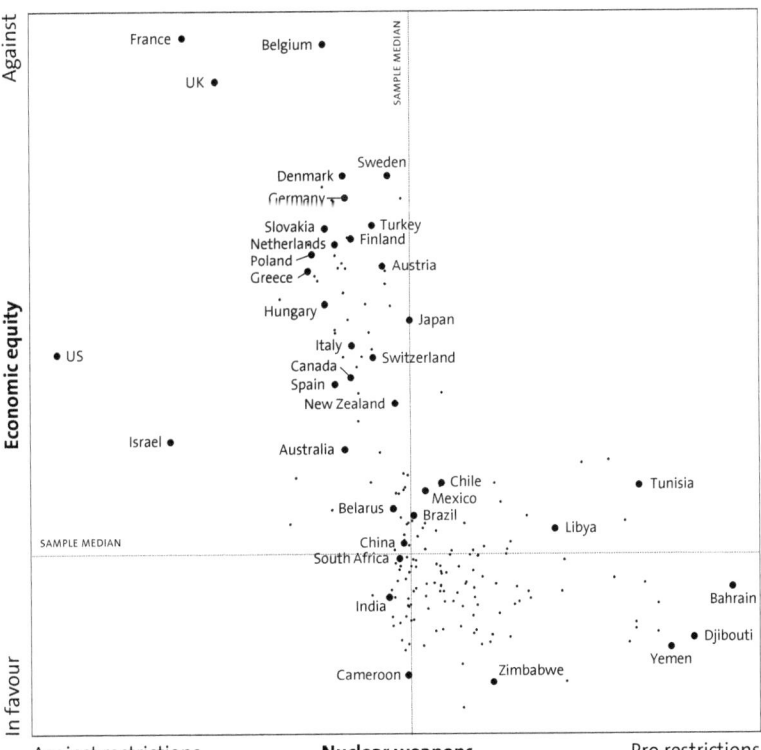

- The first dimension, plotted along the horizontal axis of Figure 5.5a, deals with the Palestinian question most directly, and sees the US and Israel facing most other countries. A set of Arab countries are located at one extreme, and European and other advanced countries place themselves around the middle of the scale.
- The second dimension (vertical axis of Figure 5.5a) has to do mainly with conventional weapons control, and sees European countries at one, and 'rogue states' at the other extreme, with the US and other advanced countries much less supportive of conventional weapons control than Europe.
- The third dimension, plotted along the horizontal axis of Figure 5.5b, reflects issues around nuclear weapons. Advanced countries with nuclear weapons (US, the UK, France and Israel) oppose, quite intransigently, a set of resolutions that would affect them, with some developing countries at the other extreme, and non-nuclear European countries located closer to the centre.
- The fourth dimension (vertical axis of Figure 5.5b) is mainly about tensions between advanced countries and developing and underdeveloped countries, and deal substantively with issues of international economic equity, i.e. fairness.

One could conclude that, since the end of the Cold War, the UNGA has been dealing mainly with security issues (one unresolved regional conflict, conventional and nuclear weapons) and with the ridge between developed and developing or underdeveloped economies, with the developed on one side, the developing on the other.

Even if we set aside the Palestine and the nuclear weapons issues, their influence in terms of positioning is very strong and carries over into the way countries vote on many other issues, thereby 'contaminating' voting behaviour throughout. The only dimension that seems more related to responsible sovereignty is the one dealing with conventional weapons control and transparency in armaments. As shown in Figure 5.5a, this dimension sees a division between some advanced countries that support conventional weapons control and some which oppose it. The UNGA seems 'stuck' in a situation in which carry-over conflicts from the Cold War era and complex North-South conflicts (dimension 4) still dominate how coalitions form and disagreements manifest themselves.

United Nations treaty ratification–GR3 (Strengthening externality management) and GR4 (Promoting issue-focus and result-orientation). Treaty ratifications are indications of a need to cooperate for improved externality management (GR3) and to do so with a focus on specific issues or policy fields (GR4). The data come from the UN Treaty Collection, and cover all treaties either signed or ratified between 1998 and the first months of 2012. The UN categorises treaties in twenty-nine chapters based on their subject matter / policy area.

Figure 5.6 displays the estimated positions of each country based on a two-dimensional ideal point model of treaty ratification. The two dimensions predict ratification of treaties, dealing, as it turns out, with different subject matters: legal matters and resource management, respectively. The first dimension, plotted on the vertical axis, explains ratification of treaties that deal with legal matters: among the 20 treaties that are associated most strongly with this latent dimension, seven are from chapter XVIII (Penal matters), seven are from chapter IV (Human rights), and four are from chapter XXVI (Disarmament). One is from chapter XII (Navigation) and deals with a rather special issue, the arrest of ships.

The second dimension, plotted on the horizontal axis, has to do with the management of natural resources: among the twenty treaties that are associated most strongly with this dimension, fifteen belong to chapter XXVII (Environment); of the remaining five, one is from chapter XXI (Law of the sea) and two are from chapter XIX (Commodities) and deal respectively with tropical timber and food aid.

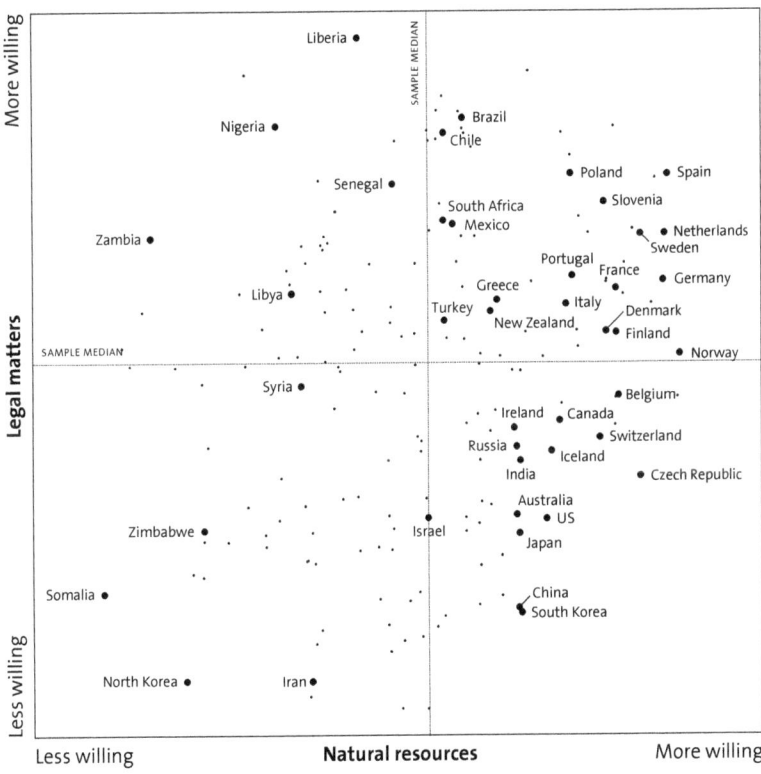

Figure 5.6 **Estimates of the latent willingness to ratify treaties belonging to one of two groups (legal matters and natural resources) based on an ideal-point model of UN treaty ratifications (1998–2012)**

Countries towards the upper right-hand corner of Figure 5.6 are more likely to ratify both kinds of treaties, whereas countries in the lower left corner are more likely to ratify none. As we can see, however, there is considerable variation in the positions of the countries: the propensity to ratify treaties varies, and not all countries are equally likely to enter binding international commitments. There is also a substantial number of countries that are selective in the types of treaties they ratify: some like the US, Japan and Australia are more like to ratify natural resources than legal-related treaties, while others, among them many African countries, reveal the opposite pattern.

Overall, we suggest that treaty signing and ratifications reveal a less than perfect picture: of the 80 treaties we consider, the median number of ratifiers is 26, around 13% of all the countries that potentially could sign and ratify a given treaty. From another perspective, the median country signed and ratified 27.5% of all the treaties under consideration in our analysis. This finding lends credence to others who found that UN organisations like UNESCO suffer from an erosion in treaty ratification and implementation[11].

UN peacekeeping operations and international security–GR4 (Promoting issue-focus and result-orientation) and GR5 (Recognising and promoting synergies). Peacekeeping has become a major function of the United Nations, the European Union, NATO and the Organisation of African Unity. Especially the UN relies on voluntary member states' contributions to support peacekeeping operations. Some suggest, based on spending data, that the burden of peacekeeping missions is shouldered disproportionately by richer countries (Khanna, Sandler, and Shimizu 1998, Shimizu and Sandler 2002). By contrast, some developing countries (Pakistan, India, Bangladesh, Nigeria, Nepal, Jordan and Ghana) contribute a significant proportion of the UN peacekeeping troops.

This pattern might reflect two different motivations: on the one hand, the willingness of countries to increase their geopolitical standing and there-

Table 5.5 **Peacekeeping contributions and patterns**

Pattern Contributions	Resource Attraction	Dual	Status Attraction
Extensive	High resource seekers	'Best of both worlds' seekers	'Empty corner'
Limited	Moderate resource seekers	Politically handi-capped 'best of both worlds' seekers	Moderate status seekers
None	Potential and actual free-riders		

fore contribute to the production of global public goods like peacekeeping; on the other, peacekeeping is a source of revenue, given fixed reimbursement schedules and spare military capacity[12]. Compared to countries with more expensive armies, for which the UN reimbursements would constitute just a small (and possibly negligible) portion of the defence budget, peacekeeping missions might indeed be attractive to poorer countries with either smaller or under-financed standing armies.

To explore this pattern, we employed two indicators: On the horizontal axis of Figure 5.7 is a measure of GDP on a log scale, based on Penn World Table data (Heston, Summers, and Aten 2012); on the vertical axis is a measure of contributions in kind (i.e., military personnel) to UN peacekeeping missions adjusted by differences in the population of countries.[13]

Of the 198 UN member states, about one-third (37%) do not contribute to peacekeeping efforts at all. They are classified as free-riders in Table 5.5. There are also few very large countries making large contributions–the nearly empty upper right-hand corner in Figure 5.7–a fact that probably has to do with the avoidance of seemingly overt power politics by major military

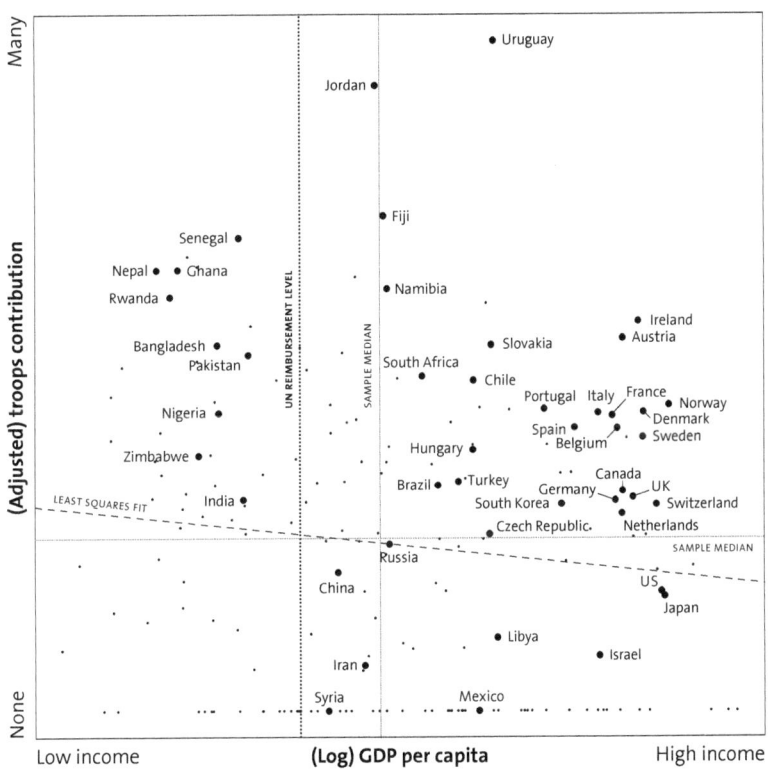

Figure 5.7 **Adjusted troop contributions to UN peacekeeping missions (1989–2011) and size of economy**

INTRODUCING A NEW GENERATION OF GOVERNANCE INDICATORS

powers. Most countries that are part of peacekeeping efforts are in or close to the middle category of 'best of both worlds', and exercise a policy that may seek to combine national self-interest with public goods contributions.

In general, the data do not highlight the existence of a clear relationship between income and contribution, in either direction. Yet, it is remarkable that several African countries are among the top contributors. Furthermore, in general, a sizable group of the countries that contribute the most in adjusted terms have GDP per capita lower than the reimbursement per soldier (around 1000 US$). Indeed, 19 countries among those whose population-adjusted contribution is in the top 25% of all contributions have GDP per capita below 1000 US$ as of the late 2000s. These can be classified as 'resource seekers'.

Among the large emerging economies, only South Africa seems to contribute (in population-adjusted terms) more than the traditionally 'multilateralist' countries of Western Europe (France, Italy, Sweden, Belgium, Denmark).

In conclusion, the record on governance requirements in terms of responsible sovereignty is higher for peacekeeping than it was in the case of the Kyoto Protocol, and is similar in terms of overall achievement to trade policies. The finding suggests that a subset of countries does indeed make contributions to global public goods–and seek cooperative arrangements accordingly–when such contributions can be aligned with national self-interest in terms of power or material as well as financial benefits. Alas, as we have seen in the case of both trade disputes and peacekeeping operations, too few countries are following such policies. Free-riding tendencies and bullying remain pronounced. As an overall assessment, we suggest the value of 67%, i.e. the number of countries grouped as 'best of both worlds' seekers (according to the most optimistic definition) as a fraction of all countries.

Alternatively, being somewhat more cynical, we can classify as pursuers of resources those countries that are among the top contributors and have incomes per capita well below the reimbursement level, and as pursuers of the 'best of both worlds' only the countries that have incomes above the reimbursement level and are among the top 25% of contributors. There are 31 countries that could fall into this latter category. This would lead to a ratio of 2.2 free-riders to 1 contributor: this is the ratio between the 69 countries that one could classify as free-riders and the 31 countries acting on their 'enlightened self-interest'.

Governance Performance System

For the Governance Performance System, we are able to look at the country level to explore the role of government and civil society, thereby exploring two 'actors', though corporate data would have completed the picture of the multi-actor indicator system we aim at over time. We estimate three indexes, based on the variables included in the National Governance Dashboard (see

Table 5.3 above for sample indicators[14]). We then use these indexes to explain variation in governance performance and legitimacy across countries.

The first index measuring efficacy captures knowledge resources located outside of the government apparatus, including the public sector and state agencies. It assesses whether a country has a vibrant set of think tanks and a well-funded and internationally-recognised academic sector. The index is a weighted average of the measures reported in the full dashboard as measures of expertise.

The second index measures effectiveness and captures the Weberian nature of government as a functioning, impartial bureaucracy and the presence of intellectual resources within the state administration. Again, the index is a weighted average of the measures reported in the full dashboard under the rubric of capacity measures.

The third index measures the strength of the civil society and relates to the existence of a civil society with a high level of civic engagement, a strong organisational infrastructure, and an egalitarian recruitment. Here too, the index is a weighted average of the measures reported in the full dashboard under the label civil society.

We use these indexes to predict country performance and legitimacy. For both, we rely on measures collected and published by third parties as well as summaries of perceptions of government quality we estimate from surveys:

- Transparency: For resource-rich countries, we have a score of transparency in revenue management, compiled by Revenue Watch (2010); for a larger set of countries, we also use the Open Budget Survey, an expert survey compiled by the International Budget Partnership (2010) on the public availability of budget information and other accountability measures in 94 countries.
- Confidence: We estimate a confidence score in government elites (defined as the executive, the legislative, and political parties) and in government services (defined as the education system, the police, and the civil services) from individual-level data in the World Values Survey and in regional survey collections (Asia Barometer, Latino Barometro, Afrobarometer).

Do efficacy and effectiveness of the public sector and a strong civil society contribute to better governance outcomes and generate more confidence? We explored this question with the help of the variables above, and as a fuller analysis including cities is presented in Stanig (forthcoming), we limit ourselves to only selected results here.

Figure 5.8 looks at efficacy, i.e. the extent to which governments can rely on knowledge resources. In terms of transparency (Figure 5.8a), there are major findings: first, the great majority of countries rank low in terms of efficacy, which simply means that they rarely have adequate recourse to governance-relevant knowledge and information. In fact, in both figures that relate to efficacy, all but a few countries cluster close to the left-hand end of

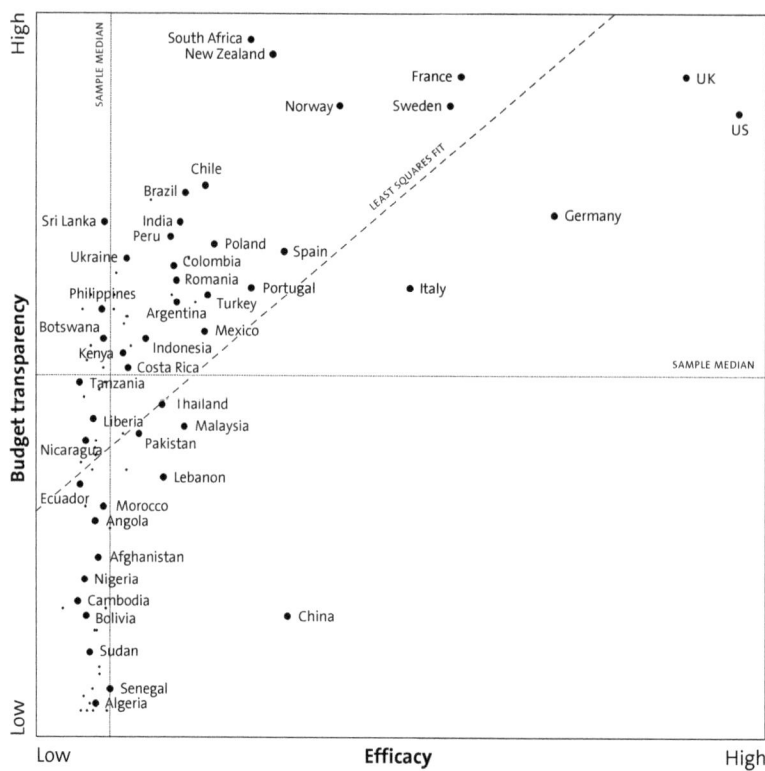

Figure 5.8a/b **Efficacy, transparency, and legitimacy**

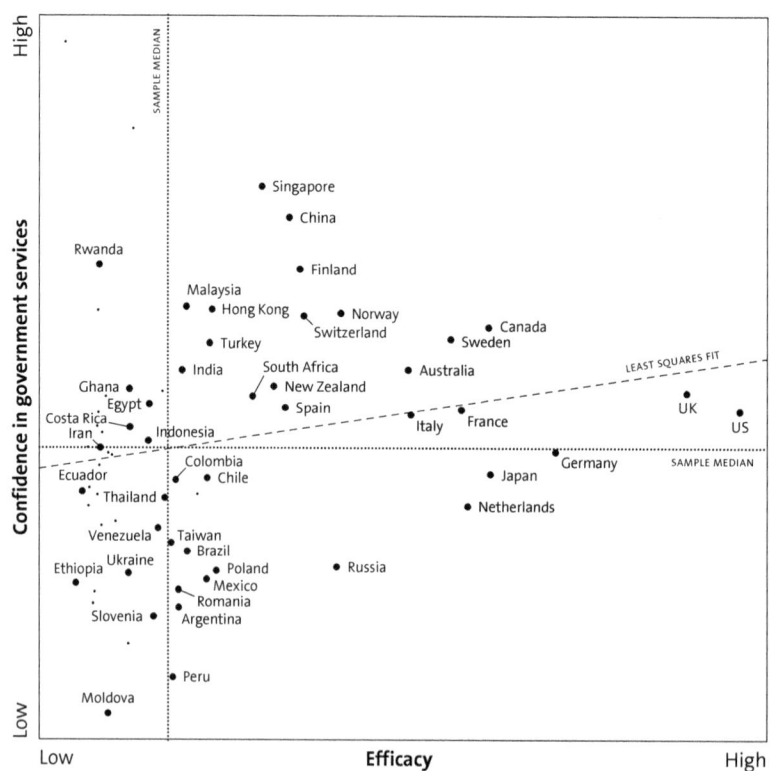

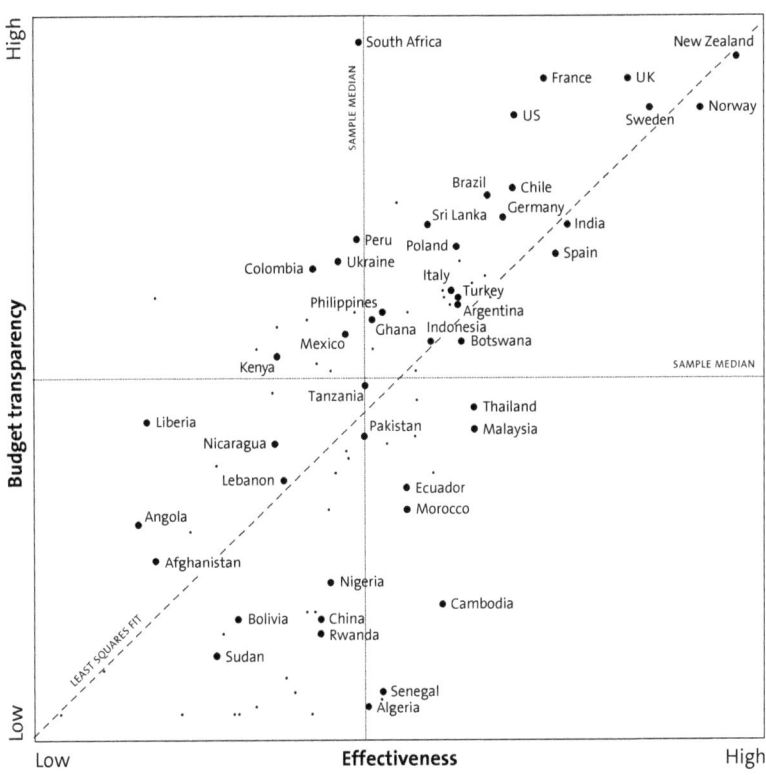

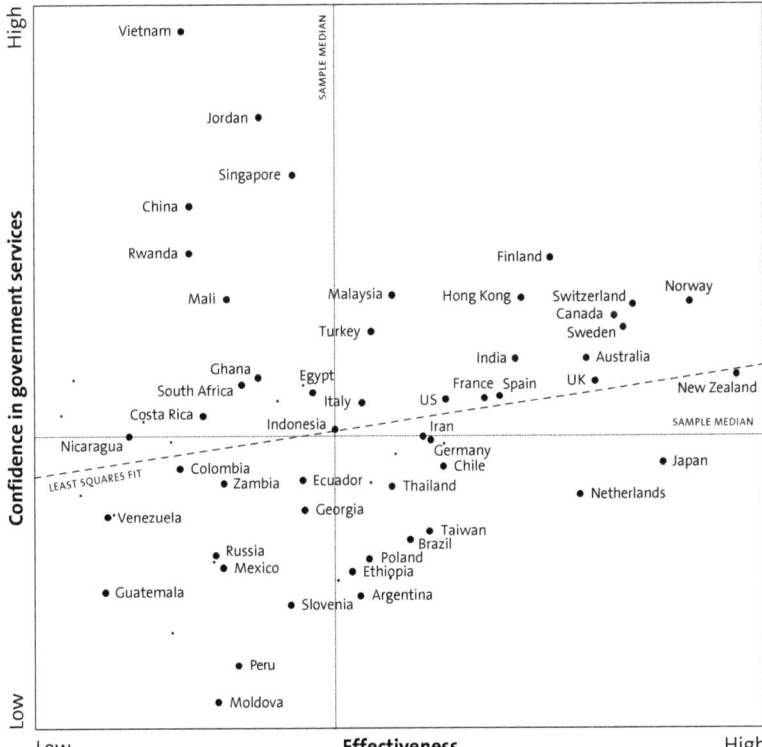

Figure 5.9a/b **Effectiveness, transparency, and legitimacy**

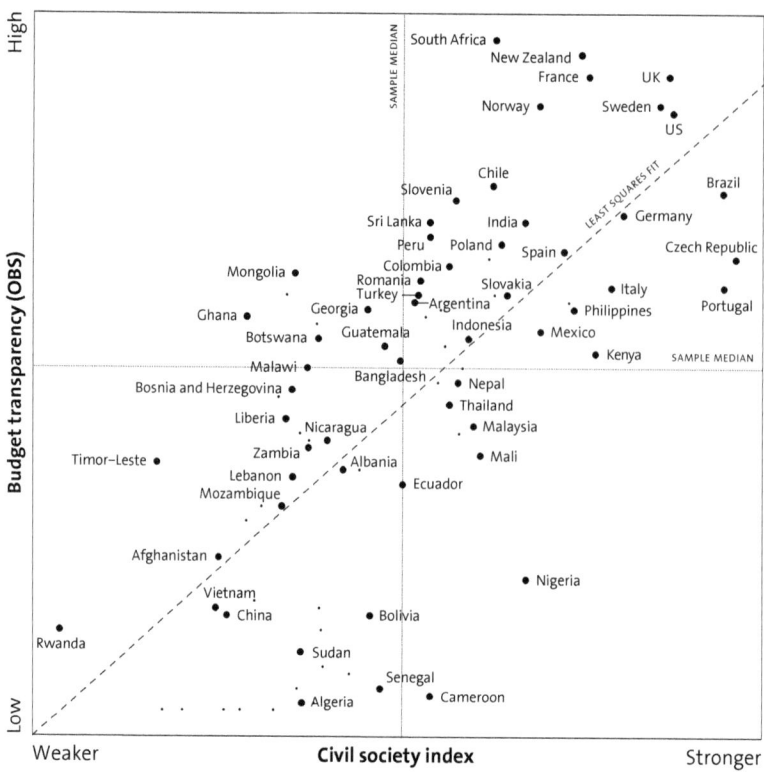
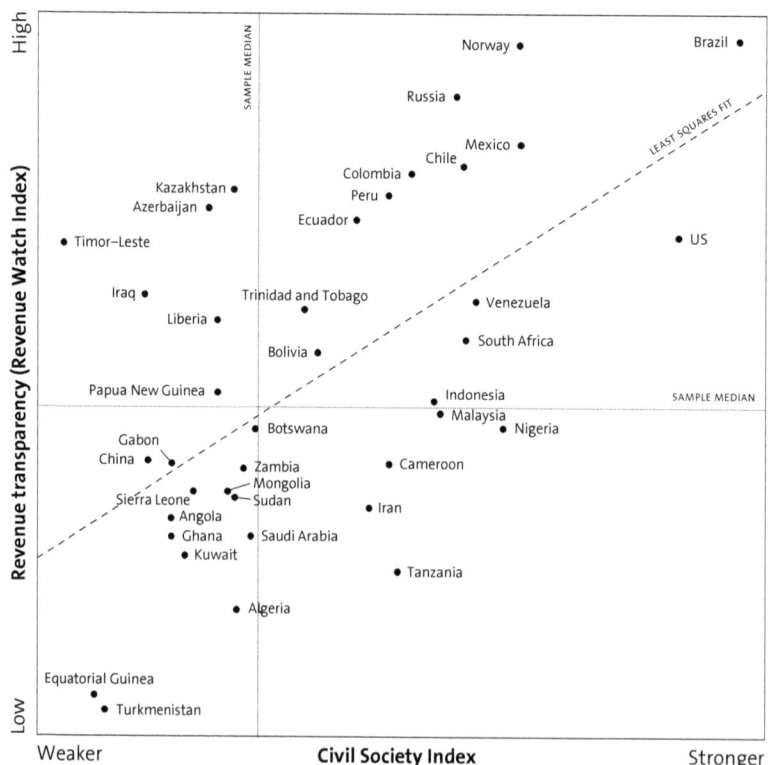

Figure 5.10a/b **Civil society strength and transparency**

the scale. Second, for more efficacious countries we do observe higher rankings in terms of transparency, but the relationship seems weak and not well pronounced. In other words, even if efficacy is in place, its impact on more transparent governance is not necessarily the case.

This is different for effectiveness (Figure 5.9a), which reveals a strong relationship with transparency. More effective administrations are also more transparent ones. What is more, the strength of civil society, too, reveals a strong impact on transparency (Figures 5.10a and 5.10b): more transparent public sectors are associated with vibrant civil societies. What is more, less than is the case for efficacy, fewer countries cluster at the low end of the effectiveness and civil society scale. At the same time, there is a significant overlap among countries located in the upper right-hand (e.g. Germany, UK, New Zealand, US) and lower left-hand (e.g. Nicaragua, Sudan, Liberia) corners of Figures 5.9a and 5.10a.

The governance performance model includes a feedback mechanism between efficacy and effectiveness and confidence, or, we could say, legitimacy. Figure 5.8b reveals a funnel pattern, whereby countries tend to converge slightly above the median in terms of confidence in government services as efficacy increases–keeping in mind most countries included rank rather low when it comes to both efficacy and confidence. This means that more efficacious governments are more likely to enjoy higher degrees of confidence than countries with fewer knowledge resources that can be devoted to governance. However, as the funnel pattern indicates, the confidence payout of efficacy has a declining gradient.

Effectiveness shows a different and altogether less pronounced pattern (Figure 5.9b), as a number of governments in countries like China, Rwanda, Vietnam or Singapore located in the upper left-hand corner enjoy high confidence despite less effective service delivery, a result probably due to political factors. Yet overall, taking these countries out of the figure, there is a slight tendency that more effective government services yield greater confidence.

Governance Innovations System

Finally, we take a look at innovations at the city level. If cities are, ideally, spaces in which equality of opportunity is provided, do they achieve that goal? And are more meritorious cities also more innovative? For this purpose, we compared the perceived meritocracy[15] and patent applications per capita[16] for 18 cities, and obtained the rather striking pattern displayed in Figure 5.11. There were no cities ranking very high in per capita patents that are perceived as less meritocratic; conversely, there are only a very few cities (Auckland, Sydney, Hamburg) perceived as more meritocratic but with a lower number of patents per capita. There is a pronounced cluster of less innovative and less meritocratic cities and a spread among more innovative and more meritocratic ones in the upper right-hand corner of Figure 5.11. The message seems clear: cities perceived by their inhabitants as 'closed shops' are less innovative.

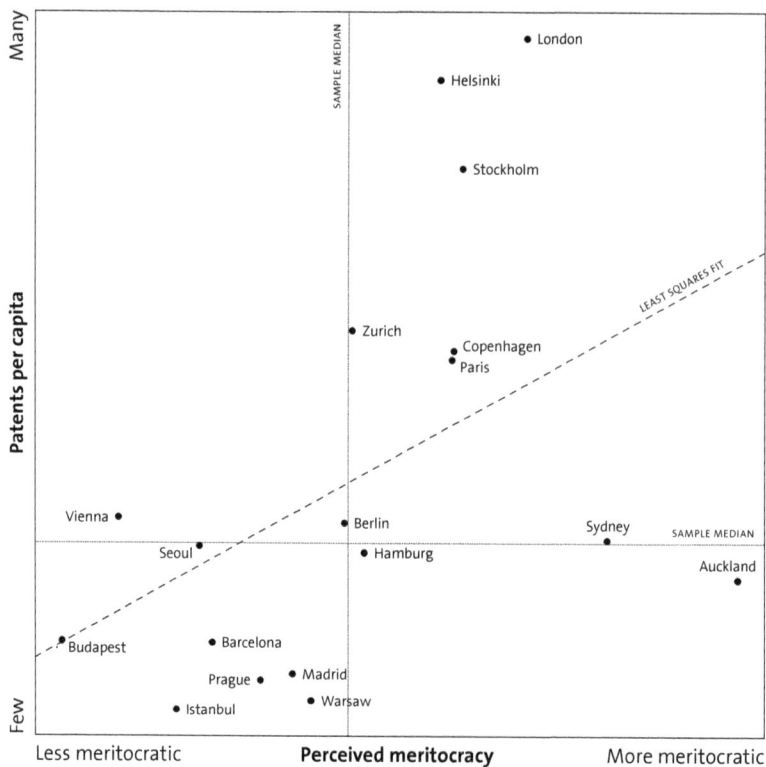

Figure 5.11 **Patent applications per capita and perceptions of meritocracy**

Conclusion

Of course, we were only able to introduce the main facets of the three indicator systems and present only a small part of the analysis based on the data available; once more we invite readers to the Report website. The main purpose of this chapter was to make the case for a new generation of governance indicators–indicators that are conceptually embedded in three frameworks of readiness, performance, and innovativeness.

The way ahead is clear: for one, a fuller operationalisation of each system is called for, as is the development of a larger set of tested indicators and improved data coverage. This implies a way of tracking governance readiness over time along the various dimensions of governance requirements, and a better way of capturing the causality relations and feedback mechanisms in the governance performance model. As part of these efforts, we will build links to other governance indicator systems, especially the Ibrahim Index of African Governance, the World Bank Institute, Revenue Watch, and the

Bertelsmann Stiftung. All approaches face similar challenges in terms of data coverage and availability. For this Report, improving the data situation on governance innovations is a next big step—and the topic of the next edition.

Endnotes

1. Kaufmann, Kraay and Zoido-Lobatón (1999); Kaufmann, Kraay and Mastruzzi (2010); http://info.worldbank.org/governance/wgi/index.asp; http://www.transparency.org/research/cpi/overview; http://www.revenuewatch.org/rwindex2010/index.html; Schwab (2011); http://reports.weforum.org/global-competitiveness-2011-2012/; http://www.bti-project.org/home/index.nc; http://www.prosperity.com/; http://www.moibrahimfoundation.org/en/section/the-ibrahim-index
2. See Stanig and Kayser (forthcoming) for a critical review of the governance indicators field.
3. On methodological nationalism, see Rössel (2012) and Beck (2007).
4. See Deutsch (1963), Anheier (2004; 2007); also: Pignataro (2003) and Brown and Corbett (1997) on similar sets of criteria that are more geared towards indicator assessments.
5. Fuller descriptions of the dashboards are found in Stanig (forthcoming) and Stanig and Kayser (forthcoming). The datasets with the dashboards, along with methodological notes, are available at www.governancereport.org
6. The 'dashboard' metaphor is taken from Stiglitz, Sen and Fitoussi (2010); a seminal discussion about disaggregated indicator suites as an alternative to composite indexes is found in UNESCO and UNRISD (1997). The advantages and limitations of dashboards compared to aggregate indexes are discussed in detail in Stanig and Kayser (forthcoming).
7. 38 countries, plus the European Community, have committed to binding targets to reduce emissions under the Protocol. Additionally, Malta and Turkey report emissions data, but do not have set targets; Canada had targets but officially withdrew in 2012; the US has targets, but has not ratified the Protocol so far.
8. The figures are based on the data on openness published in the Penn World Table (Heston, Summers, and Aten 2012), except for the European Union, for which we use Eurostat figures http://epp.eurostat.ec.europa.eu/tgm/refreshTableAction.do?tab=table&plugin=1&pcode=tet00018&language=en (accessed July 2012).
9. We consider the EU as a single entity for this purpose, and only consider extra-EU trade. This is because intra-union disputes do not go through the WTO dispute mechanisms, and because complaints related to extra-European trade with Europe, that go through the WTO, are—or should be—recorded as complaints involving Europe. We recode those erroneously filed to EU individual countries as EU complaints.
10. Ideal point models are a standard approach used in political science to summarise and explain voting behaviour in legislatures. See Clinton and Jackman (2009) for an overview of available methods to estimate latent 'ideological' positions based on roll-call votes, and Voeten (2000; 2004) for applications to the UN General Assembly. An explanation of model selection, i.e. why and how we arrived at a four-dimensional model, and the technical details about model identification are found in Stanig (forthcoming).
11. See the International Regulatory Frameworks indicator suite (pp. 586-595) in Anheier and Isar (2008).

12 Bove and Elia (2011) relate troop contributions to the availability of manpower.
13 The scores displayed on the vertical axis are based on a simple statistical adjustment (linear regression) that makes it possible to account for the fact that larger countries tend, on average, to contribute more troops than smaller countries. Our adjusted score is, in substance, an estimate of the contributions that countries would make if all countries were of the same size.
14 See Stanig (forthcoming) and Stanig and Kayser (forthcoming) for more detail on the fuller set of indicators and corresponding data sources.
15 Measured as the difference between responses to survey items that ask how important to get ahead in life are education, ambition, and hard work rather than knowing the right people, having political connections, and paying bribes.
16 The patent application data comes from OECD (2010b).

VI. Recommendations and Conclusion

by HELMUT K ANHEIER

This inaugural edition of the Governance Report explored the state of governance from many angles as befits our understanding of governance as a multi-level, multi-actor approach to solving a recognised collective issue or problem. The opening chapters introduced conceptual frameworks for governance performance and readiness, and provided a foundation for developing a new generation of indicators. Both the frameworks and the indicator systems will be further developed and refined in future editions.

Here we propose what we regard as realistic and feasible recommendations that can be tracked and assessed in terms of achievements over time. We are also conscious that any such set of recommendations ought not address governments alone and begin with 'Governments are called upon...'. Rather, and in line with the general thrust of this Report, recommendations are targeted not only at public policymakers but also at academics, corporate leaders and civil society representatives. We invite our readers to contribute to the Report's website where we hope these recommendations and others might not only lead to lively discussion but also to further the debate.

> *For governance, such interdependencies have opened up opportunities, but also involve risks; they invite competition as well as cooperation.*

Seven Recommendations

The first chapter highlighted the deepening interdependencies among actors at all levels and across policy fields ranging from trade and migration to the environment and climate change, and from health to security issues. For governance, such interdependencies have opened up opportunities, but also involve risks; they invite competition as well as cooperation. As emphasised in Chapter 2, there is indeed growing awareness of this interdependence, especially at the global level, and of the spill-ins and spill-outs across levels, actors and fields. Indeed, reforms appear to have advanced most in respect to national-level externality management and the introduction of issue-focus as an added performance criterion.

However, as also confirmed in Chapter 3 in the fiscal and financial field, most actors, especially national governments, have been, and are, slow to react to these changing conditions in key policy areas, and, by and large, do not exhibit the governance readiness required to find and enact lasting solutions. Governments appear to have been particularly slow to pursue positive-sum strategies and to recognise the global public domain as a new, added policy space. This was clearly seen in financial policy, a field ready for first order governance solutions based on first principles to solve the kinds of fundamental trade-offs Chapter 3 identified. Inert behaviour became apparent in central institutions like the UN General Assembly, as Chapter 5 showed. Indeed, innovations of many kinds at first and second order governance levels[1] are much needed to overcome stalemate if the UN is to regain relevance for addressing the new and pressing governance problems of a post Cold War world.

In contrast to a lacklustre UN record in terms of reform towards greater governance readiness, there are many approaches and attempts underway to improve governance elsewhere–at different levels across policy fields. As Chapter 4 argued, many are worth reporting, and some hold promise in terms of replication and scalability. Yet, striking was the absence of first order and first principle innovations given the threat of punctuated equilibriums, especially in the aftermath of the 2008 financial crisis. Second order governance innovations, however, seemed almost plentiful, and with some potential of making existing systems more efficacious and effective. Not surprisingly, given the central role of the public sector, most innovation initiatives seem to stay within existing governance moulds. Chapter 4 also indentified the pivotal role of civil society as innovator, often in cooperation with public agencies. Such cross-sector collaboration, triggered as it were by civil society rather than government, appears as a fertile ground for finding ways to improve governance.

Finally, even though the indicator systems introduced in Chapter 5 remain to be fully developed, the initial analysis, however incomplete, brought about some important findings that suggest implications for policy. For one, some treaties designed to help manage interdependencies are clearly troubled, with the Kyoto Protocol as prime example. Despite some improvements among 'the usual suspects', the basic design failure of the Protocol was to disregard the importance of positive-sum strategies especially for key stakeholders and effective sanctions, which in turn encouraged too many to either free-riding or 'do nothing', wait-and-see approaches.

As a result, progress has been mostly involuntary and lack of progress largely wilful–a sign of treaty failure by erosion. For such cases it may well be best to go back to first principles and consider if it were better to review what went wrong and what can be done to rescue, abandon and restart the treaty. By contrast, other treaties seem to entice governments into cooperation while guarding national self-interest, as the WTO and peacekeeping examples have shown. Here, the right incentives for watchdog behaviour and reducing free-riding as well as effective sanctions are needed, largely though second order innovations.

Greater interdependence among the various governance actors, levels and policy fields requires not only awareness of its existence, but the actual pursuit of positive-sum solutions. In terms of national governments and the global challenges they face, this entails rethinking national sovereignty along the lines of responsible sovereignty, as outlined in Chapter 2. Adopting such a notion would imply that states took the outside world into account in making national policy; and where an issue could be more effectively addressed through international cooperation, they would–in their enlightened national self-interest–seek international cooperation and make sure that this cooperation works.

Governments would opt for win-win or mutually beneficial bargains when possible so that all concerned parties 'crowd in'–rather than, what often happens today, 'crowd out'. Of course, finding solutions that locate and embed enlightened self-interest in win-win situations requires a proactive policy stance and an elevation of such outcomes as the preferred option. Hence:

Recommendation 1: There is a great need for policy analysts to find positive-sum solutions to public good problems, and to inform, even educate, policymakers and publics accordingly.

To demonstrate to policy makers that fields marked by global public goods are also those with high policy interdependence–and a potential for positive-sum strategies and investments in sustainable growth and development–Chapter 2 calls for the development of a systematic approach to public policy with the notion of responsible sovereignty in its centre.

Yet we see Recommendation 1 in a realistic light: a focus on positive-sum games which we encourage contrasts with some of the main lessons from Chapter 3. Especially during post-crisis periods, the issue is 'to clean up the mess', and in seeking a way out, countries engage in distributive rather than positive-sum games. Pre-crisis, however, and in line with the proactive policy stance suggested here, positive-sum approaches are more likely: everyone benefits from financial stability. In other words, the creation of policy space for positive-sum approaches requires settlement of the trade-offs Chapter 3 identified, and settling them demands answers to 'who pays', 'who loses', and 'who benefits'. The art of politics is to find solutions that make positive-sum thinking more likely in the future–and not out of some notion of altruism but because under conditions of interdependence such approaches strengthen rather than weaken governance readiness.

This is where the notion of responsible sovereignty becomes central. The term was originally articulated by Deng et al. (1996) and further expanded by ICISS (2001) and Jones, Pasqual and Stedman (2009). Initially, it primarily meant that national governments are legally obliged to ensure basic standards of security, personal freedom and welfare of citizens, and prevent the export of security threats from within their territory. If a state fails in these duties, the international community has a responsibility to intervene and to protect people in that country.

However, as Chapter 2 makes clear, sovereignty as responsibility came mainly to refer to weaker developing nations, failing and failed states and to cases of human rights violation. Yet, the notion of responsible sovereignty proposed here applies to states strong and weak, developed and developing alike, as the governance requirements specify. In other words, it applies to Germany and Greece, as it does to the United States and Zimbabwe. Responsible sovereignty is about managing interdependence, not only about how to deal with failed and failing states.

Fully exploring the potentials and limitations of responsible sovereignty would require a major intellectual effort in the political economy of public goods under the prevailing conditions of interdependence. It would go significantly beyond the conventional notion of sovereignty and could help policymakers make sense of the steps needed to undertake governance reforms like those that global challenges require–and, if needed, to design treaties that stand a greater chance of achieving intended policy outcomes.

Recommendation 2: A major intellectual effort is needed to modernise the notion of conventional sovereignty by replacing it with the concept of responsible sovereignty, taking interdependence rather than the singularity, and indeed insularity, of the nation state as its starting point.

Chapter 2 put forth the proposition that sovereignty and openness can indeed be combined if deepening policy interdependence and commitment to cooperate are matched by enhanced mutuality of benefit. The Chiang Mai Initiative Multilateralisation in Chapter 4 highlighted that pooling sovereignty enhances rather than reduces national sovereignty. How could such examples be made more suggestive to policymakers as the 'default setting' rather than the exception of international relations? For the various components of governance readiness, Box 6.1 offers a number of examples, building on Table 2.1 in Chapter 2.

One way of advancing the notion of responsible sovereignty to 'centre stage' is to have it taken up by the very world body that suffers from the excessive use of conventional sovereignty: the United Nations. In fact Chapter 2 proposed to set up an international high-level commission to that effect:

Recommendation 3: The UN Secretary-General should consider establishing a high-level commission on responsible sovereignty, charged with developing the concept and its policy implications.

For states, responsible sovereignty and multilateralism are closely linked: under conditions of policy interdependence, so a principle credo of the Report, more multilateralism helps states regain and maintain their policy-making sovereignty. Yet when it comes to major policy frameworks, multilateralism has not seen much progress in recent decades, although specialised, issue-focused treaties[2] and regional developments took place, mostly in

Box 6.1 Responsible Sovereignty and the Improvement of Governance Readiness

The governance requirements laid out in Chapter 2 offer examples of how the principle of responsible sovereignty can be put into practice. Here we propose some ways this can be done at different levels and by different actors:

GR1: Averting the risk of dual—market and state—failure

Measures must be put in place to discourage the free-riding of governance actors and encourage their willingness to cooperate. At the transnational level, this might include compliance monitoring systems equipped with adequate sanctions. Transparency in such agreements, also at other levels, would help stakeholders and watchdogs understand what is expected of each party and who is keeping commitments.

GR2: Correcting fairness deficits

Proper incentives must be created to ensure that all parties are genuinely motivated to support, and act on, what was jointly decided. This requires clear rules of participation, which are implemented fairly and transparently, and goals that can be supported by strengthening regional collaboration among states.

GR3: Strengthened externality management

Actors must be more watchful about the effects that their policy actions and their consumption and production choices have on others. This is so not only at the nation-state level, but also within corporations, along the lines of social responsibility strategies and reporting that take into account suppliers' actions, environmental impact, and other externalities.

GR4: Promoting issue-focus and result-orientation

Issue-focus must be added to today's set of organisational criteria in order to ensure that all required inputs fall in place. Essential is the 'modernisation' of central ministries to enable them to act across borders. At the same time, result-orientation must be strengthened through a variety of mechanisms, e.g. pay-for-performance contracts in social services such as those supported by social impact bonds reviewed in Chapter 4.

GR5: Recognising and promoting synergies

Synergies among problems and their solutions must be recognised and promoted, requiring strategic leadership that spots early warning signals. Here is where civil society organisations, mixed-membership entities such as the World Economic Forum, and others can take the lead in creating and shaping debate. At the same time, a serious debate about a modernised UN system that reflects the realities of the twenty-first rather than mid-twentieth century is called for.

GR6: Active acceptance of policy interdependence

Governance actors must recognise policy interdependence and pursue positive-sum solutions, where appropriate but also where such solutions might not be evident from the outset. This calls for a new multilateralism.

Europe (e.g., Lisbon Treaty of 2007) but also in Asia (ASEAN charter of 2007; Shanghai Cooperation Organization, 2007) and Latin America (Constitutive Treaty of the Union of South American Nations, 2008). While it may be premature to speak of a crisis of multilateralism, the troubling fact remains that no new major comprehensive multilateral treaty addressing one of the major challenges to individual well-being and global threats has been successfully concluded and enacted for over a decade! The absence of major treaties stands in marked contrast to the 1990s, when several were negotiated and signed[3], and treaty failure rather than success threatens to become a hallmark of multilateralism in the early twenty-first century.

In the language of the performance model introduced in this Report, such failures and deficiencies point to weaknesses in effectiveness. In other words, even when countries and international organizations have the resources in place to design an overarching framework for addressing a policy problem, they fail to do so—either because of disagreements about how to implement and monitor treaties and subsequent programs or because of misaligned incentives and sanctions. Hence the weak performance of multilateralism is not only a problem of efficacy; it is ultimately about effectiveness.

Deficiencies in both efficacy and effectiveness, as we have argued, can trigger downward spirals in performance and legitimacy. To help stem such a development, and to improve effectiveness, we propose to develop new forms of multilateralism that are less centred on the nation state and lodged with international organisations like the UN and more in line with the notion of governance as a multi-actor, multi-level system that underlies this Report.[4] Could it be that a new multilateralism based on diversity of actors and levels, including regions, may hold more promise than the nation state–global approach of the past, as Van Langenhove (2011) suggests?

Recommendation 4: A systematic assessment of the potentials and weaknesses of devolved approaches to multilateralism should be undertaken, and major regional organisations like the EU, SCO, OAS or OAU should be encouraged to do so.

Yet, similar paradigm changes are required of actors at other levels as well. A key example of 'responsible sovereignty' as applied more broadly to all actors in governance processes is the Rhine River System reviewed in Chapter 1. All stakeholders, whether corporate, governmental or civil society, whether national or local, had to think in terms of positive-sum solutions in order for the river system to survive, let alone thrive as it does today. The world needs more examples of this kind, and policy analysts are invited to search for potential cases where such approaches could be developed and applied.

Indeed, many of the most promising governance innovations we are tracking involve new combinations in the types of actors or levels collaborating, often in some form of partnership, as the civil society–government cooperations reviewed in Chapter 4. This underscores the importance of understanding governance as a multi-level and multi-actor process. However, we cannot get to the positive-sum solutions required if we assume that one particular actor alone is responsible for solving a certain challenge (e.g. 'government is responsible for the provision of public goods'), that a challenge has to be tackled on a specific level (e.g. 'global challenges need global-level action'), or 'that markets are best left alone'.

Put differently: finding positive-sum solutions requires new ways of thinking and a move away from simplistic notions that equate the national interest with some sort of purely self-interested maximisation of power, influence or resources. It also necessitates new thinking in the corporate world. The financial and economic crisis has amply demonstrated that maximising short-term shareholder return on investments at the expense of other and longer term responsibilities can lead to rather negative outcomes–both in terms of private and public goods. Indeed, we view the preoccupation with short-term investor profits–preached and exercised for many decades by major corporations, banks, rating agencies and some governments alike–as the late twentieth century business sector analogue to the nineteenth century notion of the national interest as maximising the power of sovereign states.

The world no longer fits such simplifying and ultimately misleading approaches, if it ever did. Civil society organisations, too, are called upon to contribute to make sure states can move towards responsible sovereignty. We are reminded of Gellner's (1994) powerful description that saw NGOs in the role of counterbalancing the state's tendency to dominate society, and the market's tendency to 'atomise' citizens into consumers. We are also reminded of Keane when he describes civil society 'as a complex and dynamic ensemble of legally protected non-governmental institutions that tend to be non-violent, self-organising, self-reflexive, and permanently in tension with each other and with the state institutions that "frame", constrict and enable their activities' (1998: 6).

Chapter 5 did point out that a vibrant civil society enhances public sector transparency and accountability. Enlisting NGOs in a collaborative effort–indeed project–to find positive-sum solutions under the umbrella policy of responsible sovereignty does not mean that we enter some non-ideological, conflict-free zone. Nor does it mean that zero-sum outcomes are no longer required. To the contrary, needed are new platforms and vehicles for conflicting parties to express themselves and seek settlement in terms of positive and zero sums. Dahrendorf's (1961) fundamental insight still holds: modern societies are both more conflict-prone and 'smarter', and it applies here and does so to the fullest. They are more resilient and carry greater potential because they seek ways to find acceptable solutions to conflicts that may involve complicated trade-offs of the kind analysed in Chapter 3. Modern societies can turn potentially divisive conflicts into productive solutions, thereby adding to both stability and legitimacy.

In light of the urgency of action that today's governance challenges require, we emphasise that efforts on multiple levels by different actors, ideally working collaboratively, are perhaps the most promising approach for improving governance readiness and performance. The roles of national and international governmental actors at the nation-state and global levels examined in this Report, and especially in the innovations chapter, made clear that governance and governance innovation indeed involve combinations of different kinds of actors (civil society, corporations) and applications of solutions borrowed from one sector or level in other situations (Norwegian fund borrowing socially responsible investment ideas from the business world).

> **Recommendation 5: Collaboration among actors across levels and fields is to be encouraged to bring about governance innovations. We propose a systematic search for areas where such collaboration happens–and does not happen, but could, and why.**

Among countries, governance readiness is clearly lacking in many respects, as Chapter 2 has argued and Chapter 5 has shown for a selected number of issues. Voting at the UN General Assembly was a clear case of how countries exercising 'old style' sovereignty are caught in a self-inflicted stalemate that built up over decades and now may well threaten the long-term viability of the institution. At the same time, there are also positive signs and indications that responsible sovereignty is not only possible and feasible but that it ultimately pays off, as the WTO and peacekeeping examples in Chapter 5 showed.

The recommendations so far can also be put in the form of a single question: how can we encourage positive-sum strategies? To some extent simply by pointing out that the national interest is best realised through co-operation, even in fields characterised by high-level competition as in the case of monetary policy or great conflict potential as in security matters. Yet who would do the pointing out? Let's consider both questions in turn.

In some instances, challenges are acute threats and come with signals so strong and clear that they coerce actors into collective action–with NATO and the Warsaw Pact during the Cold War as prime examples. In many other cases, however, signals are complex, more subtle and on longer timelines– as the euro debt crisis reveals. Here, early warning systems can alert policymakers in advance, and preset incentives and sanctions can keep actors aligned and reduce free-riding. In both cases, however, it seems that governments alone cannot be expected 'to do the job', i.e. to read signals and to devise and enact policies encouraging positive-sum outcomes. What is more, governments are too frequently unable or unwilling to read their own signals, as Chapter 3 made clear when addressing the question of what can be done to dampen governments' temptation to overspend.

At least for the great majority of countries, as Chapter 5 has shown, governments simply do not have the efficacy and effectiveness in place to be responsible sovereigns in the face of today's interdependencies.

Recommendation 6: There is a strong need to strengthen governmental and nongovernmental capacity in terms of efficacy–managing information, creating knowledge, and finding solutions to policy problems.

Do governments actually have a solution in mind, or some response adequate to the policy challenges of an interdependent world?[5] If yes, how do we know it is the right one, and will it achieve what is intended without undue unintended consequences? If no, what can be done to arrive at efficacious proposals? At one level, this question calls for the development of an adequate infrastructure of institutions concerned with generating social science and policy-relevant information and knowledge. At another, it points to the important role of civil society, which, as Chapters 4 and 5 have shown, contributes significantly to innovations and improved governance performance in terms of transparency and accountability. Hence, increasing efficacy is no longer the sole and primary responsibility of governments but requires private sector input–from civil society like think tanks and Internet platforms as well as from corporate 'universities' and consultancy firms.

The lessons to be drawn from Chapter 3 on how major countries dealt with the succession of financial crises after 2008 are stark: the capacity to cope with governance challenges is about preventing such crises from happening in the first place, and making countries less prone to them. This capacity was not fully developed and triggered secondary shocks that amplified the impact of the disjuncture between globalised financial markets, financial market integration in the EU, and national systems of supervision, the separation of central banking functions from supervisory functions, and ailing cross-border financial institutions. There was a lack of attention to systemic supervision to safeguard the stability of the entire financial system and to the interconnection between micro and macro financial supervision, as well as a lack of awareness of the interconnection among monetary policy, macroeconomic imbalances, and financial stability.

These are important findings and with many implications. For one, we have to recognise that with very few exceptions single national governments, and very likely also the international organizations they create and control, no longer have sufficient expertise and knowledge to manage interdependencies–if they ever had in recent decades, as, again, the financial crisis of 2008 and the many intelligence failures in security policy reveal. As we are unlikely to have some form of world government in the foreseeable future– and may indeed not want one, even if we could, as a recent Brookings report by Altinay (2012) suggests–it is also unlikely that some supranational body would emerge to fill the efficacy gap.

In other words, we will need to live and, for better or worse, make do with largely inefficacious and likely also more or less ineffective nation states for some time to come, even given regional forms of government like the EU. However, these nation states have to come to terms with a reality that is different from the era that ushered in their creation.

As Chapter 2 suggests, responsible sovereignty as both concept and first order governance decision could help achieve two seemingly contradictory demands put on nation states: managing interdependence and serving the national interest. We do not see responsible sovereignty as some idealistic dream or soft compromise. To the contrary: it requires alertness, an astute reading of signals, and stewardship with a strategic eye for positive-sum solutions that advance the national interest. Responsible sovereignty is an essential element of good governance in an interdependent world. In other words, to be a responsible sovereign demands certain capacities in terms of efficacy and effectiveness.[6]

Some policy domains like the environment are largely outside the full reach of the nation state; others have partially escaped a nation-state frame some time ago, for example, migration, finance, communication, and technological advancement. In such instances, innovations are needed around the governance of global public goods, which are hampered by a certain backwardness of economics and economic teaching. The focus of standard theories of public economics remains the national economy almost exclusively, and, therefore, there is little on the economics of meeting global challenges taught at undergraduate and graduate levels; conventional textbooks in economics seem to live in a world of seemingly independent national economies that trade in private goods. That some goods are global and others are commons reaching above and beyond national economies has yet to enter mainstream economics teaching as a topic of equal weight to corporate finance. While some studies have emerged that deal with particular issue areas like global warming or a particular communicable disease, conventional macroeconomics seems curiously unaffected by the fundamental fact of economic interdependence.[7]

> **Recommendation 7: Social science curricula are to be adjusted and revised to take account of the new realities and help educate a new generation of policy experts, administrators and managers who not only understand interdependence and its challenges but embrace its opportunities.**

Already, states are able to enjoy policymaking sovereignty only to the extent that they commit to cooperate in meeting global and trans-border challenges that might otherwise turn into global or regional crises; to strengthen their national-level management of cross-border spillovers; and to contribute their fair share to protect any states' sovereignty. As Chapter 2 argues, not many states are willing to make these commitments–but go on to exercise sovereignty nonetheless–with the frequent disappointing outcomes that Chapter 5 pointed out when looking at the performance of some international treaties and protocols. Yet the notion of responsible sovereignty goes beyond these three commitments: the difference is that responsible sovereignty offers a new governance paradigm–a first order governance decision that allows policymakers to make sense of interdependencies and establishes a new default of policymaking. Yet as long as governance reforms like those that especially global challenges require are being viewed from the perspective of the conventional, nineteenth century notion of sovereignty, they are easily captured by established political elite and party politics–and therefore readily avoided, ignored and opposed.

We have seen that such a proactive policy stance to interdependence is limited to too few countries. Clearly, no one expects all countries to become equally responsible in all fields, and it may well be easier for a country like Norway or Costa Rica to become a responsible sovereign than let's say for a superpower like the United States or any of the BRIC countries. Yet the governance requirements discussed in Chapter 2 and partially explored empirically in Chapter 5 make clear that more countries could be more responsible–and that they could well afford to do so and indeed be better off in the long run–if they moved away from the first order governance premise that the national interest is best served through competition and going it alone rather than through cooperation and proper management of interdependence.

In this first edition of the Report, we refrain from naming countries that fall into one category of responsible sovereignty or another.[8] The indicator system introduced and partially explored in Chapter 5 does not yet yield the solid analytics and evidence needed for such an exercise. But it has become clear that being a responsible sovereign is not the exclusive province of major powers, developed or emerging market economies, resource-rich and resource-poor states, or large or small countries. Across all nation states, more can be done.

Even when actors demonstrate governance readiness, they still face a number of trade-offs inherent in finding solutions and acting upon them in today's interdependent world. Chapter 3 honed in on three of these trade-offs that arise particularly in fiscal and financial governance: liquidity vs. moral hazard; accountability vs. effectiveness; domestic politics vs. international commitments. Some of these trade-offs, especially accountability vs. effectiveness and internal vs. external commitments, emerge in other policy areas as well. Furthermore, we can see them not only at the global level, but also the local level, affecting not only national leaders, but also civil society and corporate actors. Nonetheless, the assumption is that actors will find it easier to address these trade-offs the more governance-ready they are.

Concluding Comment

Throughout, the Report made clear that there are no quick fixes in the form of some technocratic solution or another to solve key public problems, in global finance or in other policy fields characterised by interdependence. This is so, in part, because there are no true apolitical technocrats, as the role of the IMF, the ECB or the Bundesbank in the euro crisis shows. Perhaps more important, as Chapter 3 argues, is that the actors themselves determine which part of a given trade-off they prefer–and any such preferences reveal political preferences, not merely technocratic ones.

Nevertheless, as we have seen in various chapters, governance actors at all levels are not sitting still, but are indeed seeking ways to handle such trade-offs, to improve governance and, ultimately, policy outcomes. They are taking advantage of 'policy windows' that open in such times of uncertainty. Yet, we found that most of these approaches focus mainly on improving efficacy and effectiveness at the level of second order governance questions, i.e., designing and implementing solutions, setting incentive structures, and monitoring–certainly steps in the right direction. Few, however, tackle first order governance questions, involving problem-framing and allocating rights and responsibilities, or offer first principle solutions that both capture the underlying problem and propose a solution. In fact, there seems at present to be no overarching plan or vision guiding governance innovation and change. Especially given this void, the notion of responsible sovereignty appears as a reasonable and achievable way forward.

Endnotes

1. As presented and applied in Chapters 1 and 4, first order governance decisions are primarily about politics and matters of principles, and second order governance decisions more about policies and specific issues.
2. For example, World Health Organisation Framework Convention on Tobacco Control (2003), signed by 168, and ratified by 176 member states.
3. United Nations Framework Convention on Climate Change (1992): signed by 165, ratified by 195 member states; Convention on the Prohibition of the Development, Production, Stockpiling and Use of Chemical Weapons and on their Destruction (1997): signed by 165, ratified by 188; Kyoto Protocol to the United Nations Framework Convention on Climate Change (1997): signed by 83, ratified by 191; Rome Statute of the International Criminal Court (1998): 139 signed, 121 ratified.
4. See Keohane, Macedo and Moravcsik (2009); Muldoon et al. (2010); Hampson and Heinbecker (2011); Altinay (2012).
5. Some basic statistical data systems have seen much improvement in recent decades, especially population statistics and national income accounts. For example, 174 out of 192 countries had their census in or after 2000 (90.6%). 89 out of 192 countries had their census in or after 2005 (46.4%). All but a few countries submit national income accounts (http://unstats.un.org/unsd/nationalaccount/sna.asp). In part, the improvement in national statistical capacity is the result of efforts like Paris21 (http://www.paris21.org/). At the same time, such statistical capac-

ity, while improved, is part of the measure of efficacy employed in Chapter 5, and only but underscores the need for investment in policy-relevant information and knowledge systems.

6   We do not mean, however, that all actions are to be based on positive-sum outcomes. Clearly, some will require zero-sum thinking and for good reasons. The point of the argument here is rather that more positive-sum policies are more possible and feasible than could be realised.

7   Critiques of mainstream macroeconomics can be found, for instance, in Krugman (2009) and Stiglitz (2010).

8   In future editions, we plan to extend the system to major corporations and CSOs.

References

Albrow, M., and Anheier, H. (2006). 'Violence and the Possibility of Global Civility', in M. Glasius, M. Kaldor, and H. Anheier (eds), *Global Civil Society 2006/2007*. London: Sage, 1-17.

Altinay, H., (ed) (2012). 'Global Governance Audit', Washington, D.C.: The Brookings Institution. Global Economy & Development Working Paper 49.

Anheier, H. K. (2004). *Civil Society: Measurement and Policy Dialogue*. London: Earthscan.

Anheier, H. K. (2005). *Nonprofit Organizations: Theory, Management, Policy*. New York, Abingdon: Routledge.

Anheier, H. K. (2007). 'Bringing Civility Back in – Reflections on Global Civil Society', *Development Dialogue*, 49:41-50.

Anheier, H. K., and Daly, S. (ed) (2007). *The Politics of Foundations: A Comparative Analysis*. New York, Abingdon: Routledge.

Anheier, H. K., and Isar, Y. R. (eds) (2008). *The Cultural Economy*. The Cultures and Globalization Series, Volume 2. London: Sage Publications.

Anheier, H. K., and Seibel, W. (2001). *The Nonprofit Sector in Germany: Between State, Economy, and Society*. Manchester, New York: Manchester University Press.

Archibugi, D., and Iammarino, S. (2002). 'The Globalization of Technological Innovation: Definition and Evidence', *Review of International Political Economy*, 9:98-122.

Axelrod, R. (1984). *The Evolution of Cooperation*. New York: Basic Books.

Bandura, R. (forthcoming). *Composite Indicators and Rankings: Inventory 2011*. Brussels: European Commission Joint Research Centre.

Barrett, S. (2007). *Why Cooperate? The Incentive to Supply Global Public Goods*. New York: Oxford University Press.

Bearce, D. H., and Hallerberg, M. (2011). 'Democracy and De Facto Exchange Rate Regimes', *Economics & Politics*, 23:172-94.

Beattie, A. (2010). 'Steep Path to a Modern-day Plaza Accord', *Financial Times*, 16 September, http://www.ft.com/intl/cms/s/0/5be5e788-c1ba-11df-9d90-00144feab49a.html(accessed 28 August 2012).

Beck, U. (2007). 'The Cosmopolitan Condition: Why Methodological Nationalism Fails', *Theory, Culture & Society*, 24:286-90.

Biersteker, T. J. (2002). 'State, Sovereignty and Territory', in W. Carlsnaes, T. Risse, and B. A. Simmons (eds), *Handbook of International Relations*. London: Sage Publications, 157-76.

Borins, S. (2000). 'What Border? Public Management Innovation in the United States and Canada', *Journal of Policy Analysis and Management*, 19:46-74.

Bove, V., and Elia, L. (2011). 'Supplying Peace: Participation in and Troop Contribution to Peacekeeping Missions', *Journal of Peace Research*, 48:699-714.

Bown, C. P. (2012a). *Global Antidumping Database*. Retrieved from http://econ.worldbank.org/ttbd/gad/.

Bown, C. P. (2012b). *Global Countervailing Duties Database*. Retrieved from http://econ.worldbank.org/ttbd/gcvd/.

Bräutigam, D. (2004). 'The People's Budget? Politics, Participation and Pro-poor Policy.' *Development Policy Review*, 22(6): 653-68.

Brinkley, D. G., and Hackett, C. (ed) (1991). *Jean Monnet: The Path to European Unity*. London: Palgrave Macmillan.

Brown, B., and Corbett, T. (1997). 'Social Indicators and Public Policy in the Age of Devolution', Institute for Research on Poverty Special Report 71.

Brown, M., Peter, M., and Wehrmüller, S. (2009). 'Swiss Franc Lending in Europe', *Aussenwirtschaft (Swiss Review of International Economics)*, 64:167-82.

Buergenthal, T. (2001). 'Proliferation of International Courts and Tribunals: Is it Good or Bad?', *Leiden Journal of International Law*, 14:267-75.

Carin, B. (2012). 'G20 Rapid Response: The G20 and Climate Change', http://www.cigionline.org/publications/2012/6/g20-rapid-response-g20-and-climate-change (accessed 28 August 2012).

Chang, R. (1999). 'Understanding Recent Crises in Emerging Markets', *Federal Reserve Bank of Atlanta Economic Review*, second quarter: 6-16.

Chinn, M. D., and Frieden, J. A. (2011). *Lost Decades: The Making of America's Debt Crisis and the Long Recovery*. New York: W.W. Norton.

Chiu, E. M. P. et al. (2012). 'The Discipline Effects of Fixed Exchange Rates: The Distinction between Hard and Soft Pegs', *Global Economic Review*, 41:1-31.

Christensen, C. M. (1997). *The Innovator's Dilemma: When New Technologies Cause Great Firms to Fail*. Boston: Harvard Business Press.

Clark, W. R., and Hallerberg, M. (2000). 'Mobile Capital, Domestic Institutions, and Electorally Induced Monetary and Fiscal Policy', *American Political Science Review*, 94:323-46.

Clinton, J. D., and Jackman, S. (2009). 'To Simulate or NOMINATE?', *Legislative Studies Quarterly*, 34:593-621.

Conceição, P. (2006). 'Accommodating New Actors and New Purposes in International Cooperation: The Growing Diversification of Financing Mechanisms', in I. Kaul, and P. Conceição (eds), *The New Public Finance: Responding to Global Challenges*. New York: Oxford University Press, 269-80.

Conceição, P., and Mendoza, R. U. (2006). 'Identifying High-Return Investments: A Methodology for Assessing When International Cooperation Pays - and For Whom', in I. Kaul, and P. Conceição (eds), *The New Public Finance: Responding to Global Challenges*. New York: Oxford University Press, 327-56.

Cooper, R. N. (1971). 'Currency Devaluation in Developing Countries', Princeton University, International Finance Section, Essays in International Finance No. 86.

Copelovitch, M. S., and Singer, D. A. (2008). 'Financial Regulation, Monetary Policy, and Inflation in the Industrialized World', *Journal of Politics*, 70:663-80.

Crabtree, J. (2003). 'Civic Hacking: A New Agenda for E-democracy', *Open Democracy*, 6 March, http://www.opendemocracy.net/media-edemocracy/ article_1025.jsp (accessed 29 August 2012).

Crockett, A. (1997). 'The Theory and Practice of Financial Stability', Princeton University, International Finance Section, Essays in International Finance No. 203.

Dahrendorf, R. (1961). *Gesellschaft und Freiheit. Zur soziologischen Analyse der Gegenwart*. München: Piper.

Danninger, S. (2002). 'A New Rule: "The Swiss Debt Brake"', IMF Working Paper 02/18.

Davies, H. (2010). 'Global Financial Regulation after the Credit Crisis', *Global Policy*, 1:185-90.

DB (Deutsche Bank) Climate Change Advisors (2011). *Global Climate Change Policy Tracker: Winners and Losers*. Frankfurt: Deutsche Bank.

De Larosière Group (2009). *The High Level Group on Financial Supervision in the EU*. Report, 25 February, Brussels, http://ec.europa.eu/internal_market/finances/docs/de_larosiere_report_en.pdf (accessed 31 August 2012).

Deng, F. M. et al. (1996). *Sovereignty as Responsibility: Conflict Management in Africa*. Washington, D.C.: The Brookings Institution.

Deutsch, K.W. (1963). *The Nerves of Government: Models of Political Communication and Control*. New York: The Free Press.

DiMaggio, P. J., and Powell, W. W. (1983). 'The Iron Cage Revisited: Institutional Isomorphism and Collective Rationality in Organizational Fields', *American Sociological Review*, 48:147-60

DiMaggio, P. J., and Powell, W. W. (ed) (1991). *The New Institutionalism in Organizational Analysis*. Chicago: University of Chicago Press.

Dolls, M., Peichl, A., and Zimmermann, K. F. (2011). 'A Challenge for the G20: Globally Stipulated Debt Brakes and Transnational Independent Supervisory Councils', IZA Policy Paper 33.

Drazen, A. (2002). 'Fiscal Rules from a Political Economy Perspective', Paper prepared for the IMF-World Bank Conference on Rules-Based Fiscal Policy in Emerging Market Economies, 14-16 February 2002, Oaxaca, Mexico.

Dreher, A., and Vaubel, R. (2004). 'The Causes and Consequences of IMF Conditionality', *Emerging Markets Finance and Trade*, 40:26-54.

Drori, G. S., Meyer, J. W., and Hwang, H. (2006). *Globalization and Organization: World Society and Organizational Change*. Oxford: Oxford University Press.

Dubash, N. K., and Florini, A. (2011). 'Mapping Global Energy Governance', *Global Policy*, 2(Special Issue):6-18.

Eichengreen, B. (1996). *Globalizing Capital: A History of the International Monetary System*. Princeton: Princeton University Press.

Eichengreen, B. (ed) (2004). *Capital Flows and Crises*. Cambridge: MIT Press.

Eichengreen, B., and Park, B. (2012). *The World Economy After the Global Crisis: A New Economic Order for the 21st Century*. Singapore: World Scientific Books.

Elson, A. (2012). 'Global Financial Reform – Where Do Things Stand?', *World Economics*, 13:155-70.

Enderlein, H., Wälti, S., and Zürn, M. (2010). *Handbook on Multi-level Governance*. Cheltenham: Edward Elgar.

Ezzat, H. R., and Kaldor, M. (2006). '"Not Even a Tree": Delegitimising Violence and the Prospects for Pre-emptive Civility', in M. Glasius, M. Kaldor, and H. K. Anheier (eds), *Global Civil Society: 2006/7*. London: Sage Publications, 18-41.

Feld, L. P., and Kirchgässner, G. (2006). 'On the Effectiveness of Debt Brakes: The Swiss Experience', CREMA Working Paper 2006-21.

Fidler, D. P. (2010). *The Challenges of Global Health Governance*. New York: Council on Foreign Relations (International Institutions and Global Governance Program).

Fleming, M. J. (1962). 'Domestic Financial Policies under Fixed and under Floating Exchange Rates', *IMF Staff Papers*, 9:369-80.

Foot, R., MacFarlane, S. N., and Mastanduno, M. (eds) (2003). *US Hegemony and International Organizations*. New York: Oxford University Press.

Frankel, J. A. (2005). 'Contractionary Currency Crashes in Developing Countries', NBER Working Paper 11508.

Frankel, J. A., and Wei, S.-J. (2004). 'Managing Macroeconomic Crises: Policy Lessons', NBER Working Paper 10907.

Freund, C. (2005). 'Current Account Adjustment in Industrial Countries', *Journal of International Money and Finance*, 24:1278-98.

Gellner, E. (1994). *Conditions of Liberty: Civil Society and Its Rivals*. London: Hamish Hamilton.

Gersick, C. J. G. (1991). 'Revolutionary Change Theories: A Multilevel Exploration of the Punctuated Equilibrium Paradigm', *Academy of Management Review*, 16:10-36.

Glasius, M. (2006). *The International Criminal Court: A Global Civil Society Achievement*. Oxford: Routledge.

Grimes, W. W. (2011). 'The Asian Monetary Fund Reborn? Implications of Chiang Mai Initiative Multilateralization', *Asia Policy*, 11:79-104.

Group of Thirty (2009). *Financial Reform: A Framework for Financial Stability*. Special Report, Washington DC, http://www.group30.org/images/PDF/Financial_Reform-A_Framework_for_Financial_Stability.pdf (accessed 28 August 2012).

Hallerberg, M. (2004). *Domestic Budgets in a United Europe: Fiscal Governance from the End of Bretton Woods to EMU*. Ithaca: Cornell University Press.

Hallerberg, M., Strauch, R., and von Hagen, J. (2007). 'The Design of Fiscal Rules and Forms of Governance in European Union Countries', *European Journal of Political Economy*, 23:338-59.

Hamilton, A. (1787). The Federalist No. 28: 'Idea of Restraining the Legislative Authority in Regard to the Common Defense Considered (continued)', *Independent Journal*, 26 December, http://www.constitution.org/fed/ federa28.htm (accessed 31 August 2012).

Hampson, F. O., and Heinbecker, P. (2011). 'The "New" Multilateralism of the Twenty-First Century', *Global Governance: A Review of Multilateralism and International Organizations*, 17:299-310.

Henning, C. R. (2009). 'The Future of the Chiang Mai Initiative: An Asian Monetary Fund?', Peterson Institute for International Economics Policy Brief 09-5.

Heston, A., Summers, R., and Aten, B. (2012). *Penn World Table Version 7.1*. Center for International Comparisons of Production, Income and Prices at University of Pennsylvania. Retrieved from http://pwt.econ.upenn.edu/php_site/pwt_index.php

Heydon, K., and Woolcock, S. (2009). *The Rise of Bilateralism: Comparing American, European and Asian Approaches to Preferential Trade Agreements*. Tokyo: United Nations University Press.

HLPE (High Level Panel of Exports on Food Security and Nutrition) (2011). *Land Tenure and International Investments in Agriculture: A Report by the High-level Panel of Experts on Food Security and Nutrition of the Committee on World Food Security*. Rome: HLPE.

'Hong Kong in Honduras' (2011). *The Economist*, 10 December, http://www.economist.com/node/21541392 (accessed 29 August 2012).

Hood, C. (1995). 'Contemporary Public Management: A New Global Paradigm?' *Public Policy and Administration*, 10:104-17.

Hopkins, R. (2008). *The Transition Handbook: From Oil Dependency to Local Resilience*. Totnes: Green Books.

Howarth, D. (2001). 'Comparing Public Administrative Reform in France and the UK', *Public Policy and Administration*, 16:1-8.

ICISS (International Commission on Intervention and State Sovereignty) (2001). *The Responsibility to Protect: Report of the International Commission on Intervention and State Sovereignty*. Ottawa: International Development Research Centre.

IEA (International Energy Agency) (2011). *World Energy Outlook 2011*. Paris: IEA.

IMF (International Monetary Fund) (2011). *World Economic Outlook Database: September 2011*. Retrieved from http://www.imf.org/external/pubs/ft/weo/2011/02/weodata/index.aspx

IMF (International Monetary Fund) (2012a). *Modernizing the Legal Framework for Surveillance – Building Blocks Toward an Integrated Surveillance Decision*. Washington, D.C.: IMF.

IMF (International Monetary Fund) (2012b). *Quota Formula Review – Data Update and Further Considerations*. Washington, D.C.: IMF.

IMF (International Monetary Fund) (2012c). *Spillover Report*. Washington, D.C.: IMF.

International Budget Partnership (2010). *Open Budgets. Transform Lives. The Open Budget Survey 2010*. Washington, D.C.: International Budget Project.

Jenkins, J. C. (2006). 'Nonprofit Organizations and Political Advocacy', in W. W. Powell and R. Steinberg (eds), *The Nonprofit Sector: A Research Handbook*. 2nd edition. New Haven, London: Yale University Press.

Jessop, B. (2011). 'Metagovernance', in M. Bevir (ed), *The Sage Handbook of Governance*. London: Sage Publications, 106-23.

Jones, B., Pasqual, C., and Stedman, S. J. (2009). *Power and Responsibility: Building International Order in an Era of Transnational Threats*. Washington, D.C.: Brookings Institution Press.

Judt, T. R. (2010). *Ill Fares the Land*. London: Penguin.

Kanter, R. M. (1983). *The Change Masters: Innovation & Entrepreneurship in the American Corporation*. New York: Simon & Schuster.

Kaufmann, D., Kraay, A., and Mastruzzi, M. (2010). 'The Worldwide Governance Indicators: Methodology and Analytical Issues', World Bank Policy Research Working Paper 5430.

Kaufmann, D., Kraay, A., and Zoido-Lobatón, P. (1999). 'Governance Matters', World Bank Policy Research Working Paper 2196.

Kaul, I. (2006). 'Blending External and Domestic Policy Demands: The Rise of the Intermediary State', in I. Kaul, and P. Conceição (eds), *The New Public Finance: Responding to Global Challenges*. New York: Oxford University Press, 73-108.

Kaul, I., and Mendoza, R.U. (2003). 'Advancing the Concept of Public Goods', in I. Kaul et al. (eds), *Providing Global Public Goods: Managing Globalization*. New York: Oxford University Press, 78-111.

Keane, J. (1998). *Civil Society: Old Images, New Visions*. Stanford: Stanford University Press.

Keohane, R. O., Macedo, S., and Moravcsik, A. (2009). 'Democracy-Enhancing Multilateralism', *International Organization*, 63:1-31.

Khanna, J., Sandler, T., and Shimizu, H. (1998). 'Sharing the Financial Burden for U.N. and NATO Peacekeeping, 1976-1996', *Journal of Conflict Resolution*, 42:176-95.

Khanna, P. (2011). *How to Run the World: Charting a Course to the Next Renaissance*. New York: Random House.

Kinderman, D. (2008). 'The Political Economy of Sectoral Exchange Rate Preferences and Lobbying: Germany from 1960-2008, and Beyond', *Review of International Political Economy*, 15:851-80.

Kingdon, J. W. (1995). *Agendas, Alternatives, and Public Policies*. 2nd ed. New York: Addison, Wesley Longman.

Kooiman, J., and Jentoft, S. (2009). 'Meta-governance: Values, Norms and Principles, and the Making of Hard Choices', *Public Administration*, 87(4): 818-836.

Krugman, P. (2009). 'How Did Economists Get it So Wrong?', *New York Times Magazine*, 2 September, http://nytimes.com/2009/09/06/magazine/06Economic-t.html?pagewanted=all (accessed 31 August 2012).

Lamy, P. (2012). 'Multilateralism is at a Crossroads', Speech delivered at the Humboldt-Viadrina School of Governance in Berlin on 26 June 2012, http://www.wto.org/english/news_e/sppl_e/sppl239_e.htm (accessed 28 August 2012).

Le Guernigou, Y. (2009). 'City Fears as Sarkozy Hits Out at Anglo Saxon Model', *The Scotsman*, 2 December, http://www.scotsman.com/business/city-fears-as-sarkozy-hits-out-at-anglo-saxon-model-1-770491 (accessed 28 August 2012).

Lindblom, C. E. (1959). 'The Science of "Muddling-Through"', *Public Administration Review*, 19:79-88.

Linz, J. J., and Stepan, A. (1978). *The Breakdown of Democratic Regimes*. Baltimore: Johns Hopkins University Press.

MacKinnon, R. (2012). *Consent of the Networked: The Worldwide Struggle for Internet Freedom*. New York: Basic Books.

Madison, J. (1788). The Federalist No. 51: 'The Structure of the Government Must Furnish the Proper Checks and Balances Between the Different Departments', *Independent Journal*, 6 February, http://constitutions.org/fed/federa51.htm (accessed 31 August 2012).

Malone, D. M. (2007). 'Security Council', in T. G. Weiss, and S. Daws (eds), *The Oxford Handbook on the United Nations*. Oxford: Oxford University Press, 117-35.

McKinnon, R. I. (1963). 'Optimum Currency Areas', *The American Economic Review*, 53:717-25.

Meyer, J. W., and Rowan, B. (1977). 'Institutionalized Organizations: Formal Structure as Myth and Ceremony', *American Journal of Sociology*, 83:340-63.

Millard, J. (2010). 'Government 1.5 – is the Bottle Half Full or Half Empty?', *European Journal of ePractice*, 9:1-16.

Minkoff, D., and Agnone, J. (2010). 'Consolidating Social Change: The Consequences of Foundation Funding for Developing Social Movement Infrastructures', in H. K. Anheier, and D. Hammack (eds), *American Foundations: Roles and Contributions*. Washington, D.C.: The Brookings Institution Press, 347-67.

Mitchell, D. J. (2012). 'How the Swiss "Debt Brake" Tamed Government', *Wall Street Journal*, 25 April, http://online.wsj.com/article/SB10014240527023034590045773616229271999902.html (accessed 29 August 2012).

Moore, M. H. (2005). 'Break-Through Innovations and Continuous Improvement: Two Different Models of Innovative Processes in the Public Sector', *Public Money & Management*, 25(1): 43-50.

Mueller, M. L. (2010). *Networks and States: The Global Politics of Internet Governance*. Cambridge: MIT Press.

Muldoon, Jr., J. P., et al. (eds) (2011). *The New Dynamics of Multilateralism: Diplomacy, International Organizations, and Global Governance*. Boulder: Westview Press.

Mundell, R. A. (1961). 'A Theory of Optimum Currency Areas', *The American Economic Review*, 51:657-65.

Mundell, R. A. (1963). 'Capital Mobility and Stabilization Policy under Fixed and Flexible Exchange Rates', *Canadian Journal of Economics and Political Science*, 29:475-85.

Nkonya, E., et al. (2011). 'The Economics of Desertification, Land Degradation, and Drought: Toward an Integrated Global Assessment', ZEF Discussion Paper on Development Policy 150.

Norris, F. (2009). 'The Upside to Resisting Globalization', *The New York Times*, 5 February, http://www.nytimes.com/2009/02/06/business/06norris.html (accessed 28 August 2012).

North, D. C. (1990). *Institutions, Institutional Change and Economic Performance*. Cambridge: Cambridge University Press.

Norwegian Ministry of Finance (2011). *The Management of the Government Pension Fund in 2010*. Report No. 15 to the Storting.

Nye, Jr., J. S. (2010). *The Future of Power*. New York: Public Affairs.

OECD (Organisation for Economic Co-operation and Development) (1995). *Governance in Transition, Public Management Reforms in OECD Countries*. Paris: OECD.

OECD (Organisation for Economic Co-operation and Development) (2010a). *Perspectives on Global Development 2010: Shifting Wealth*. Paris: OECD.

OECD (Organisation for Economic Co-operation and Development) (2010b). *Regional Statistics and Indicators*. July 2010. Retrieved from http://stats.oecd.org/Index.aspx?DataSetCode=REG_INNO_TL2.

OECD (Organisation for Economic Co-operation and Development) (2011). *Towards Green Growth*. Paris: OECD.

OECD (Organisation for Economic Co-operation and Development) (2012). *OECD Economic Outlook Vol. 2012/1*. Paris: OECD Publishing.

Painter, C. (1999). 'Public Service Reform From Thatcher To Blair: A Third Way', *Parliamentary Affairs*, 52:99-112.

Parsons, W. (2006). 'Innovation in the Public Sector: Spare tyres and fourth plinths', *The Innovation Journal: The Public Sector Innovation Journal*, 11(2).

Pignataro, G. (2003). 'Performance Indicators', in R. Towse (ed), *A Handbook of Cultural Economics*. Cheltenham: Edward Elgar, 366-72.

Pollitt, C., and Bouckaert, G. (2000). *Public Management Reform: A Comparative Analysis*. New York: Oxford University Press.

Quaglia, L. (2007). 'The Politics of Financial Service Regulation and Supervision Reform in the European Union', *European Journal of Political Research*, 46:269-90.

Quaglia, L. (2008). 'Committee Governance in the Financial Sector in the European Union', *Journal of European Integration*, 30:565-80.

Reinhart, C. M., and Reinhart, V. R. (2008). 'Capital Flow Bonanzas: An Encompassing View of the Past and Present', NBER Working Paper 14321.

Reinhart, C. M., and Rogoff, K. S. (2009). *This Time Is Different: Eight Centuries of Financial Folly*. Princeton: Princeton University Press.

Reisen, H. (2010). 'The Multilateral Donor Non-System: Towards Accountability and Efficient Role Assignment', *Economics: The Open-Access, Open-Assessment E-Journal*, 4: 2010-5, http://www.economics-ejournal.org/economics/journalarticles/2010-5 (accessed 28 August 2012).

REN21 (Renewable Energy Policy Network for the 21st Century) (2011). *Renewables 2011 Global Status Report*. Paris: REN21 Secretariat.

Revenue Watch Institute and Transparency International (2010). *Revenue Watch Index 2010*. New York: Revenue Watch Institute.

Romanelli, E. (1991). 'The Evolution of New Organizational Forms', *Annual Review of Sociology*, 17:79-103.

Romanelli, E., and Tushman, M. L. (1985). 'Organizational Evolution: A Metamorphosis Model of Convergence and Reorientation', in L. L. Cummings and B.M. Staw (eds), *Research in Organizational Behavior, Volume 7*. Greenwich: JAI Press, 171-222.

Romanelli, E., and Tushman, M. L. (1994). 'Organizational Transformation as Punctuated Equilibrium: An Empirical Test', *The Academy of Management Journal*, 37:1141-66.

Romer, P. M. (2010). 'Technologies, Rules, and Progress: The Case for Charter Cities', Center for Global Development Essay.

Rössel, J. (2012). 'Methodological Nationalism', in H. K. Anheier, and M. Juergensmeyer (eds), *Encyclopedia of Global Studies*. Thousand Oaks: Sage Publications, 1152-5.

Salamon, L. M. (1995). *Partners in Public Service: Government-Nonprofit Relations in the Modern Welfare State*. Baltimore: Johns Hopkins University Press.

Sandler, T. (2004). *Global Collective Action*. Cambridge: Cambridge University Press.

Scharpf, F. (1999). *Governing in Europe: Effective and Democratic?* Oxford: Oxford University Press.

Schumpeter, J. A. (1950). *Capitalism, Socialism, and Democracy.* 3rd ed. New York: Harper & Brothers.

Schwab, K. (ed) (2011). *The Global Competitiveness Report 2011-2012.* Geneva: World Economic Forum.

Scott, W. R. (1995). *Institutions and Organizations.* Thousand Oaks: Sage Publications.

Shimizu, H., and Sandler, T. (2002). 'Peacekeeping and Burden-Sharing, 1994-2000', *Journal of Peace Research*, 39:651-68.

Simmons, B. A. (1994). *Who Adjusts? Domestic Sources of Foreign Economic Policy During the Interwar Years.* Princeton: Princeton University Press.

Simon, N. (2011). *International Environmental Governance for the 21st Century: Challenges, Reform Processes and Options for Action on the Way to Rio 2012.* SWP (German Institute for International Security Affairs) Research Paper 1.

Sinn, H.-W., and Wollmershäuser, T. (2011). 'Target Loans, Current Account Balances and Capital Flows: The ECB's Rescue Facility', CESifo Working Paper 3500.

Skidmore, D. (2012). 'The Obama Presidency and US Foreign Policy: Where's the Multilateralism?', *International Studies Perspectives*, 13:43-64.

Stein, E. H., and Streb, J. M. (2004). 'Elections and the Timing of Devaluations', *Journal of International Economics*, 63:119-45.

Stanig, P. (forthcoming). 'Governance Beyond the Nation-state: Estimating Governance Indexes at the Sub-national and Trans-national Level', in Hertie School of Governance (ed), *Governance Challenges and Innovations: Financial and Fiscal Governance.* Oxford: Oxford University Press.

Stanig, P., and Kayser, M. (forthcoming). 'Measuring Governance: A Proposal', Hertie School of Governance (ed), *Governance Challenges and Innovations: Financial and Fiscal Governance.* Oxford: Oxford University Press.

Stern, N. (2007). *The Economics of Climate Change: The Stern Review.* Cambridge: Cambridge University Press.

Strezhnev, A., and Voeten, E. (2012-08). *United Nations General Assembly Voting Data.* Retrieved from http://hdl.handle.net/1902.1/12379 (accessed 31 August 2012).

Stiglitz, J. E. (2010). *Freefall: America, Free Markets, and the Sinking of the World Economy.* New York: W. W. Norton & Company.

Stiglitz, J. E., Sen, A., and Fitoussi, J.-P. (2010). *Mismeasuring Our Lives: Why GDP Doesn't Add Up.* New York: The New Press.

Subacchi, P., and Pickford, S. (2011). 'Legitimacy vs Effectiveness for the G20: A Dynamic Approach to Global Economic Governance', Chatham House International Economics Briefings Paper 2011/01.

Sussangkarn, C. (2010). 'The Chiang Mai Initiative Multilateralization: Origin, Development and Outlook', Asian Development Bank Institute Working Paper 230.

TERI-KAS (The Energy and Resources Institute and Konrad-Adenauer-Stiftung) (2011). *Energy Security: Managing Risks, Balancing Concerns and Developing Frameworks.* 5th TERI-KAS International Energy Dialogue, 24-26 October 2010, Surajkund. New Delhi: Office of the Konrad-Adenauer-Stiftung in India.

Timmer, H., et al. (2011). *Global Development Horizons 2011: Multipolarity—The New Global Economy.* Washington, D.C.: The World Bank.

Touffut, J.-P. (ed) (2009). *Changing Climate, Changing Economy.* Cheltenham: Edward Elgar.

Tushman, M. L., and O'Reilly, C. A. (2002). *Winning Through Innovation: A Practical Guide to Leading Organizational Change and Renewal*. Boston: Harvard Business School Press.

UN (United Nations) (2005). 'Tunis Agenda for the Information Society', 18 November. http://www.itu.int/wsis/docs2/tunis/off/6rev1.html (accessed on 28 August 2012).

UN (United Nations) (2010). *Report of the Secretary-General's High-Level Advisory Group on Climate Change Financing*. New York: United Nations.

UNBISNET (United Nations Bibliographic Information System) [website]. http://unbisnet.un.org/ (accessed May 2012).

UNESCO and UNRISD (United Nations Educational, Scientific and Cultural Organization and United Nations Research Institute for Social Development) (1997). *Towards a World Report on Culture and Development: Constructing Cultural Statistics and Indicators*. Report of the Workshop on Cultural Indicators of Development, 4-7 January 1996, Royaumont Foundation.

UNFCCC (United Nations Framework Convention on Climate Change) [website]. *Greenhouse Gas Inventory Data*. Retrieved from http://unfccc.int/ghg_data/ghg_data_unfccc/time_series_annex_i/items/3814.php (accessed 15 May 2012).

UNICEF (2012) *Committing to Child Survival: A Promise Renewed, Annual Report 2012*. New York: UNICEF.

United Nations Human Rights Council (2010). *Report of the Special Rapporteur on the Right to Food, Olivier De Schutter; Addendum: Large-scale Land Acquisitions and Leases: A Set of Minimum Principles and Measures to Address the Human Rights Challenge*. Document A/HRC/13/33/Add.2.

United Nations Peacekeeping [website]. http://www.un.org/en/peacekeeping/resources/statistics/ (accessed 16 March 2012).

United Nations Treaty Collection [website]. http://treaties.un.org/Home.aspx?lang=en (accessed 12 April 2012).

Van Asselt, H., and Fariborz, Z. (2012). 'Connect the Dots: Managing the Fragmentation of Global Climate Governance', Earth Systems Governance Working Paper 25.

Van Langenhove, L. (2011). 'Multilateralism 2.0: The Transformation of International Relations', 5 May, http://unu.edu/publication/articles/multilateralism-2-0-the-transformation-of-international-relations.html (accessed 31 August 2012).

Vaubel, R. (1991). 'The Political Economy of the International Monetary Fund: A Public Choice Analysis', in R. Vaubel, and T. D. Willett (eds), *The Political Economy of International Organizations*. Boulder: Westview Press, 204-44.

Véron, N. (2012). 'Financial Reform after the Crisis: An Early Assessment', Peterson Institute for International Economics Working Paper 12-2.

Vestergaard, J., and Wade, R. (2012). 'The Governance Response to the Great Recession: The "Success" of the G20', *Journal of Economic Issues*, 46:481-90.

Vidal, J. (2010). 'How Food and Water are Driving a 21st-century African Land Grab', *The Observer*, 7 March, http://www.guardian.co.uk/environment/2010/mar/07/food-water-africa-land-grab (accessed 28 August 2012).

Voeten, E. (2000). 'Clashes in the Assembly', *International Organization*, 54:185–215.

Voeten, E. (2004). 'Resisting the Lonely Superpower: Responses of States in the United Nations to U.S. Dominance', *The Journal of Politics*, 66:729-54.

Volz, U. (ed) (2011). *Regional Integration, Economic Development and Global Governance*. Cheltenham: Edward Elgar.

von Weizsäcker. E., et al. (2009). *Factor Five: Transforming the Global Economy Through 80% Improvements in Resource Productivity*. London: Earthscan.

WEF (World Economic Forum) (2011). *Global Risks 2011*. Geneva: WEF.

WEF (World Economic Forum) (2012). *Global Risks 2012*. Geneva: WEF.

Weischer, L. et al. (2011). *Grounding Green Power: Bottom-Up Perspectives on Smart Renewable Energy Policy in Developing Countries*. Washington, D.C.: German Marshall Fund in collaboration with World Resources Institute and Heinrich-Böll-Stiftung.

Weiss, T. G., and Thakur, R. (2010). *Global Governance and the UN: An Unfinished Journey*. Bloomington: Indiana University Press.

Wheatley J. (2010). 'Brazil Raises Taxes on Foreign Inflows to 4%', *Financial Times*, 4 October, http://www.ft.com/intl/cms/s/0/0a5d4b48-cffe-11df-bb9e-00144feab49a.html#axzz24pw8Lajl (accessed 28 August 2012).

Whipp, L., and Garnham, P. (2010). 'Tokyo Currency Move Surprises Markets', *Financial Times*, 15 September, http://www.ft.com/intl/cms/s/0/d0e59c4c-c0e6-11df-99c4-00144feab49a.html#axzz24pw8Lajl (accessed 28 August 2012).

Wijen, F., et al. (eds) (2012). *A Handbook of Globalisation and Environmental Policy, Second Edition: National Government Interventions in a Global Arena*. Cheltenham: Edward Elgar.

Willett, T. D. (2002). 'Toward a Broader Public-Choice Analysis of the International Monetary Fund', in D. M. Andrews, C. R. Henning, and W. Pauly (eds), *Governing the World's Money*. Ithaca: Cornell University Press, 60-77.

Wood, T., and Murray, W. E. (2007). 'Participatory Democracy in Brazil and Local Geographies: Porto Alegre and Belo Horizonte Compared.' *European Review of Latin American and Caribbean Studies*, 83:19-41.

Woods, N. (2010). 'Global Governance after the Financial Crisis: A New Multilateralism or the Last Gasp of the Great Powers?', *Global Policy*, 1:51-63.

World Bank (1991). 'Managing Development: The Governance Dimension.' Discussion Paper 34899.

World Bank (2008). *Public Sector Reform: What Works and Why? An IEG Evaluation of World Bank Support*. Washington, D.C.: The World Bank.

WTO (World Trade Organization) (2011). *World Trade Report 2011: The WTO and Preferential Trade Agreements: From Co-existence to Coherence*. Geneva: WTO.

Yermo, J. (2008). 'Governance and Investment of Public Pension Reserve Funds in Selected OECD Countries', OECD Working Paper on Insurance and Private Pensions 15.

Zelner, B. A., Henisz, W. J., and Holburn, G. L. F. (2009). 'Contentious Implementation and Retrenchment in Neoliberal Policy Reform: The Global Electric Power Industry 1989-2001', *Administrative Science Quarterly*, 54(3):379-412.

Zürn, M. (1998). *Regieren jenseits des Nationalstaates: Globalisierung und Denationalisierung als Chance*. Frankfurt: Suhrkamp.

Zürn, M. (2000). 'Democratic Governance Beyond the Nation State', *European Journal of International Relations*, 6(2):183-221.

Zürn, M. (2011). 'Vier Modelle einer globalen Ordnung in kosmopolitischer Absicht', *Politische Vierteljahresschrift*, 52:78-118.

About the Contributors

Helmut K. Anheier (PhD, Yale) is Dean and Professor of Sociology of the Hertie School of Governance (Berlin, Germany). He also holds a chair of Sociology at Heidelberg University and serves as Academic Director of the Center for Social Investment there. Previously, he was Professor of Public Policy and Social Welfare at UCLA's School of Public Affairs and Centennial Professor at the London School of Economics (LSE).

William Roberts Clark (PhD, Rutgers) is Professor of Political Science at the University of Michigan (USA). His research explores how political and social institutions can simultaneously be the product of human choice and an important determinant of human behaviour. His publications include *Capitalism, Not Globalism: Capital Mobility, Central Bank Independence, and the Political Control of the Economy* (University of Michigan Press, 2003).

Mark S. Copelovitch (PhD, Harvard) is Assistant Professor in the Department of Political Science and the Robert M. La Follette School of Public Affairs at the University of Wisconsin-Madison. Copelovitch examines international political economy and international organisations, focusing on the politics of global financial governance, capital flows and financial crises, and the political economy of exchange rates and monetary institutions.

Mark Hallerberg (PhD, UCLA) is Professor of Public Management and Political Economy and Director of the Fiscal Governance Center at the Hertie School of Governance. He is the author of *Domestic Budgets in a United Europe: Fiscal Governance from the End of Bretton Woods to EMU* (Cornell University Press, 2004) and co-author (with Rolf Strauch and Jürgen von Hagen) of *Fiscal Governance: Evidence from Europe* (Cambridge University Press, 2009).

Inge Kaul (Dr. rer. soc., Konstanz University) is an adjunct faculty member at the Hertie School of Governance. She served as the first director of the *Human Development Report* office of the United Nations Development Program (UNDP) and later as director of UNDP's Office of Development Studies. Her research focuses on the identification of factors that facilitate or impede policy responses to global challenges, and thus, successes and failures of global governance.

Mark Kayser (PhD, UCLA) is Professor of Applied Methods and Comparative Politics at the Hertie School of Governance. His research focuses on comparative and international political economy, with an emphasis on domestic political institutions, elections, redistribution, and political intervention in the economy.

Sabrina Korreck is a Research Associate at the Hertie School of Governance. She studied economics, political science and sociology in Potsdam and completed the Advanced Studies Program at the Kiel Institute for the World Economy.

Lucia Quaglia (PhD, University of Sussex) is Professor of Political Science at the University of York and Research Fellow at the Hanse-Wissenschaft-Kolleg. Her research interests range from economic governance in the European Union, Euroscepticism, Europeanisation, and EU presidencies, as well as comparative European politics and public policy, to elites studies.

Piero Stanig (PhD, Columbia University) is Research Fellow in Governance and Methodology at the Hertie School of Governance and a member of the Technical Committee of the Ibrahim Index of African Governance. His research interests span comparative voting behaviour and public opinion, the political economy of corruption, and statistical methodology for political science.

Stephanie Walter (PhD, ETH Zürich) is Junior Professor for International and Comparative Political Economy at the Institute for Political Science, Heidelberg University (Germany). Her research deals primarily with the influence distributional conflicts, policy preferences, and institutions have on economic policy decision-making.

The manufacturer's authorised representative in the EU for product safety is Oxford University Press España S.A. of el Parque Empresarial San Fernando de Henares, Avenida de Castilla, 2 – 28830 Madrid (www.oup.es/en or product. safety@oup.com). OUP España S.A. also acts as importer into Spain of products made by the manufacturer.

www.ingramcontent.com/pod-product-compliance
Ingram Content Group UK Ltd.
Pitfield, Milton Keynes, MK11 3LW, UK
UKHW021320180426
11947UKWH00015B/1340